Lecture Notes in Computer Science 6229

Commenced Publication in 1973
Founding and Former Series Editors:
Gerhard Goos, Juris Hartmanis, and Jan van

Efthimios Tambouris   Ann Macintosh
Olivier Glassey (Eds.)

Electronic Participation

Second IFIP WG 8.5 International Conference, ePart 2010
Lausanne, Switzerland, August 29 – September 2, 2010
Proceedings

 Springer

Volume Editors

Efthimios Tambouris
University of Macedonia
Naousa, Greece
E-mail: tambouris@uom.gr

Ann Macintosh
The University of Leeds
Leeds, UK
E-mail: a.macintosh@leeds.ac.uk

Olivier Glassey
IDHEAP
Lausanne, Switzerland
E-mail: olivier.glassey@idheap.unil.ch

Library of Congress Control Number: 2010932604

CR Subject Classification (1998): J.1, H.4, C.2, H.5, H.3, D.2

LNCS Sublibrary: SL 3 – Information Systems and Application, incl. Internet/Web
and HCI

ISSN   0302-9743
ISBN-10   3-642-15157-4 Springer Berlin Heidelberg New York
ISBN-13   978-3-642-15157-6 Springer Berlin Heidelberg New York

springer.com

© IFIP International Federation for Information Processing 2010
Printed in Germany

Typesetting: Camera-ready by author, data conversion by Scientific Publishing Services, Chennai, India
Printed on acid-free paper   06/3180

Preface

The International Conference on eParticipation is supported by IFIP WG 8.5 (International Federation for Information Processing Working Group 8.5 on Information Systems in Public Administration). Organized annually, it is a show-case for research and practice in the multidisciplinary field of eParticipation.

ePart is committed to reviewing research advances and case studies in social and technological scientific domains, seeking to demonstrate new concepts, methods, styles and enabling technologies of eParticipation. It brings together researchers from a wide range of academic disciplines and provides the scientific community with a platform for discussing and advancing the latest research findings.

ePart 2010 continued the success of the last ePart conference. The ePart 2009 proceedings contained 16 completed, research papers published by Springer in LNCS vol. 5694 and 20 ongoing research, project and development papers published by Trauner Druck.

This year the ePart 2010 Springer proceedings brings together 19 completed, comprehensive research papers from researchers around the globe. The papers have been clustered around the following headings:

- Foundations and Visionary
- eParticipation Initiatives
- Understanding and Evaluating eParticipation
- Information and Communication Technologies and eVoting

Included in this volume are papers that introduce new participation models based on advanced information and communication technologies, investigate the potential of social networking, present evaluation frameworks and assessment outcomes, critically analyze eParticipation initiatives around the globe, and demonstrate how cutting-edge technology can facilitate eParticipation. Accepted papers on ongoing research and general development issues, on case and project descriptions, as well as workshop abstracts continue to be published by Trauner Druck in a complementary proceedings volume. The volume, edited by the Chairs of both the ePart and EGOV conferences, illustrates the close links ePart has with EGOV, our sister conference focusing on eGovernment research.

All ePart papers were blind reviewed by at least three reviewers from the ePart 2010 Program Committee with the assistance of additional reviewers. We would like to acknowledge their professionalism and enthusiasm which enabled authors to further improve their papers. We would also like to thank Maria Wimmer, Co-chair of EGOV, for her valuable assistance and support with the organization of ePart 2010.

ePart 2010 was hosted by the Swiss Graduate School of Public Administration (IDHEAP) at the University of Lausanne/Switzerland. As well as preparing students for senior positions in public administrations, IDHEAP provides expert advice to administrations, political leaders, and the national government of Switzerland. We would like to thank IDHEAP for its excellent organization of this conference and also thank all the local institutions for their support.

August/September 2010   Efthimios Tambouris
                                                            Ann Macintosh
                                                            Olivier Glassey

Organization

Conference Chairs

Ann Macintosh   The University of Leeds, UK
Efthimios Tambouris   University of Macedonia, Greece
Olivier Glassey   University of Lausanne, Switzerland

PhD Colloquium Chairs

Sharon Dawes   Center for Technology in Government,
     University at Albany, NY/USA
Björn Niehaves   ERCIS, Universität Münster, Germany

Program Committee and Reviewers

Georg Aichholzer   Austrian Academy of Sciences, Austria
Kim Viborg Andersen   Copenhagen Business School, Denmark
Lasse Berntzen   Vestfold University College, Norway
Yannis Charalabidis   National Technical University of Athens,
     Greece
Fiorella de Cindio   University of Milan, Italy
Clelia Colombo   Generalitat of Catalonia, Spain
Simon Delakorda   Institute for Electronic Participation, Slovenia
Annelie Ekelin   Blekinge Institute of Technology Sweden
Olivier Glassey   Institut de Hautes Etudes en Administration
     Publique, Switzerland
Tomas Gordon   Fraunhofer Institute for Open Communications
     Systems, Germany
Dimitris Gouscos   University of Athens, Greece
Mary Griffiths   University of Adelaide, Australia
Ake Grönlund   Örebro University, Sweden
Konstantinos Koskinas   Panteion University, Greece
Patrizia Lombardi   Politecnico di Turin, Italy
Euripides Loukis   University of the Aegean, Greece
Ann Macintosh   Leeds University, UK
Ursula Maier-Rabler   Salzburg University, Austria
Peter Mambrey   Fraunhofer FIT, Germany
Rony Medaglia   Copenhagen Business School, Denmark
Jeremy Millard   Danish Technological Institute, Denmark

David O'Donnell   Intellectual Capital Research, Institute of
                                  Ireland, Ireland
Peter Parycek   Danube University Krems, Austria
Cristian Peraboni   Università degli Study di Milano, Italy
Vassilios Peristeras   DERI, University of Ireland, Ireland
David Price   Thoughtgraph Ltd., UK
Øystein Sæbø   University of Agder, Norway
Efthimios Tambouris   University of Macedonia, Greece
Konstantinos Tarabanis   University of Macedonia, Greece
Ella Taylor-Smith   International Teledemocracy Center,
                                  UK
Maria Wimmer   University of Koblenz-Landau, Germany
Scott Wright   University of East Anglia, UK
Alexandros Xenakis   Panteion University, Greece

Additional Reviewers

Eleni Panopoulou
Evangelos Kalampokis
Gudrun Haindlmaier
Nikos Loutas
Stefan Huber

Table of Contents

Foundations and Visionary

eParticipation Initiatives

Understanding and Evaluating eParticipation

Information and Communication Technologies and eVoting

Towards a Systematic Exploitation of Web 2.0 and Simulation Modeling Tools in Public Policy Process

Yannis Charalabidis[1], George Gionis[2], Enrico Ferro[3], and Euripidis Loukis[1]

[1] University of the Aegean, Gorgyras Str., Karlovassi 83200, Greece
{yannisx,eloukis}@ aegean.gr
[2] National Technical University of Athens, 9 Iroon Polytechniou, Athens 15780, Greece
gionis@epu.ntua.gr
[3] Istituto Superiore Mario Boella, 61Via Boggio, Turin 10138, Italy
ferro@ismb.it

Abstract. This paper describes a methodology for the systematic exploitation of the emerging web 2.0 social media by government organizations in the processes of public policies formulation, aiming to enhance e-participation, in combination with established simulation modeling techniques and tools. It is based on the concept of 'Policy Gadget' (Padget), which is a micro web application combining a policy message with underlying group knowledge in social media (in the form of content and user activities) and interacting with citizens in popular web 2.0 locations in order to get and convey their input to policy makers. Such 'Padgets' are created by a central platform-toolset and then deployed in many different Web 2.0 media. Citizens input from them will be used in various simulation modeling techniques and tools (such as the 'Systems Dynamics'), which are going to simulate different policy options and estimate their outcomes and effectiveness. A use case scenario of the proposed methodology is presented, which outlines how it can be used in 'real life' public policy design problems.

Keywords: e-participation, web 2.0, social media, public policy, simulation, system dynamics.

1 Introduction

The design of public policy in most domains is a 'wicked' problem, since it is characterised by high complexity and many stakeholders with different and heterogeneous views of the problem, values, concerns and interests; such problems do not have mathematically 'optimal' solutions and pre-defined algorithms for calculating them, but only 'better' and 'worse' solutions, so they cannot be solved by formal methodologies and require 'second generation' approaches based on deliberation among stakeholders [1] – [4]. These approaches include several circles of deliberation, in which the stakeholders interact, raise issues concerning the problem under discussion, propose solutions and argue about advantages and disadvantages of them, finally resulting in a better understanding of the problem. From a knowledge management perspective in such deliberations valuable 'tacit knowledge' possessed

E. Tambouris, A. Macintosh, and O. Glassey (Eds.): ePart 2010, LNCS 6229, pp. 1–12, 2010.

by the stakeholders is transformed into 'explicit (codified) knowledge' [5] - [6], which can be processed, disseminated and combined with other relevant knowledge that public organizations possess, in order to formulate better policies and regulations for addressing social needs and problems and deliver better services to citizens and enterprises.

For these reasons a new model of democracy has emerged, which is termed "participatory democracy" [7] – [11], and combines decision making by citizens' elected representatives with citizens' participation, with the latter not replacing but supporting and enhancing the former. A key principle of this model is that "the equal right to self-development can only be achieved in a participatory society, a society which fosters a sense of political efficacy, nurtures a concern for collective problems and contributes to the formation of a knowledgeable citizenry capable of taking a sustained interest in the governing process" (Held 1987, [9], p. 262). Row and Frewer (2004) [11] define public participation as 'the practice of consulting and involving members of the public in the agenda-setting, decision-making and policy forming activities of organizations or institutions responsible for policy development'. The development and increasing penetration of information and communication technologies (ICT), and Internet in particular, in many countries enables the extensive application of the above principles through electronic media, which has been termed as e-participation [12] – [15]. According to the OECD [12], [13] e-participation is defined as the use of ICTs for supporting the provision of information to the citizens concerning government activities and public policies, the consultation with the citizens and also their active participation.

However, despite the high public investments that have been made in many countries by government organizations for developing 'official' e-participation websites aiming to inform citizens on various public policies under formulation and have various types of interactions and consultations with them, their use by the citizens has been in general limited and below the initial expectations [16]; most of these official e-participation spaces were largely unknown to the general public due to the high costs of promotion and the slow pace of dissemination, while the topics dealt with were sometimes distant from people's daily problems and priorities, so that content contributions by non experts was inhibited. These problems, in combination with the high heterogeneity of citizens in terms of political interests, educational level and technological skills, and at the same time the emergence of the new Web 2.0 social media necessitate government to exploit the numerous users-driven Web 2.0 virtual spaces, which have been launched through citizens initiatives with dramatic success in terms of adoption and usage, for widening and enhancing e-participation. Web 2.0 initially had a big impact on the social life of people, and later on several private sector industries, such as advertising and media; however, recently there has been some first evidence that Web 2.0 applications are relevant for supporting various tasks in many different domains of government, including public participation [17].

In this direction this paper describes a methodology for the systematic exploitation of the emerging Web 2.0 social media, in combination with the 'established' simulation modelling techniques and tools, by central and local government organizations in the processes of public policies formulation. Though in recent literature are presented some guidelines and frameworks for the exploitation of Web 2.0 by private sector firms [18], [19], something similar for the public sector is missing. In particular, the proposed methodology aims at bringing together two well established domains, the mashup architectural approach of Web 2.0 for creating web applications (termed as Policy Gadgets - Padgets) and the simulation modelling techniques and tools for analyzing complex system behaviour, such as System Dynamics [20].

The paper is structured in seven sections. In section 2 the background and foundations of the proposed methodology is outlined, which includes results from previous research on the use of web 2.0 in government and simulation modelling. Then in section 3 the fundamentals of our methodology are presented, while in section 4 the architecture of the central platform for creating and deploying Padgets is described. Section 5 presents an application scenario of the proposed methodology, which outlines how it can be used in 'real life' public policy design problems. Finally, section 6 summarizes the conclusions and the next steps we are going to take for validating the proposed methodology.

2 Background

2.1 Web 2.0 and Government

Web 2.0 is defined as a set of technologies, applications and values [17], [21]. In particular, from the technological point of view, the building blocks of Web 2.0 are a number of new technologies, such as Ajax, XML, Open API, Microformats, Flash/Flex, which have been developed and introduced aiming to increase the usability, integration and re-use of web applications. Based on these technologies some applications have been developed, which enable easy content creation and publishing, information sharing and collaboration, such as Blog, Wiki, Podcast, RSS feeds, Social networks, Massive Multiplayer Online Games, etc. These applications share some common values. They build on the knowledge and skills of the user, and enable the user to build content and services (termed as the 'user as producer' value), reducing the content and services producer and consumer dichotomy. User contributions can be made more meaningful and rich through collaboration and networking among users, while the quality control filtering relies strongly on peer review by other users (termed as the 'collective intelligence' value). Also, applications are first released in beta format in order to include early user feedback, and very often are continuously improved (this termed as the 'perpetual beta' value), rather than following a linear development process. Finally in Web 2.0 usability is highly important, because the success of these applications rely critically on the quantity and quality of users' contributions, so their take-up is not only an index of success, but often a condition for their continued existence (this termed as the 'extreme ease of use' value).

Web 2.0 was initially used by people for personal and social communication, while later it was used by several private sector industries, such as advertising and media, and had an important impact on them. In recent literature are presented some guidelines and frameworks for the exploitation of Web 2.0 by private sector firms for marketing purposes [18], [19]. Recently, there has been some first evidence [17] that Web 2.0 applications are already being used in government, not only for 'soft' issues, such as public relations and public service announcements, but also for 'core' tasks, such as intelligence services, reviewing patents, knowledge management, cross-agency collaboration, public services evaluation by citizens, regulation, law enforcement and public participation. These applications of Web 2.0 in government aim to and result in a more active 'user' role, having as users both civil servants and citizens. However, a comprehensive methodology and toolset for exploiting systematically web 2.0 social media by government organizations is missing.

Focusing now on the area of public participation, previous research [16] has found that numerous e-participation experiments has been documented in Europe and abroad, which have used different technologies and various methodologies to purport to highly heterogeneous policy goals, however their usage by the citizens has been in general limited, much lower than expectations, and some important weaknesses have been identified:

- public administrations expected citizens to make the first step: to move forward from their own online environments to government websites for participating in public debates;
- the designated "official" spaces were largely unknown to the general public, mainly due to the high costs of promotion and the slow pace of dissemination;
- the topics discussed were sometimes distant from people's daily problems and priorities, so that content contributions by non experts was inhibited;
- the tools adopted were not appropriate, or at least usable only by a rather reach and educated minority;
- the methodologies used for e-participation were not scalable, so they could only be adopted in pilot trials with a limited impact;
- and also the distribution of online users behavior was not taken into account (only a small minority of Internet users is willing to actively produce content or offer reviews/feedbacks).

For the above reasons it is concluded that a change of approach in the implementation of e-participation by government is necessary, taking into account and exploiting the development and high penetration of Web 2.0 and mobile communications. In particular, the increased capabilities for Internet users to create content and the birth of social networks have driven the development of more and more virtual spaces for the expression of political views, problems and needs. At the same time the pervasive diffusion of mobile Internet in most citizens' groups (even in less rich and educated ones, who make limited use of Internet) deserves a more careful consideration from e-participation designers. Therefore governments should become more aware of the social complexity, and at the same time the wealth of information that is already available and is continuously developed in citizens-initiated Web 2.0 social media, in order to increase the quantity, quality and inclusiveness of e-participation; they should make a step towards citizens rather than expecting the citizenry to move their content production activity onto the "official" spaces created for e-participation.

2.2 Simulation Modelling

Modeling has been used for long time as a way of understanding complex social and technical systems, estimating their evolution/performance and addressing their problems that, especially when prototyping or experimenting with the real system is too costly or impossible [22]. We can distinguish between analytical and simulation modeling. Simulation modeling is a good approach for complex systems and problems, in which time dynamics is important and an analytical solution is difficult. A simulation model may be considered as a set of rules (expressed in various forms, such as equations, flowcharts, state machines, cellular automata) that define how the system behaves and evolves with time. There are four basic paradigms of simulation modeling, which differ mainly in the level of abstraction and detail and also in the way they model time (using continuous or discrete time):

- Dynamic Systems: It is actually the ancestor of System Dynamics, which is used for the detailed modeling (at a low abstraction level) in continuous time of mechanical, electrical, chemical, and other technical systems, as part of their design process.
- System Dynamics: It has been initially developed for analyzing from a high level of abstraction in continuous time the information-feedback characteristics of industrial activities and examine how various types of amplification, time delays and organizational structures affect performance. However, latter it has been extensively used for modeling and analyzing many other types of systems, such as urban, social, ecological, etc. System Dynamics models a real-life activity as a set of 'stocks' (of quantities gradually accumulated, e.g. people, money, material, etc.), 'flows' between these stocks and also 'information' that determines the levels of these flows.
- Discrete Events Modeling: It is used for modeling at a medium or low level of abstraction systems which are characterized by discrete events that determine their evolution and performance.
- Agent Based Modeling: It is based on modeling the behavior of the individual 'agents' forming the systems, which are defined as objects characterized by pro- and re-activeness, spatial awareness, ability to learn, social ability and "intellect". Therefore the behavior at the system level is not defined, but emerges as a result of many individual agents, each following its own behavior rules, living together in some environment and communicating with each other and with the environment.

From these four basic paradigms of simulation modeling Systems Dynamics (being described in detail in [20], [23], [24]) seems more appropriate for analyzing public policies, since this usually i) requires high level views of complex social or economic systems in continuous time, and ii) such systems include various individual processes with 'stocks' (e.g. users and non-users of various services or new technologies, employed and unemployed citizens, citizen groups of various income levels, etc.) and 'flows' among them, which are influenced by public policies. For this reason Systems Dynamics has been successfully used in the past for estimating the evolution of a number of critical variables for society, such as unemployment, economic development, taxation income, technologies penetration, pollution, poverty, etc. and for the analysis of various types of public policies, e.g. [25] – [30]. Systems dynamics focuses on understanding initially the basic structure of a system and then based on it understanding the behavior it can produce (e.g. exponential growth or S-shared growth of the basic variable).

3 Methodology Fundamentals

The proposed methodology in based on the background and foundations presented in the previous section, and brings together two well established domains: the mashup architectural approach of web 2.0 for creating web applications (gadgets) and the methodology of simulation modelling for analyzing complex systems behaviour. Its main objective is to design, develop and deploy a prototype central toolset that will allow policy makers to create graphically micro-applications, which are then going to be deployed in many different web 2.0 social media (each of them can have a different audience, so that we can finally reach appropriate groups of citizens, which are quite different from the ones who visit and use the official government-initiated e-participation websites) in order to convey policy messages to their users and interact with them. Similarly to the approach of gadget applications in web 2.0 – i.e. using data and services from heterogeneous sources to create and deploy quickly applications that provide value added services – the project introduces the concept of 'Padget' (Policy Gadget) to represent a micro web application that combines a policy message with underlying group knowledge in social media (in the form of content and user activities) and interacts with end users in popular web locations (such as social networks, blogs, forums, news sites, etc) in order to get and convey their input to policy makers.

In particular, as we can see in Figure 1 a Padget is composed of four elements:

Fig. 1. The elements of a Padget

• A <u>policy message</u>, which could be a public policy in any stage, e.g. a policy white paper, a draft policy plan, a legal document under formulation, a law in its final stage, an EU directive under implementation, etc.

• An <u>interface</u> that will allow users to interact with the policy gadget; this interface will be relevant to the Padget objective – for example it may give users the capability to access policy documents, be informed on relevant news, stipulate opinions, vote on some issues, upload material, tag other people opinions or content as relevant, get location based information, etc.

• Relevant <u>group knowledge</u>, in the form of relevant content and users' activities that have been produced in external social media, forums, blogs, wikis, social networks, etc., which concerns the above policy, is properly annotated in order to indicate its relation with a particular web 2.0 location and constitutes the context of the Padget.

• A <u>decision support model</u>, which includes simulation modelling methods and tools (such as Systems Dynamics), using as input the above data from the interaction of the Padget with the public, and giving as output the effect of specific policies on critical performance indicators that are of interest to the policy maker.

Additionally, any Padget will include a privacy statement informing the citizen as a potential user about what kind of personal data will be collected, how it will be used and processed, and what will happen to it after the expiration of the Padget.

Such a Padget can be deployed in many different web 2.0 social media. In particular, we are going to target the following categories of media (and from each category choose the most appropriate ones taking into account the particular public policy under discussion and the audience we would like to involve in the discussion):

- Platforms for Communication, such as Blogs, Internet forums, Presence applications, Social networking sites, Social network aggregation sites and event sites.
- Platforms for Collaboration, such as Wikis, Social bookmarking (or Social tagging) sites, social news and Opinion sites.
- Platforms for Multimedia and Entertainment, Photo sharing, Video sharing, Livecasting and Virtual World sites.
- Platforms for News and Information, such as Goggle News, Institutional Sites with high number of visitors (i.e. EU, Human Rights and WWF sites) and newspaper sites.
- Platforms for Policy Making and Public Participation, such as governmental organisations forums, blogs, petitions, etc.

Each of them usually provides open APIs in the form of Web services for communicating with it; these programming interfaces are characterized by their simplicity and are often based on existing standards such as HTTP, URL/URI, XML, etc. The application field of Web services is very extensive, but in the context of Web 2.0 are mainly used REST web services. The reason for this is that in web2.0 the Internet is viewed as a collection of resources, which can be easily retrieved or manipulated with REST-based interfaces.

With respect to the decision model, it should be mentioned that it will receive as input the alternative policy scenarios and actions that have been planned by decision makers in combination with existing data referring to the policy issue (studies, statistical data, background information) and also data gathered by Padgets' interaction with end users (opinion polls, survey results etc.) e.g. referring to the adoption rate of the planned policy actions among citizens and other stakeholders. Based on the operation of a simulation engine, embedded in the Padget decision model the potential policy outcomes will be estimated in a hypothetical basis of applying them over a specific time period. These outcomes, after aggregation with existing background information about the particular policy issue, will be used as input for simulating policy actions related to the next steps of the policy making process; this procedure is going to be repeated several times (according to the alternative policy scenarios duration and the policy making process stages), creating thus several loops, in order to end up to the final outcomes and impact of each policy scenario and finally give the decision makers a basis for making the best possible decision. This will also enable the development of hybrid scenarios and policies if needed, in order to manage the particular social problem or need in a better way.

4 Central Platform Architecture

The central platform will provide capabilities for creating graphically Padgets and deploying them in many different Web 2.0 media. Its architecture is shown in Figure 2. It consists of several modules, which are partly dependent on each other and easily expandable. These modules can be divided into two categories: the first one includes internal and 'non-visible' modules, such as the composition module, while the second category includes 'visible' modules responsible for the interaction with the Padgets designers and administrators, such as the Web module and REST-module.

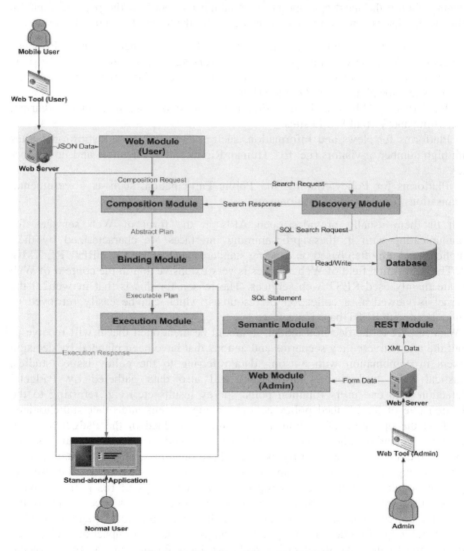

Fig. 2. Architecture of the central platform

In particular the main modules of the central platform are:

Semantic Module: In this module the new language for semantic service description will be implemented; all semantic information will be stored in a database, so this module provides an interface for managing the semantic information in the database.

Discovery Module: The main task of this module is to find all services, which fit to a request; thereby different search strategies can be implemented.

Composition Module: This module is implementing a scheduling algorithm for automatic service composition; it tries to create all plans for a request (request composition), which are leading to a goal. In order to complete its task, this module communicates constantly with the discovery engine and sends in each composition step a search query.

Binding Module: This module converts abstract plans into executable plans; for this purpose it searches and integrates specific services.

Execution Module: It receives as input the plans from the previous module and executes them.

Web Module: This module provides a web interface to communicate with the system. On the client side the user can create a Padget graphically via a Web-Tool, which will be transformed in a suitable format and send to the server. On the server side the Web module receives the request and forwards it to the Composition-module. Then comes the binding module, and at the end the execution module. The Padget is shown on the client side.

REST Module: This module provides a RESTfull interface, which can communicate to the Semantic module.

Standalone Application: Is an installable application with a graphical interface to create and deploy Padgets in blogs, wikis and communities.

5 An Application Scenario

A simple and typical application scenario of the proposed methodology in the policy making processes, based on the use of the above central platform, would start from a policy maker or policy making group wanting to "harvest society's input" in order to take decisions about a future policy to be introduced, or to evaluate whether an already implemented policy aligns with the society or needs modifications. The steps to be taken are shown in Figure 3:

I) The policy maker uses the platform capabilities to Design an appropriate Padget through a graphical drag-and-drop user interface, similar to the one of existing mashup editors for creating gadget applications.

II) The Padget is then Published via the platform to a number of appropriate (in terms of the audience we want to consult for the particular public policy) Web 2.0 social media and becomes available to the public. There will be a variety of choices for deploying the Padget through the central platform according to the its objective and targeted audience. For example it can be deployed to a social network in the form of a specific policy application, as an embedded petition, poll or social tagging application in the sidebar of a popular blog, wiki or forum, or even in the platform's own registry.

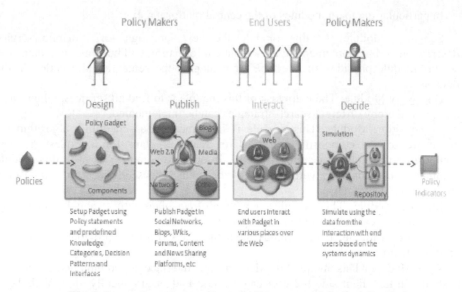

Fig. 3. Steps of a typical application of the proposed methodology

III) The Padget Interacts with the public in all these web locations. This means that users can access it, see its policy message, access the related content and using the Padget's interface interact with it, i.e. relate stipulate opinions, add material, vote and even create relations to other existing similar Padgets. The above will be performed in a privacy preserving manner in accordance with the privacy preferences of users.

IV) At the last stage the Padget helps the policy maker to Decide and form a better understanding of the public policy at stake. For this purpose simulation modelling techniques and tools will be used, such as System Dynamics, which will use as input the data from the interaction of the Padget with the public and simulate how the specific policy (or even a number of alternative policies) will affect a number of critical performance/effectiveness indicators.

6 Conclusions

In the previous sections, a methodology has been described that allows the systematic and centralised exploitation of the 'emerging' Web 2.0 social media, in combination with the 'traditional' simulation modelling techniques and tools, in order to support participatory policy making activities. The proposed methodology allows for a broader, deeper and more inclusive citizens' e-participation in the formulation of significant public policies, by taking advantage of the emerging and highly used web 2.0 social media and involving various different groups who do not usually visit the official e-participation stages of government organizations. This novel e-participation approach enables the government to make a step towards citizens, going to the web locations each group is using for interaction, rather than expecting the citizens to move their content production activity onto the "official" spaces created for e-participation. In this way more valuable 'tacit knowledge' on important social problems and needs, and policy options for addressing them, which is possessed by various stakeholders can be transformed into 'explicit (codified) knowledge'.

This methodology will be further validated in the PADGETS project (its full title being 'Policy Gadgets Mashing Underlying Group Knowledge in Web 2.0 Media - www.padgets.eu) supported by the Seventh Framework Programme (ICT for Governance and Policy Modelling research initiative) of the European Commission. For this purpose initially an analysis will be made of the domain of Web 2.0 social media for news sharing, social networking, publishing and broadcasting, communication and collaboration, followed by identification of standards, interfaces and APIs that allow for interacting with these platforms and tools. Based on the conclusions of these analyses the detailed design will be finalised of the central platform for creating and deploying Policy Gadgets as well as of the ways of exploiting Padgets for providing decision support to policy makers and enabling a more socially-rooted, citizen-centric policy making. Finally the proposed methodology and the above technological tools will be validated through a number of pilots in real life conditions, so that their added value in the policy making process can be assessed and possible improvements of them.

References

1. Rittel, H.W.J., Weber, M.M.: Dilemmas in a general theory of planning. Policy Sciences 4, 155–169 (1973)
2. Buckingham Shum, S.: The Roots to Computer Supported Collaborative Argument Visualization. In: Kirschner, P.A., Buckingham Shum, S., Carr, C.S. (eds.) Visualizing Argumentation: Software Tools for Collaborative and Educational Sense-Making, pp. 3–20. Springer, London (2003)
3. Girle, R., Hitchcock, D., McBurney, P., Verheij, B.: Decision Support for Practical Reasoning: A Theoretical and Computational Perspectiv. In: Reed, C., Norman, T.J. (eds.) Argumentation Machines: New Frontiers in Argument and Computation, pp. 55–83. Kluwer Academic Publishers, Dordrecht (2003)
4. Karacapilidis, N., Loukis, E., Dimopoulos, S.: Computer-supported G2G collaboration for public policy and decision making. Journal of Enterprise Information Management 18(5), 602–624 (2005)
5. Nonaka, I.: A Dynamic Theory of Organizational Knowledge Creation. Organization Science 5(1), 14–37 (1994)
6. Cohendet, P., Steinmueller, W.E.: The Codification of Knowledge: a Conceptual and Empirical Exploration. Industrial and Corporate Change 9(2), 195–209 (2000)
7. Pateman, C.: Participation and Democratic Theory. University Press, Cambridge (1970)
8. Barber, B.: Strong Democracy. University of California Press, Berkeley (1984)
9. Held, D.: Models of Participation. Polity Press, Cambridge (1987)
10. Rowe, G., Frewer, L.J.: Public Participation Methods: A Framework for Evaluation. Science, Technology & Human Values 25(1), 3–29 (2000)
11. Rowe, G., Frewer, L.J.: Evaluating Public-Participation Exercises: A Research Agenda. Science, Technology, & Human Values 29(4), 512–557 (2004)
12. Organization for Economic Co-operation & Development (OECD): Engaging Citizens Online for Better Policy-making. Policy Brief, Paris (2003)
13. Organization for Economic Co-operation & Development (OECD): Promise and Problems of e-Democracy: Challenges of Online Citizen Engagement. Paris (2004)

14. Macintosh, A.: Characterizing E-Participation in Policy Making. In: Proceedings of the 37th Hawaii International Conference on System Sciences (2004)
15. Timmers, P.: Agenda for eDemocracy – an EU perspective. European Commission (2007)
16. Ferro, E., Molinari, F.: Making Sense of Gov 2.0 Strategies: No Citizens, No Party. In: Prosser, A., Parycek, P. (eds.) Proceedings of EDEM 2009 (2009)
17. Osimo, D.: Web 2.0 in Government: Why and How? JRC Scientific and Technical Reports. European Commission, Joint Research Centre, Institute for Prospective Technological Studies (2008),
    http://ftp.jrc.es/EURdoc/JRC45269.pdf (retrieved)
18. Constantinides, E.: Social Media/Web 2.0 as Marketing Parameter: An Introduction. In: Proceedings of 8th International Congress Marketing Trends (2009)
19. Constantinides, E.: Connecting Small and Medium Enterprises to the New Consumer: The Web 2.0 as Marketing Tool. In: Global Perspectives on Small and Medium Enterprise. IGI Global, Hershey (2010)
20. Kirkwood, C.W.: System Dynamics Methods – A Quick Introduction. Arizona State University,
    http://www.public.asu.edu/~kirkwood/sysdyn/SDWork/work-f.pdf (retrieved)
21. O' Reilly, T.E.: What is web 2.0 (2005),
    http://www.oreillynet.com/pub/a/oreilly/tim/news/2005/09/30/what-is-web-20.html (retrieved)
22. Borshchev, A., Filippov, A.: From System Dynamics and Discrete Event to Practical Agent Based Modelling: Reasons, Techniques, Tools. In: Proceeding of 22nd International Conference of the System Dynamics Society, Oxford, England (2004)
23. Forrester, J.: Industrial Dynamics: A Major Breakthrough for Decision Makers. Harvard Business Review 36(4), 37–66 (1958)
24. Forrester, J.: Industrial Dynamics. MIT Press, Cambridge (1961)
25. Liu, C.Y., Wang, W.T.: System Dynamics Approach to Simulation of Tax Policy for Traditional and Internet Phone Services. In: Proceedings of the 23rd International Conference of the System Dynamics Society, Boston (2005)
26. Homer, J.B., Hirsch, G.B.: System Dynamics Modelling for Public Health: Background and Opportunities. American Journal of Public Health 96(3), 452–458 (2006)
27. Robert, Y.C., Leslie, V.C.: Demonstrating the utility of system dynamics for public policy analysis in New Zealand: the case of excise tax policy on tobacco. System Dynamics Review 22(4), 321–348 (2006)
28. Schwaninger, M.S., Ulli-Beer, S., Kaufmann-Hayoz, R.: Policy Analysis and Design in Local Public Management - A System Dynamics Approach. In: Handbook of Transdisciplinary Research, pp. 205–221. Springer, Heidelberg (2007)
29. Zamanipour, M.: A System Dynamics Model for Analyzing the Effects of Government Policies: A Case Study of Iran's Cell Phone Market. In: Proceedings of the 27th International Conference of the System Dynamics Society, Albuquerque, New Mexico, USA (2009)
30. Teekasap, P.: Cluster Formation and Government Policy: System Dynamics Approach. In: Proceedings of the 27th International Conference of the System Dynamics Society, Albuquerque, New Mexico, USA (2009)

Don't Vote, Evolve!

Pietro Speroni di Fenizio and Derek Paterson

CISUC, Department of Informatics Engineering,
University of Coimbra, Coimbra, Portugal
speroni@dei.uc.pt,
cellers@gmx.com
http://cisucpt.dei.uc.pt/ecos/

Abstract. We present an alternative form of decision making designed using a Human Based Genetic Algorithms. The algorithm permits the participants to tackle open questions, by letting all of them propose answers and evaluate each others answers. A successful example is described and some theoretical results are presented showing how the system scales up.

Keywords: e-Democracy, Voting Theory, Pareto Front, Genetic Algorithms, Multi-Criterion Decision Making.

1 Introduction

The word "democracy" comes from the Greek "dēmokratia", "dēmos" meaning "the people" and "-kratia" meaning "power, rule". It literally means "rule of the people" [1]. The word has come to mean a government where either directly or indirectly the citizens decide, through voting, what should be done. Is this the only option? As technology advances the possibilities with which the core idea of democracy can be implemented, expand. It becomes then necessary to investigate, also formally, these new possibilities. Voting Theory is the branch of Mathematics which studies the different ways in which people can express their preferences, and how these preferences can be integrated to reach a final result [2]. But Voting Theory is based upon the assumption that we know what the options are, and inevitably the result of a vote is always selecting one alternative, among the many. And leave those who did not like the winning alternative unhappy with the result.

The amount of information that the citizens send to the government through voting each election is incredibly low. If we are able to chose between m candidates, each citizen is sending $\log_2(m)$ bits of information every few years. How could a government be able to represent correctly the desire of the citizens with such a tiny amount of information? But this represented correctly the amount of information that could be exchanged in the 18th century, when travel was done on horse, and modern democracies were designed. Now we are able to transmit a much broader amount of information. Apart from voting for our representatives, we have many other tools: from polls, to debates on television, to blogs, discussion boards, and wikis. Recently governments around the world have started to

E. Tambouris, A. Macintosh, and O. Glassey (Eds.): ePart 2010, LNCS 6229, pp. 13–25, 2010.

open up their data and become transparent to the scrutiny of the public [3, 4].
Also some government have started posting online the laws they are about to
implement, letting people comment on them [5]. All this is positive and permits
a much broader integration between the representatives and the represented.

But the politicians can ignore all this, and still the only moment when people
are directly affecting their government is during an election. And, although the
tool might have in the meantime progressed from a paper ballot into an electronic
form of voting, the essence of it hasn't changed. We are still only sending $\log_2(m)$
bits of information every election.

How could the citizen more directly participate in the governance process? We
are not suggesting here a form of direct democracy, in fact quite the opposite;
what we are trying to suggest in this paper is that our ability to design the
democracy of the 21st century suffers an endemic lack of imagination. Now that
we have a tool, the internet, that permits an instantaneous, and cheap, transfer
of information between the citizens and the governing body, we don't know how
to use it. We should go back to the basic idea behind dēmos-kratia, and rethink
the whole process through. What this paper wants to suggest is a fundamentally
new system. This by introducing two ideas which are not new in science, but are
new in political science...

2   Evolving and Selecting Ideas

2.1   Evolving

Our basic critique of Voting Theory is that by assuming that the alternatives
are easy to find out sets up the stage for its too limited results. Not only are
the people who decide these alternatives given an unbalanced amount of power
with respect to the voters, but also the best alternative that can be reached
is one which has been decided beforehand by them. What if there existed an
alternative solution to the problem at hand which has not yet been considered?
A solution which could aggregate a wide majority, or even a consensus. Finding
and agreeing on such solution would be a worthwhile goal of the integrated
system we are designing.

To do this we need to reframe the basic problem. Instead of finding the alternative among a finite set of options (thus asking a *closed* question: "which
among those alternatives would you prefer?"), we should look for the answer to
an *open* question: "what is the solution to this problem... ?". When we reframe
our question in this way, Voting Theory is not anymore the field to apply; we
should, instead, use Genetic Algorithms[6]. Genetic Algorithms (GA), which are
both a tool and the field that studies them, aim to look at the best solution in a
space of potential alternative solutions. This space can be very wide, sometimes
infinite, and it is assumed that not all possible solutions can be tested. The solution, instead, is found through further approximations. Each solution can be
tested at a small (but never null) cost. Through those tests the algorithm receives
a feedback on how well each solution satisfies the requirements that is trying to
meet (i.e. technically it calculates the *fitness* of the solution). Solutions that

behave poorly (have a low fitness) are discarded; good solutions (solutions with a high fitness) are retained and modified (technically *mutated* and *recombined* - in the interest of brevity we will consider both operations here as *mutations*), to generate new possible solutions. Two elements are important in this process: the production and the evaluation of the solutions. Usually in GAs the evaluation and the mutations are done in an automatic way. Automatically calculating the fitness of a solution to a question in a political context is not just an unsolved problem, but probably an unsolvable one too. Similarly given a solution, finding alternative similar solutions is equally challenging. This is maybe why no one has suggested using GA in a political context. Recently a new type of Genetic Algorithm was proposed: a Human Based Genetic Algorithm [7][8][9]. In such algorithm humans beings provide the fitness of a solution, and given a set of solutions provide alternative solutions. For such algorithm to succeed we need a semi-continuous dialogue between the participants and the computer. The computer asking for possible solutions from each participant, then, after collecting those solutions, presenting them to the participants again, asking them to evaluate them. This evaluation is then used by the computer to assess the fitness of the existing solutions, to decide which solutions should be discarded and which should be kept. The surviving solutions are then fed back to the participants, asking them to produce new solutions, mutating these surviving ones. To establish such process in a political context we would need a strong participation between the citizen and the government. Exactly what the internet permits, and what many citizens are now demanding!

To test these ideas the authors have set up a website where users can ask questions, and participate in finding the solution to the questions asked. We are going to show some of the results later.

2.2   Selecting

Which solutions should be maintained from one generation to the next? The trivial (and sub-optimal!) strategy would be to define how many solutions should be kept, in advance, and then sum up the votes that each solution receives. The top n solutions would then be copied to the next generation. We can either let people vote for one solution each, or vote for all the solutions they support. A number of problems arise with either of these strategies. If the participants are allowed to write their own proposals, and only vote for one solution, the temptation will be high for each person to just vote for their own solution. Also if the solution a person prefers has a low probability to be selected, a person might switch their vote to a less desired outcome, but an outcome where his vote has a higher chance to be useful. This leads to the behavior of *strategic voting*, voting in a way that does not represents the voter real desires, to let an acceptable outcome be the result of the voting process. A better solution is to let everybody vote for all the solutions they agree to, a form of voting called *approval voting*[10]. The problem with this form of voting is that if we let everybody vote for each possible solution, then similar solutions will be supported by a group of people of similar size (often comprised of the same people). Thus if we take

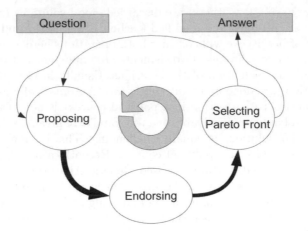

Fig. 1. Scheme of the genetic algorithm procedure. A question is asked. All the participants propose their answer. Then all the participants endorse the answers they support. Out of those proposals the Pareto Front is selected, and extracted. If those proposals achieve consensus, we have our answer. If not they are presented back to the community, asking the participants to be inspired by them to produce new proposals.

the n most popular solutions, they will probably be very similar, representing the same group of people. Instead people who did not agree with one of them might not agree with the others as well. Thus the resulting set of solutions will not represent the whole community. Instead a sub-community will be overrepresented while other participants will be totally ignored. In Voting Theory this is often considered an unavoidable evil. But if we are not aiming to find which among a set of choices is better, but we want to set up a process that eventually leads us to find a proposal that has the widest possible support, ignoring some participants means to loose important information.

The logic behind the idea of summing up the votes is that each person is equally important. But when we are summing up the votes we are also losing information. If we have n people selecting the proposal to support among m alternatives, each of them sends 1 message among 2^m possible, thus each citizen sends $\log_2(2^m) = m$ bits of information. And considering that we have n citizen that are voting we are sending $n * m$ bits of information. But how much information is received? When we sum up the votes we end up knowing for each proposal how many people approve it. And since we are permitting each person to vote for multiple proposals, then the amount of information that we have received for each proposal will be $\log_2(n)$. Considering that we know this for each of the m proposals, the total amount of information received will be $m \log_2(n)$. In other words by summing up the votes we drop information from $n * m$ to $m \log_2(n)$. What went wrong? By summing up the votes we are ignoring any information which correlates one proposal to another. In other words we ignore information of the kind: everybody who voted for proposal A, also voted for proposal B. But what would be the alternative?

Instead of using as fitness the sum of the votes that each proposal has received, we could consider fitness as a point in a multidimensional space. The number of dimensions will be the number of participants. The fitness will then be a boolean vector of size n, which we shall call the voting vector of the proposal. Such vector will have a 1 in the t position if the t participant has supported the proposal, and a 0 if not. A proposal that has reached consensus will be represented by a vector of all 1s. Then instead of selecting the proposal that has more votes (more 1s) we take the *Pareto Front* in this multidimensional space.

Pareto Fronts (PF) are particular subsets that are calculated starting from the concept of dominance. PF have been used in economy and in Multi-Criterion Decision Making[11]. Recently they have also been suggested as a tool in genetic algorithms and co-evolutionary learning[12]. To take the Pareto Front we must first define a function of dominance. We shall say that a proposal A *dominates* a proposal B if they have different voting vectors $v_A \neq v_B$, and in every dimension t, $v_A^t \geq v_B^t$. Since we have chosen to use only boolean vectors this is equivalent to saying that the set of people that support B must be a proper subset of the set of people that support A. Note that the procedure can be generalised, permitting each participant to evaluate each proposal by ranking it or evaluating each proposal by assigning it an integer. The Pareto Front will be the set of proposals that are not being dominated by any other proposal.

Let's look at some of the consequences of our selection choice: (1) the most popular proposal will always be in the Pareto Front; (2) for each participant at least one of the proposal he supports must be in the Pareto Front; as a corollary of (2) we have (3) each user who wants to have some particular proposal present in the Pareto Front must simply vote for only that proposal; but, vice-versa, (4) if a proposal is in the Pareto Front and is supported by only one person, that person cannot support any other proposal that is supported by any other participant. In other words nothing stops users to only vote for their own proposals to make sure they make it to the Pareto Front. But this asocial behavior will not go unspotted. Sometimes it is acceptable, (for example in the rare situation when a person really believes that their proposal is the only acceptable solution), but if repeated in time can lead to the other people ignoring that person and trying to reach a consensus without her.

Also note that we did not need to set the number of proposals that would be maintained from one generation to the other. This number is implicit in the definition of Pareto Front and will change from generation to generation. The only time a single proposal is selected is when everybody has voted for it. On the other hand, it is possible to have multiple solutions that all reach consensus if everybody votes for them. While keeping the Pareto Front unbounded might seem dangerous (what if too many proposals reach the next generation? Will the system explode?), recent results suggest that although no apparent limit is present, as long as the people vote following their values (and not in a random way), the Pareto Front will still be bounded. More about this in the Results section.

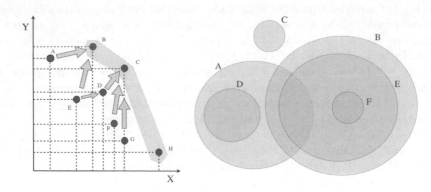

Fig. 2. Left Domination and Pareto Front in a 2 dimensional space. Each dot represents a possible solution. X and Y can either represent the Subjective Evaluation of those solutions by two participants or their Objective Evaluation (like it is being done in Multi-Criterion Decision Making[11, 15]). The Solutions B, C and H are not dominated by any other solution and thus represent the Pareto Front. **Right**. If the evaluation becomes boolean (support/ignore), then each solution can be represented as a set. Dominance becomes set inclusion, and the Pareto Front becomes the set of sets that are non dominated (in the image the sets A B, and C).

3   Testing the Idea

Applying those two ideas we coded a website, Vilfredo goes to Athens (available at http://vilfredo.org), to test them. The website permits the users to ask questions and participate in evolving proposals to the questions asked. From a formal point of view, once a question is asked it goes through a series of rounds called generations. Each generation is divided into a proposing phase and an evaluation phase. In the proposing phase the users are allowed to write their own proposals. In the evaluation phase they can evaluate all the proposals that have been submitted. This is done by clicking a button next to all the proposal each user likes, and ignoring the others. Thus there is no "I do not like" button. Ignored proposals are considered having being rejected. The Pareto Front of the proposal (as described above) is then extracted and presented to the users as representative of the whole community. If a consensus has been reached it is declared and the question is moved into the "solved questions" area. If instead a consensus has not been reached the users are invited to read the Pareto Front proposals and write new ones. In particular they are invited to try to bridge different ideas, and rewrite existent proposals, especially proposals they could not support, in a way they would be acceptable for them. Note that no further aid or limits are given to the participants, other than presenting them with a blank slate and the list of the previous Pareto Front. They can ignore those suggestion, as well as use them.

Testing the website we soon discovered that it was necessary to fine tune the process to allow the procedure to work better. We shall list here the elements which we found important, with an explanation on how they affected the procedure.

- During the proposing phase, proposals being written are not revealed to the participants. This prevents users from copying each other's ideas. While copying each other's ideas could be seen as a positive element, we want to make sure that the ideas in the Pareto Front are more likely to be used than others.
- During the evaluation phase, proposals are presented in an anonymous format. No information about the author is presented. This forces users to rely on the actual content of a proposal, without being able to support something out of trust with the author. And, more importantly, this gives the possibility for everybody to have their proposal evaluated on an equal ground.
- When the evaluation is over, all the information about the authorship and who supported which proposal is revealed. This permits users to see which participants are only voting for their own proposals. Interestingly, we observed that this behavior drastically diminished after this information was made public.

Soon the website was used to bootstrap its own creation, with participants discussing, proposing and voting on the features of the website itself. Although the website was public, it did not attract a huge attention, and as such the number of users that have registered is around a hundred (137 on the 16 of May 2010), and the number of different users that were participating at any one period of time, was less than 20. Many of the question did not attract a wide participation, ending up with only 2 or 3 participants agreeing on an answer. Discussing why this is so, goes beyond the scope of this paper. And of course further tests should be completed, possibly with the aid of workers in the psychology and sociological field to ascertain if the participants found the process satisfactory. For now we will instead focus on one the most popular question that was asked. The question was open to the public, but it was not publicised, which led to a very little turn over of participants during the process.

3.1   The Wall of Text Question

We shall now present an example of a question which was discussed: 'How should we handle the "wall of text" problem?'. The wall of text was the situation where a user proposal was so long that would slow down the process for everybody (since most people would wait to have read that proposal before voting any proposal). The question was presented and after 4 generations, and 61 proposals (of which 41 were original), the community reached a consensual agreement. It should be noted that although the process seemed fast, each generation took two weeks time, of which one week in proposing and one week in voting. So the final result took about two months to complete. The final result had an abstract and the main text consisted of three points (an excerpt is presented here for brevity, the full data can be seen at [13]):

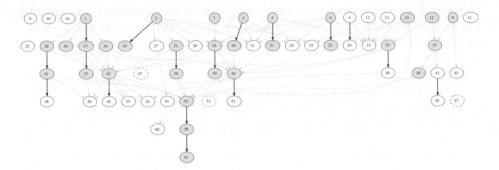

Fig. 3. Proposals submitted and voted in the "Wall of text" question. Sixty-one proposals were considered. After 4 generations a consensus was found. Each proposal is shown as a node. Proposals in the same generation are at the same height. Proposals that made it into the Pareto Front are copied to a new proposal in the next generation, and connected with a black arrow (making the actual number of original proposals to be 44). Grey arrows indicate a connection in the content (ideas that made it from one proposal to the next). Nodes with a dotted border are comments, (i.e. proposal not meant to be voted, but only presented by users to explain why a particular proposal is not acceptable. Making the actual number of real proposals 41). Dotted links represent a critique (the lower proposal criticize the higher proposal). By following the lines we can see that 29 proposals (with greyed background) out of 61 (or 19 out of 41) had their idea, or part of their idea, integrated in the final proposal.

1. Proposals longer than 1,000 characters require an abstract. Abstracts are hard-limited to 500 characters. (These numbers could be tweaked.)
2. Give visual feedback about the quality of writing of the proposal body, perhaps in the form of a bar across to top of the input box which contains a gradation from green to red. [...]Metrics for the difficulty score could include: SMOG score; Length of proposal - weighted heavily; Number of other proposals by same author on same question [...]; Possibly "readability-votes" by other users; Possibly others;
3. Proposals are presented in order of their difficulty score. [...] And we confront it with some of the proposals presented in the first generation (the number refers to the actual proposal in Fig 2): (1) Writing an abstract of the proposal. (2) Shorter proposals appear in the first places of a ranking. There are two new buttons: I understand, I don't understand. Negative understanding points sink the proposal in that ranking. (3) Prizes or reputation points for the succinct writer. (5) Rating systems. The idea being, that people will write more concisely to get a higher rating. (7) [...]include a Dismiss button with one or two reason options. Select Reason for dismissal: Spam; Too Long; Irrelevant; Difficult to understand. Main point would be to get feedback to [the] proposer. It could be used with or without limiting character input. (12) It's fine as it is. No limit should there be on the length of proposals! (15) Start playing with length limits. Try a very restrictive one, such as 500-1000 characters and see how burdensome it is.[...] We see how no simple voting could have produced such result: One user suggesting to

use 500 or 1000 characters limit; another to use an abstract; and a third to let proposals unbounded. The result included ideas from all three: proposals can be of any length (satisfying the third user), when they are of more than 1000 characters they need an abstract (thus satisfying the second user). Abstract which should not be longer than 500 characters (satisfying the first user). Note that the actual final proposal was much more complex as it had to satisfy more requirements.

4   Results

The main result that was observed was that the process worked better when the question asked was real and relevant. If the question was a test question, either unrealistic or such that the solution made no real difference in the life of the participants, it was harder to reach a consensus, the Pareto Front would be larger, people would get bored more easily and generally the result would just look random. When instead the question was real and relevant, the Pareto Front would never grow too much as participants would look for acceptable compromise between the winning proposals. From time to time the participants would try to recycle proposals that were eliminated, perhaps by integrating them inside winning proposals. Usually those actions were unsuccessful, but showed how the participants were trying to integrate their point of view inside the point of view of the community.

Researchers who work with Genetic Algorithms are used to running their experiments for a few hundred generations at a minimum. We could not run those experiments for such a long time. No willing volunteer would agree to participate. But in all the experiments that we made a consensus was found much sooner. Often after 3 or 4 generations. In particularly hard cases the consensus was reached after 10 or 11 generations. The answer to *which [what] is the meaning of life?* [14] could be found after only 6 generations (although the final solution was proposed on generation 4). The solution to the "wall of text" problem, presented above, needed 4 generations. And the result was unexpected by any of the participants, integrating elements from multiple people. Such good results hide a problem. When the result was hard to find, the participants would start to get bored, and often leave the question. Then the question would reach a smaller consensus. Rapid, but less meaningful. On the other hand we can assume that if the question was more important the participants would be less prone to leave. Leading to a situation where either they would find a consensus or they would eventually enter in a loop. We should discuss this last possible result in the Discussion Section.

4.1   The Subjective Pareto Front as a Subset of the Objective Pareto Front

An interesting question is: how would the system scale up? We are now going to present some mathematical results showing that under some basic assumptions, the size of the Pareto Front will be bounded, regardless of the number of people participating in the voting procedure. Let us assume that we have a question, with a number of diverse participants. We assume the participants will always vote according to their own subjective scale of values. We also assume that each person's value scale can be represented as a positive linear combination of some objective values that the participants share. In other words the participants share the same values but place different priorities upon them[1]. We can now map every proposal according to those objective values, and given any participant, we can associate to that participant a line R, linear combination of those objective values. Each user will then order all the proposals according to his values as points on the line R.

Definition 1. *Given a point A and a line $R : y = ax$, we shall define A_R, as the point where R intersects the perpendicular line that is passing through A. We shall also refer to A_{R_x} (A_{R_y}) as the x (y) co-ordinate of the A_R point.*

Now we need to formally define the Pareto Front with respect to the subjective values of the participants. To do this we start by defining the concept of dominance.

Definition 2. *Given two distinct lines R, S (with $R : y = ax$ and $S : y = bx$) with $a, b > 0$. And given two distinct points $A(a_x, a_y)$ and $B(b_x, b_y)$, we will say that A dominates B respect to (R, S) if $A_R \geq B_R$, and $A_S \geq B_S$ and we shall write it $A >_{(R,S)} B$.*

In the field of Multi-Criterion Decision Making where Pareto Fronts are commonly used[11], the standard form of dominance considered is with respect to a basis of coordinates, $(X, Y, \ldots)$. We too will say that a point A dominates a point B if $A >_{(X,Y)} B$

Definition 3. *The Pareto Front with respect to (R, S) will be the set of points that are non dominated respect to R and S.*

We need to prove that if two points $A(a_x, a_y)$ and $B(b_x, b_y)$ are in the Pareto Front with respect to the coordinates (X, Y), then they can be in the Pareto Front with respect to (R, S) (with $R : y = ax$ and $S : y = bx$) with $a, b > 0$. We shall call the Pareto Front with respect to the (X, Y) coordinates the *Objective Pareto Front*, while the Pareto Front with respect to (R, S) the *Subjective Pareto Front*. In other words we are trying to prove that the Subjective Pareto Front is contained in the Objective Pareto Front.

First we will start with an existing result from the field in Multi-Criterion Decision Making [11] [15].

---

[1] This might seem a too strong presupposition, but a simple example will convince us that it is not so. One of the political discussions that most strongly polarises public opinion is the discussion on abortion. Everywhere around the world the people divide in a pro-choice group and a pro-life group. But the people in both groups have the same values: they both believe in freedom (thus choice) and life. They just diverge on the priority. No one wants an abortion, if it can be avoided, and no one wants to be told what she must do.

Proposition 1. *Let A dominate B ($A >_{(X,Y)} B$) then given any line $R : y = ax$, A_R will be farther from the origin than B_R ($A_{R_x} > B_{R_x}$ and $A_{R_y} > B_{R_y}$).*

Proof. Let us calculate A_{R_x}. To do this we calculate the line S perpendicular to R, and passing through A. Such line will be: $S = -\frac{1}{a}x + e$ and $A_{R_x} = a * ay + ax$. Thus $B_{R_x} = a * by + bx$. Now we need to prove that $A_{R_x} > B_{R_x}$. That is: $a * a_y + a_x > a * b_y + b_x$ but this is trivial since $a > 0$ and from the fact that $A > B$ we know that either (1) $ay > by$ and $ax = bx$ or (2) $ay = by$ and $ax > bx$ or (3) $ay > by$ and $ax > bx$. In all three cases $A_{R_x} > B_{R_x}$. And since $A_{R_y} = a^2 * ay + a * ax$ and $B_{R_y} = a^2 * by + a * bx$ then $A_{R_y} > B_{R_y}$ □

Now we want to prove that if a point is in the Subjective Pareto Front it must be in the Objective Pareto Front.

Proposition 2. *Let A be a point in the Subjective Pareto Front then given two lines R, S; A is in the Objective Pareto Front.*

Proof. The Thesis is equivalent to saying that if A is not in the Objective Pareto Front, it cannot be in the Subjective Pareto Front. Or, in other words, if it is being dominated with respect to (X, Y) it will also be dominated according to (R, S). Without loss of generality let us consider two distinct points A, B. We want to prove that if $A >_{(X,Y)} B$, then $A >_{(R,S)} B$. But from Proposition 1, we know that $A_{R_x} > B_{R_x}$, and $A_{S_x} > B_{S_x}$. Thus the thesis.   □

Since the Subjective Pareto Front is a subset of the Objective Pareto Front, having more participants will not lead to an unbound growth of the Pareto Front, but just to a better approximation of the objective one. Which is, in itself, a positive result. In passing we note that this result also implies that when we need to estimate an Objective Pareto Front (a common occurrence in Multi-Criterion Decision Making [15]) we can simply ask an educated group of people to evaluate the options at hand, according to their personal preferences. And the result should naturally approximate the Objective Pareto Front.

5 Discussion

Two questions should be considered: how would such a system scale up and what should be done if a consensus is not found. Regarding the latter, we would suggest that an evolutionary system should be used as a first means trying to reach consensus on an issue. If this fails, the partial results (i.e. the final Pareto Front) should be voted on in a more traditional way. But yet in a way that permits the participants to express multiple choices, like any Condorcet method. In this option still the initial evolutionary process would not go lost, as it has helped finding a set of optimal solution among which to chose.

But how much could such a system scale up and still be practical? Of course much work needs to be done in this regard. In the Results section we have shown how the Pareto Front will generally be bounded. Still the system might explode due to the number of proposals presented by the people. In our experience we noticed that it is always easier to get people to vote for proposal made by others then to write your own proposals. Thus we do expect the number of proposals to grow at a slower rate than the number of participants. But how much slower? In any case there will be a point where it will not be possible for everybody to evaluate the proposals from everybody else. But still the system could be implemented by distributing it upon a graph, with each node being a separate, parallel, genetic algorithm, and winning solution spreading among nodes. Also, even without solving the scaling problem the system could be used to let small to medium communities self-govern. Considering that probably less than 1 in 20 people will propose something, a community of a 1000 people could use the system in its current format. Also it could be used as a very democratic way to discuss something in a context where each participant's opinion is very important. For example, what would have happened if at the *2009 United Nations Climate Change Conference*, instead of having a more traditional voting system we had a Pareto Human Based Genetic Algorithm, with each nation being a participant? Surely no one would have protested that the discussion was being held in a non-democratic way.

Finally, we would like to point out how the system presented can be used in a different context all together, for example as basis for collaborative editing of a document, but that's another story.

6   Conclusions

We investigated an alternative way to reach an agreement on an open question. We looked at this as a possible aid in the decision making process, possibly for an e-government system. In our investigation we coded for a website where users can ask open questions and try to reach a consensus over them. In alternate phases each user can propose answers to the questions posed, or chose which answers he agrees on. By selecting the Pareto Front of the approved answers we extract a subset of the answers presented that fully represents the community. If no answer has reached unanimity, the Pareto Front is offered back to the community as an inspiration to write new proposals. Although the users are invited to try to integrate and bridge the proposals in the Pareto Front, no limit is posed over what each user can suggest. We present a trial case of the website on a particular question, and showed how the different proposals build up to generate an final answer that everybody could approve. This was done through 4 generations, each divided into a proposing and a voting phase. More questions were tested, but few received the participation necessary to be considered as test cases of how the algorithm would behave. We also investigated the mathematics behind the extraction of a Pareto Front based on subjective evaluations of proposals and found under reasonable assumptions this to approximate the Pareto Front that would be extracted under an objective evaluation of such proposals. Thus suggesting that such subjective Pareto Front would not explode as the number of users increase. All together the algorithm proposed showed to be a possible alternative to more traditional forms of voting to reach an agreement on a solution. It's drawback seem to be how the increased participation risks lowering the number of people willing to participate...

References

1. Merriam Webster online dictionary, page (2010), http://www.merriam-webster. com/dictionary/democracy (accessed March 3, 2010)
2. Taylor, A., Pacelli, A.: Mathematics and Politics: Strategy, Voting, Power and Proof. Springer Book, Heidelberg (2008)
3. Data gov., http://www.data.gov/ (accessed March 03, 2010)
4. Data.gov.uk, http://data.gov.uk/ (accessed March 03, 2010)
5. Goulandris, V.: Opengov.gr: The first 120 days of e-deliberation, http://onlinepolitics.wordpress.com/2010/02/22/ opengovgr-first-120-days-e-deliberation/ (accessed January 03, 2010)
6. Holland, J.H.: Adaptation in natural and artificial systems. In: An introductory analysis with applications to biology, control, and artificial intelligence. University of Michigan Press, Ann Arbor (1975)
7. Kosorukoff, A.: Human based genetic algorithm. In: IEEE International Conference on Systems (2001)
8. Defaweux, A., Grosche, T., Karapatsiou, M., Moraglio, A., Shenfield, A.: Automated Concept Evolution. Technical Report Vrije Universiteit Brussel, Belgium (2003)
9. Speroni di Fenizio, P., Anderson, C.: Using Pareto Front for a Consensus Building, Human Based, Genetic Algorithm. In: Proceedings of the European Conference of Artificial Life (2009)
10. Brams, S., Fishburn, P.: Approval Voting. Springer, Heidelberg (2007)
11. Ehrgott, M.: Multicriteria optimization. Springer, Heidelberg (2005)
12. Sevan, G., Ficici Jordan, B., Pareto, P.: Optimality in Coevolutionary Learning. In: Kelemen, J., Sosík, P. (eds.) ECAL 2001. LNCS (LNAI), vol. 2159. Springer, Heidelberg (2001)
13. Vilfredo goes to Athens. How should we handle the "wall of text" problem?, http://vilfredo.org/viewhistoryofquestion.php?q=67&room=Vilfredo (accessed February 28, 2010)
14. Vilfredo goes to Athens. Which is the meaning of Life?, http://vilfredo.org/ viewhistoryofquestion.php?q=14 (accessed March 03, 2010)
15. Triantaphyllou, E.: Multi-Criteria Decision Making Methods: A Comparative Study. Kluwer Academic Publishers, Boston (2000)

The Use of Expressives in Online Political Talk: Impeding or Facilitating the Normative Goals of Deliberation?

Todd Graham

University of Groningen, Department of Journalism Studies and Media, Oude Kijk in 't
Jatstraat 26, 9712 EK Groningen, The Netherlands
t.s.graham@rug.nl

Abstract. Net-based public sphere researchers have questioned whether the
internet presents the public sphere with a new opportunity for the development
of public spaces where free, equal and open deliberation among citizens can
flourish. However, much of the research has operationalized a formal notion of
deliberation thereby neglecting the expressive nature of everyday political
talk. This study moved beyond a formal notion by also investigating the use of
expressives within *The Guardian* (UK) political discussion forum. A content
analysis was employed as the primary instrument for examination. Additional
textual analyses were conducted on the use of expressives. The findings suggest
that with the exception of humour expressives tended to impede political talk
rather than facilitating it.

Keywords: Online Deliberation, Political Talk, Public Sphere, Discussion
Forum.

1   Introduction

There has been much debate concerning the internet's ability to extend the public
sphere. Much of it has focused on the potential of the internet in cultivating a public
sphere where free, equal and open communication, deliberation and exchange of
information among citizens can flourish. As a result, there has been a rise in the
number of net-based public sphere research projects, which utilize public sphere
ideals as a means of evaluating online communicative spaces.

Net-based public sphere researchers have studied online deliberation in numerous
ways within a variety of contexts from news media message boards and Usenet
newsgroups to governmentally sponsored forums. However, most studies have
operationalized a formal notion of deliberation e.g. rationality via argumentation.
Given that much of the research here focuses on everyday political talk, privileging a
formal notion neglects the expressive nature of such talk. Indeed, expressives are
inherent to political talk. Moreover, political talk is not only about e.g. argumentation
but it is also about everyday citizens talking to each other in ways that make sense to
them. This discussion is not a new one; politics has always been emotional. However,
political communication scholars and net-based public sphere researchers specifically

E. Tambouris, A. Macintosh, and O. Glassey (Eds.): ePart 2010, LNCS 6229, pp. 26–41, 2010.

still have tended neglect the role of expressives in political communication, particularly within deliberation. Neglecting expressives is not an option if our aim is to provide a better understanding of how people talk politics or if it is to assess its democratic value.

The aim of this article then is to move beyond a formal notion of deliberation by also examining the role of expressive within political talk. The focus is on how participants talk politics in online informal discussion forums. By *informal*, I am referring to those spaces that are not bound to any formal predetermined agendas such as e-consultations, but rather to forums whose primary purpose is to provide simply a communicative space for talk. By political *talk*, I am referring to everyday, informal, political conversation conducted freely between participants in these spaces, which is often spontaneous and lacks any purpose outside the purpose of talk for talk sake, representing the practical communicative form of communicative action [1, p. 327]. It is through this type of talk whereby citizens achieve mutual understanding about the self and each other, and it represents the fundamental ingredient of the public sphere.

The purpose first is a normative one; it is to examine the democratic quality of the communicative practices of participants within an online political discussion forum in light of the public sphere. It is also to move beyond a formal notion of deliberation by providing a more accurate account of how people actually talk politics in those discussions, and how humour, emotional comments and acknowledgements interact and influence the more 'traditional' elements of deliberation. Consequently, I present the following two research questions: To what extent do the communicative practices of online political discussions satisfy the normative conditions of the process of deliberation of the public sphere; and what role do expressives play within online political talk and in relation to the normative conditions of deliberation? Together, the answers to these questions present a more comprehensive account of online political talk. They seek not only to offer insight into the *quality* of such talk, but also to provide a better understanding of its *expressive* nature.

2 The Normative Conditions of the Process of Deliberation

Assessing the democratic value of political talk requires normative criteria of the public sphere. Net-based public sphere researchers have been heavily influenced by the work of Habermas. Though some have constructed different aspects of his theory of communicative rationality and the public sphere, a thorough specification is required. Thus, I offer a set of public sphere criteria: the normative conditions of the process of deliberation.[1]

Through his pragmatic analysis of everyday conversation, Habermas argues that when participants take up communicative rationality, they refer to several idealizing presuppositions. Drawing from these [1, 3, 4], six conditions are distinguished.[2] Together they provide the necessary conditions for achieving understanding during the course of political talk by placing both structural and dispositional requirements on the communicative form, process and participant.

---

[1] For a detailed account, see Graham [2].

[2] There are 11; structural autonomy and equality, discursive equality and freedom, and sincerity have been omitted due to scope of this chapter.

Rational-critical debate requires that participants provide reasoned claims, which are critically reflected upon. Such an exchange requires a sufficient level of *coherence* and *continuity*; participants should stay on the topic of discussion until understanding or some form of agreement is achieved as opposed to withdrawing. Such a process demands three dispositional requirements, three levels of achieving mutual under-standing. *Reciprocity* represents the first level. It requires that participants listen and respond to each other's questions and arguments. However, reciprocity alone does not satisfy the process; *reflexivity* is required. Reflexivity is the internal process of reflecting another participant's position against one's own. *Empathy* represents the final level of understanding. The process of deliberation requires an empathic perspective taking in which we not only seek to understand intellectually the position of the other, but we also seek to conceptualize empathically, both cognitively and *affectively*,[3] how others would be affected by the issue under discussion.

3 Expressives and Deliberation

Some democratic theorists maintain that rational discourse needs to be broadened, allowing for communicative forms such as greeting, gossip, rhetoric and storytelling [5, 6]. Others have argued that emotions and humour are essential to any notion of good deliberation [7, 8]. Indeed, when people talk politics, they not only draw from their cognitive and rational capacities, but they also draw on their emotions. It would be hard to imagine people engaging in political talk if their emotions were not there to provoke them to do so. However, past studies have tended to neglect the role of expressives. Those that do address them only identify the type and frequency of their use [9], and do little in way of providing insight into the role they play in political talk. Thus, in the analysis that follows, the use of expressives is investigated with particular attention being paid to the role they play in relation to the normative conditions. By expressives, I am referring to humour, emotional comments and acknowledgements. Humour represents complex emotional speech acts that excite and amuse for instance jokes and wisecracks. Emotional comments are speech acts that express one's feelings or attitude, while acknowledgements represent speech acts that acknowledge the presence, departure or conversational action of another person, such as greeting, thanking and complementing.

4 Methods

The forum selected was hosted by the British newspaper *The Guardian*. The Guard-ian's political talkboard is one of the most popular and oldest online communicative spaces dedicated to political talk in the UK. It hosts a multitude of participants and discussions on a diverse range of national, European and international political topics. The data gathered consisted of the individual postings and the threads in which they were situated. The selection of the data was based on a one-month period and was

---

[3] Habermas focuses on the former, the cognitive process of 'ideal role taking' [4, pp. 228--230].

taken from the sub-forum *Inside Britain*, which at the time was the most active forum.[4] The sample consisted of 30 threads containing 1215 postings.

The sample was subjected to three progressive phases of coding. Graham's [10] coding scheme, which was developed as a means of systematically describing and assessing political talk, was used. The scheme also moved beyond a formal notion of deliberation and coded for the use expressives. During the first phase, the coding categories were divided into three groups, which consisted of various types of reasoned claims, non-reasoned claims and expressive and commissive speech acts. The unit of analysis during this phase was the individual message. Once all messages were coded, phase two of the scheme began; messages that provided reasoned claims were advanced. During this phase, the coding categories were divided into two groups: *evidence type* and *argument style*. Messages were first coded for the type of evidence used, after which, selected messages were coded again for argument style. The unit of analysis during this phase was the argument. During the final phase, all messages were coded *communicative empathy*. The unit of analysis here was the individual message. For all three phases, the context unit of analysis was the discussion thread; the relationships between the messages within a single thread were analyzed. For detailed account of the individual coding categories, the coding scheme and an operationalization of the normative conditions see Graham [10, pp. 23--32].

Regarding expressives, the aim was to see how they were used during political talk and whether they tended to *facilitate* or *impede* deliberation. The above analysis represented only the first step; additional textual analyses on the use of expressives were conducted. Specifically, several separate in-depth readings on the use of expressives for each were carried out with particular attention being paid to indentifying the particular type, analyzing the social structure and examining their use in relation to the normative conditions. In each case, the selected material was read, re-read and worked through (see Graham [2, pp. 61--63] for a detailed account).

5   Talking Politics in the Guardian

Rational-critical debate requires that the discussions in part be guided by rationality and critical reflection. Regarding rationality, arguments are preferred over assertions. As Table 1 shows, there were 756 claims made by Guardian participants. Out of these claims, 84% were reasoned, which suggests that providing reasons with claims was the norm. In terms of postings, nearly half provided arguments, while only 10% contained assertions. As the results suggest, the exchange of claims (arguments and assertions), which represented approximately 59% of the postings, was the guiding communicative form. Table 1 also shows the level of disagreement and critical reflection. First, the level of disagreement was substantially higher than the level of agreement. Approximately 46% of the total claims represented some form of disagreement, while only 12% were in the form of agreement. However, disagreeing is not always accompanied by critical reflection. The level of rebuttals and refutes, on the other hand, is an indication of this. Approximately 41% of all claims (25% of the postings) represented rebuttals and refutes.

---

[4] The data was taken from all those threads originating in May 2006 and was retrieved in July 2006 at: http://politicstalk.guardian.co.uk/WebX?14@@.ee80025

Coherence requires that participants stick to the topic of discussion. The discussion threads were first analyzed and then categorized into lines of discussion. The level of coherence was established by determining the number of topic changes, and more importantly, the relevance of those changes. Overall, there were 110 lines of discussion within the Guardian's 30 threads. Participants did not diverge at all from the topic of discussion within six of these threads. That said, within the remaining 24, there were 39 lines of discussion, which consisted of only 159 postings, coded as off the topic of discussion. In other words, 87% of the postings were coherent.

Continuity requires that the discussions continue until understanding or some form of agreement is achieved as opposed to withdrawing. It was analyzed from two angles: the level of extended debate and convergence. The level of extended debate was measured via the presence of *strong-strings*. Ideally, extended debate should consist of counter-rebuttal-refute exchanges with rebuttals and refutes representing a substantial portion of those exchanges. There were 54 strong-strings. The average number was 13 with the largest totalling 42 claims. Moreover, 74% of all claims were involved in extended debate; this represented 44% of the postings. Furthermore, 89% of these claims were reasoned, and a majority came in the form of rebuttals and refutes, indicating the rational and critical nature of these exchanges.

The second indicator of continuity was convergence. Convergence represents the level of agreement achieved during the course of political talk. It was examined by coding the discussions for commissive speech acts. There were 48 commissives posted within the Guardian, representing four percent of the postings. Convergence was assessed by comparing the number of commissives with the number of lines of discussion. Ideally, a line of discussion should end in convergence. The Guardian sample consisted of 30 threads, which contained 66 coherent lines of discussion. The average number of commissives per line of discussion was 0.73. Moreover, 29% these lines (or 19 lines) contained at least one commissive. Finally, the analysis revealed that extended debate was an important ingredient in achieving convergence. In particular, 90% of commissives were a product of strong-strings exchanges.

Reciprocity requires that participants read and respond to each other's posts. In the past, this has often been assessed by determining the level of replies. However, this measurement is inadequate because it neglects the social structure of the discussions. Consequently, the level of reciprocity was assessed by determining and combining a reply percentage indicator with a degree of centralization measurement.[5] The data from both measurements for each of the 30 threads was plotted along a double axis matrix in order to assess the level of reciprocity. As Figure 1 shows, the level of replies was high. All but five threads had a reply percentage indicator of $\geq 75\%$. The percentage of replies for the whole sample was at 84%. In terms of the degree of centralization, the measurement is set on a scale of zero to one with zero representing the ideal decentralized thread and one the ideal centralized thread.

First, six of the threads were moderately to highly centralized (threads $\geq .500$). These threads resembled more a one-to-many or many-to one type of discussion rather than a web of interactions. Second, 16 threads were moderately decentralized

---

[5] The analysis is based on De Nooy et alt. [11, p. 126] degree of centralization measurement.

Table 1. The Guardian's Claim Type Usage Overview

		Claim type											
		Reasoned claims						Non-reasoned claims						Total
		Initial	Counter	Rebuttal	Refute	Affirmation	Total	Initial	Counter	Rebuttal	Refute	Affirmation	Total	
Claims[a]	Frequency	22	232	192	118	67	631	8	54	24	14	26	126	756
	% of claims	3	31	25	16	9	84	1	7	3	2	3	16	100
Postings[b]	Frequency	22	231	192	118	67	598	8	53	24	14	26	125	719
	% of postings	2	19	16	10	6	49	1	4	2	1	2	10	59

Note. A posting containing more than one of the same claim type were only counted once.

[a] n = 756 claims.

[b] n = 1215 postings.

(threads between .250 and .500).[6] Though there are still several core participants in these threads, the connections are more dispersed. Finally, eight threads were highly decentralized (threads ≤ .250). The connections between participants here were distributed more equally.

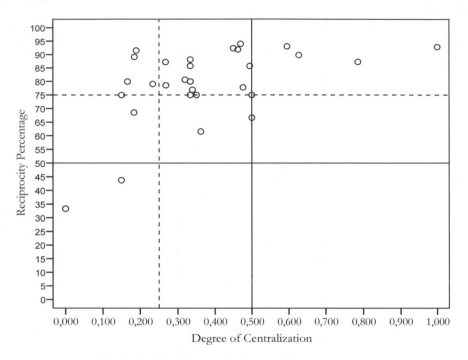

Fig. 1. The Guardian's web of reciprocity matrix results

Those threads that fell within the top left quadrant of Figure 1, the strong decentralized web quadrant, are considered to have a moderate to high level of reciprocity. Twenty-two of the 30 threads fell within this quadrant. In order to make a sharper distinction, a second set of criteria was added, represented by the dotted lines, as a means of distinguishing between those threads possessing moderate with those containing high levels of reciprocity. As is shown, there were five threads, which had a strong, highly decentralized web of interactions, in other words, an ideal level of reciprocity (threads ≥ 75% and ≤ .250). With the exception of two threads, the remaining 15 in this quadrant had a strong, moderately decentralized web of interactions, in other words, a moderately high level of reciprocity (threads ≥ 75% and between .250 and .500).

Reflexivity requires that participants reflect another participant's argument against their own. The first step in determining the level of reflexivity is to discover the type and level of evidence use because in order to relate evidence to one's own argument or an opposing argument a participant must know and to some extent understand the

---

[6] Two threads received identical scores (.333 and 75%). In the figure, they appear as one.

opposing position. There were four types of evidence identified, which were examples (43%), facts/sources (23%), comparisons (23%) and experiences (11%). Regarding the level of evidence, 43% of all reasoned claims contained supporting evidence. Rebuttals contained the highest level at half, while affirmations contained the lowest level with a third. The findings also revealed that when participants criticized opposing claims, they used supporting evidence more frequently than when they provided new, alternative or supporting arguments. However, determining the level of evidence represents only the first step in examining reflexivity. In order to determine the level of reflexivity, arguments were subject to the four criteria. When a posting or series of postings (1) provided a reasoned initial or counter claim; (2) used evidence to support that claim; (3) was responsive to challenges by providing rebuttals and refutes; (4) and provided evidence in support of that defence or challenge, they were coded as part of a reflexive argument.

There were 32 reflexive arguments consisting of 192 postings (16% of postings). Twenty-three participants were responsible for these exchanges (16% of participants). The average number of a reflexive argument was six postings. Overall, 27% of all arguments (169 arguments) were coded as reflexive. Moreover, 93% of reflexive arguments were part of strong-string exchanges or 28% of strong-string claims were reflexive, suggesting the importance of extended critical debate regarding reflexivity. The results also suggest a relationship between reflexive arguments and convergence. It seems that reflexivity, in addition to extended debate, was another important ingredient in achieving convergence. In particular, 52% of all commissives were engaged in and posted by those participants who provided reflexive arguments. The results become more revealing when all commissives, not just those posted by one of the 23 participants, are included. This reveals that 81% of all commissives occurred during reflexive exchanges.

Since deliberation is a social process, it is important that participants convey their empathetic considerations. Consequently, postings were examined for *communicative empathy*. Guardian participants rarely engaged in empathetic exchanges. In particular, there were only eight postings coded as communicative empathy. However, all eight postings were a part or a product of reflexive exchanges.

6 The Use of Expressives

Expressive speech acts appeared in 34% of the postings. The most common expressive was humour. It accounted for 43% of expressives and appeared in 15% of the postings. Overall, the analysis revealed three notable aspects on the use of humour: (1) its social function, (2) its social structure and (3) its relationship with certain variables of deliberation. The first aspect of humour was the way in which it was used. For example, humour may be used for social bonding, to express frustration and anger towards authority, criticize another or to reinforce stereotypes [12, 13]. In the Guardian, participants used humour for multiple and a variety of functions. That said, the aim here was not to provide a detailed breakdown of all the different uses, but rather, it was to detect any persistent patterns/general trends in the use of humour. There were several trends identified: participants tended to use humour to entertain; to criticize, assess or provoke thought; and/or to express hostility, anger or offence.

The most common pattern in the use of humour was *to entertain*. Humour here usually came in the form of wisecracks, jokes, sarcasm and banter.[7] There were two focuses of humour under 'to entertain'. First, humour here often focused on making fun of politicians and the Labour government in general. It usually was accompanied by malicious delight. Moreover, it tended to be less constructive in relation to the issue under discussion and more oriented towards 'having a laugh' at the expense of the subject in question. Second, a substantial portion of humour under 'to entertain' focused on good-natured teasing and the exchange of witty remarks between and about participants in the form of banter. This sort of good-natured exchange was quite common representing 65 of the 186 humorous comments. Though banter tended to create an atmosphere of playfulness, it often led the discussions off the topic. Nearly 70% of these exchanges were off the topic.

The second most common pattern was *to criticize, assess or provoke thought*. Humour has a critical function in political talk, the function of questioning, criticizing and assessing politicians, government or society in general. The participants of the Guardian used humour to do just this. The use of humour here usually came in the form of satire via the use of irony, sarcasm, parody, comparison and analogy, as the postings below illustrate:[8]

Henry: All of you old enough to remember this classic Dire Straits 80s track will appreciate that it has lost nothing of its meaning over the two decades since its original release. Despite demotion, Prescott strangely keeps his salary and perks and his choice of parliamentary skirt.
John: That ain't working, that's the way you do it, Set your own pension when you're an MP, That ain't working, that's the way you screw it, When you get caught with the secretary
Henry: Not bad, but what we need is one of those dynamic 80s power and might tracks with some really pithy and topical lyrics showing the lack of difference between Thatcherism and NuLabourism. <...sits scratching head....>
John: Look at them NuLabs, that's the way they do it, Pretending that they're not really Tories, Look at those Blairites, pretending it's the third way, Privatising hospitals and tuition fees
Richard: Let's go further back - Genesis, Selling England by the Pound.

In this thread, participants used satire via parody to criticize and assess the Labour Government. Unlike above, humour here was usually supportive and constructive to both individual arguments and to the topic of discussion.

The final pattern in the use of humour was *to express hostility, anger or offence*. This use of humour here usually came in the form of wisecracks, jokes, repartee and sarcasm. Moreover, it tended to be vulgar, offensive and usually contributed little to the discussion constructively. Rather, it often led to degrading exchanges, as the postings below show:

Charles: If Tony Blair was blown apart by a suicide bomber, I'd be over the moon and pay for drinks all around.

---

[7] The analysis is based on Shibles [13] taxonomy of humour.
[8] Forum identities have been replaced with invented ones.

Elizabeth: And no doubt you claim the moral high ground in anti-war debates. Charming.
Charles: There'd be no room on that moral high ground, [Elizabeth]. Not with Blair on top and you groupies licking his shitty arse.

In this example, a debate on the Iraq War turns into an exchange of degrading remarks when Charles, in several postings, begins to us vulgar wisecracks, sarcasm and jokes to express his anger and hostility towards Tony Blair, the British public and finally towards his fellow participants. Eventually, Elizabeth and other participants begin to take offence to Charles comments and reply accordingly.

The second aspect of humour was its social structure. As illustrated above, humour invites more humour. When a participant posted a joke, for example, it usually ignited a string of humorous comments; it was contagious. Humour here tended to stir more humour fostering lengthy exchanges or what may be called *humour fests*. Out of the 186 postings coded as humour, 86% or 160 postings were involved in humour fests. There were 32 fests. The average number was five with the largest totalling 16 postings.

The final aspect of humour was its relationship with certain variables of deliberation. As mentioned earlier, humour was used to criticize and assess politicians, government and society in general. In particular, participants used humour deliberately as a means of expressing and supporting their arguments or what may be called *rational humour*, as the posting by Mary below demonstrates:

Mary: [Edward] that news about the need Lord Kinnock being drafted in to mediate between No. 10 & 11 is quite quite barmy. They are supposed to be leaders. Instead, it's like warring schoolchildren using intermediaries,
  "Neil, tell Gordon I'm not talking to him."
  "Neil, tell Tony he's not worth talking to, he's finished here, his name is mud."
  "Neil, tell Gordon I'm not setting a date, ner ner ner ner ner."

In this thread, participants were discussing the turmoil within the Labour Party. In this posting, Mary uses humour to expose the childish behaviour taking place between Tony Blair and Gordon Brown. Her humorous skit, which is used deliberately to stress and support her argument, serves as supporting evidence (a supposed example) to her claim. Rational humour represented slightly more than a third of humorous comments (63 comments) and nearly 10% of all reasoned claims.

Humour, however, did not always contribute constructively to a discussion. First, as mentioned above, humour often led discussions off the topic; 38% of humorous comments were off the topic of discussion. A participant would post a joke and a humour fest would ensue, leading discussions off the topic. In these cases, humour acted more as a distraction. Second, though the number of degrading comments was low (85 postings), when they did occur, humour played a significant role in fostering them; nearly one third of all degrading comments were humorous or a response to humour. Humour used to express anger and hostility was the primary culprit here. As the above postings demonstrated, it often led to degrading.

The second most frequent expressive used was emotional comments, accounting for 29% of expressives and appearing in 11% of the postings. Overall, the analysis revealed three notable aspects on the use of emotions: (1) their type; (2) their social structure; and (3) their relationship with certain variables of deliberation. Expressing negative emotions was the norm. In particular, anger was the most frequent emotion expressed; 79% of emotional comments expressed some form of anger.[9] Anger here was conveyed mostly through statements of disgust, irritation, rage and exasperation.

The second aspect of emotional comments was their social structure. Similar to humour, but to a lesser degree, emotional comments fuelled more comments that were emotional in what can be called *rant sessions*. These were lengthy exchanges where participants vented their anger towards politicians in particular and the Labour Government in general. These types of exchanges were often raw and vulgar. Moreover, they tended to be polarized; they ranted together not at each other. Out of the 129 postings coded as emotional comments, 54 were involved in rant sessions. There were six sessions. The average number was nine with the largest totalling 22 postings.

The final aspect of emotional comments was their relationship with certain variables of deliberation. First, when participants expressed emotions, they were usually used in conjunction with arguments; 65% of all emotional comments were expressed via a participant's argument, or put differently, 13% of all arguments were emotional. Though emotions were used in a variety of ways within arguments, given the intense anger expressed overall, there was a tendency for these types of arguments to be abrasive and crude at times. However, these types of arguments were not ignored. Only two were neglected by fellow participants; arguments that used emotions were reciprocated. Finally, emotional comments played an important role in relation to discursive equality. Thirty-one percent of all emotional comments were used in a degrading way or 48% of all degrading comments expressed emotions.

The final expressive was acknowledgements. They accounted for 28% of expressives and appeared in 10% of the postings. There were five types of acknowledgements identified: complimenting (54%), greeting (24%), thanking (13%), apologizing (8%) and condoling (1%). Complementing was the most common acknowledgement and tended to be directed towards another's argument or position in general. Participants commonly used statements such as, "nice post", "good point", "well said", "good analysis" and "good defence". However, participants rarely complimented a participant on an opposing side of an argument; complimenting was polarized. Most complements were given in-house, between those on the same side of an argument. Participants on opposing sides of a discussion simply avoided complementing the substances of opposing claims.

7 Assessing Political Talk: The Normative Analysis

To what extent did the Guardian satisfy the normative conditions of the process of deliberation of the public sphere? Overall, the Guardian did well in light of the normative conditions. In particular, the level of rationality, critical reflection, coherence, extended debate, reciprocity, and reflexivity were moderately high to high. However, the level of convergence and communicative empathy fell well short of the normative conditions. The first condition, *rational-critical debate*, has been one of the

---

[9] It is based on Shaver's et alt. [14] categorization of primary and secondary emotions.

most common conditions of deliberation employed by past studies. The research suggests high levels of rational-critical debate within a variety of forum types, structures and contexts [9, 15, 16, 17, 18, 19, 20]. The results from the Guardian are consistent with these findings. The exchange of claims represented the guiding communicative form, which was overwhelmingly rational and regularly critical in nature, thus satisfying the normative condition.

Regarding *coherence*, research suggests directly or indirectly relatively coherent political talk [16, 18, 20] within online forums, particularly governmentally sponsored forums. The Guardian results are consistent with this, and more importantly, suggest that coherent discussions do not exclusively occur in governmentally sponsored and/or strictly moderated forums. Overall, the level of coherence was high indicating that participants regularly stuck to the topic of discussion.

Continuity was assessed by determining both the level of extend debate and convergence. Regarding the former, the analysis revealed that extend-critical debate on the issues was the norm. However, this is inconsistent with past studies, which suggest that extended debate on a single topic is uncommon [19, 21]. One possible explanation is that these studies relied upon observations rather than any systematic operationalization of extended debate as the one conducted here. There does however seem to be a link with Beierle's [22] survey research, which suggests that participants develop a sense of responsibility to participate during the course of online discussion. It seems that to a certain extent this was the case in the Guardian. In terms of convergence, the few studies available all suggest directly or indirectly that online discussions rarely achieve acts of convergence [17, 18, 22, 23]. The results from the Guardian are consistent with these findings. In particular, less than a third of the lines of discussion ended in some form of agreement. Rather, Guardian participants typically withdrew from the discussions.

Regarding *reciprocity*, much of the literature reveals that for a variety of forum types, structures and contexts high levels of reciprocity [9, 16, 18, 20, 21, 22]. The results from the Guardian are consistent with these findings. In particular, the percentage of replies was high. However, such an approach neglects the social structure of the threads. Therefore, unlike these studies, the reply percentage indicator measurement was combined with a degree of centralization measurement as a means of providing a more comprehensive indicator. The combined analysis found that a substantial portion of threads maintain a high level of decentralized social interaction, indicating that a web of reciprocity was the norm.

Reflexivity was assessed by first determining the level of evidence use and then the level of reflexive exchanges. Overall, the level of evidence use within the Guardian was substantial with close to half of all arguments providing evidence in support of their claims. Regarding the latter, the results suggest that a substantial portion of arguments were involved in reflexive exchanges, which is inline with past studies [9, 16, 18, 24].

Regarding *empathy*, the results revealed that participants simply did not engage in empathetic exchange, falling well short of the condition. One possible explanation here may have something to do with the communicative atmosphere. The Guardian forum seemed to foster a competitive communicative environment. For example, when participants did degrade, curb and/or questioned another participant's sincerity, they tended to be personal, aggressive and even malicious at times. This along with the use of expressives, e.g. acknowledgements, seemed to foster a communicative environment where achieving deeper levels of understanding and/or acts of agreement were rare.

8   Beyond the Normative Conditions of Deliberation

What role did expressives play within online political talk and in relation to the normative conditions of deliberation? Overall, the findings suggest that the use of expressives seemed to detract from the normative goals of deliberation.

Humour was the most common expressive used, appearing in 15% of the postings. This finding is consistent with past net-based public sphere research [9]. Humour was frequently used to entertain. Though humour, for the most part, created a friendly and playful atmosphere among participants, particularly across argumentative lines, it often contributed little to the political discussions. In particular, humour usually invited more humour, igniting humour fests. These fests often took control of the discussion at the expense of the political topic. In other words, it acted as an impediment to coherence. The second most common pattern in the use of humour was to criticize, assess or provoke thought. Humour here was mostly constructive to the political discussions in question. In particular, rational humour was used to enhance and support rational-critical debate. Consequently, it tended to benefit political talk. The final pattern in the use of humour was to express hostility, anger or offence. The use of humour here was typically vulgar, crude and offensive and usually contributed little to the discussion constructively, but rather, it acted at times as a vehicle of discursive inequality. Consequently, humour here functioned more as an obstacle to political talk.

The level of emotions expressed was consistent with past net-based public sphere research [9]. Unlike humour, emotional comments contributed little constructively to political talk. The primary reason for this was due to the type and intensity of the emotions expressed. Nearly 80% of emotional comments expressed some form of anger. Moreover, anger was usually raw and intense.

First, though emotional comments were often expressed via rational-critical debate, given the intense anger that was prevalent, these types of arguments tended to be abrasive, vulgar and crude. As a result, they often contributed little beneficially to the discussions. Second, often these types of arguments ignited rant sessions. Here participants engaged less in reciprocal-critical exchange and more in relieving their anger by joining in on a rant with fellow participants. Though these types of rants may have provided some form of therapeutic relief, they usually added little value, in way of understanding, to the topic under discussion. Finally, as was the case with humour, emotional comments were a vehicle of discursive inequality. Nearly a third of emotional comments were used in a degrading way. On the whole, emotional comments did more to impede deliberation than advance it.

The final expressive was acknowledgements. The most common acknowledgement was compliments. Overall, acknowledgements tended to foster a friendly communicative atmosphere. In particular, participants regularly complimented and praised each other's arguments and positions. However, there was one catch to complimenting. Participants on different sides of argumentative lines simply did not compliment one another. Complimenting was polarized. In short, unlike Barnes' et alt. [25] research on political talk via offline settings, which found that the use of greeting fostered a communicative space that enabled participants to express disagreement more productively, acknowledgements here, compliments in particular, tended to create an atmosphere that was counterproductive to deliberation.

9 Conclusion

Overall, expressives were a common ingredient of political talk within the Guardian. The findings suggest that the use of expressives tended detract from the normative goals of deliberation. These findings should caution those deliberative scholars who advocate the importance of expressives for deliberation. It seems that if one is interested in achieving normative goals, particularly within more semi-formal settings such as e-consolations, the use of expressives needs to be moderated in some fashion. However, I am not suggesting that we write expressives off as irrational or unimportant to deliberation. Humour for example played an integral role, making a distinct contribution to the use of reasoning. Moreover, the focus here was on everyday political talk, which is not bound to *politically* oriented forums as recent research suggests [26, 27, 28]. Consequently, different communicative environments may offer different insight into the use of expressives in relation to deliberation. For example, the findings suggest that the Guardian was a competitive environment, which seem to foster the use of expressives in a more impeding fashion. That said, this may not be the case elsewhere in the online communicative landscape where the discussions are less about 'battles and victories'.

Normatively speaking, one of the difficulties with the literature on the public sphere and deliberation is that there lacks concrete benchmarks as to what satisfies the normative conditions (at the level of the forum as opposed to the individual post or thread). For example, does a forum where 50% of the claims are reasoned satisfy the normative condition of rationality? Much of the literature is vague when it comes to defining what is meant by e.g. high and low quality at the level of the forum, and yet we read about this forum maintaining a high level or that forum being deliberative. There have been few attempts, by scholars to define specific benchmarks. The analysis above represents an initial step. First, for reciprocity and convergence, specific benchmarks have been provided. Second, the criteria for establishing such benchmarks were given. Finally, though explicit benchmarks were not specified, normative judgments were made, which provides a basis for future research to build upon.

Finally, given the textual focus of this study, there are limitations as to what can be said about certain conditions of deliberation and on the role of expressives. Certain conditions of deliberation require more than an analysis of the text. Though the indicators created and utilized in this study proved useful, conditions such as reflexivity ideally require a mixed method approach. They require a combination of an analysis of the text alongside methods that gauge participants' experiences, perceptions and feelings such as questionnaires and interviews. It is this mixed approach that represents the way forward for creating comprehensive indicators of deliberation for future research.

References

1. Habermas, J.: The Theory of Communicative Action. In: Reason and the Rationalization of Society, vol. 1. Beacon Press, Boston (1984)
2. Graham, T.: What's Wife Swap Got to Do with It? Talking Politics in the Net-based Public Sphere. PhD Dissertation, Amsterdam School of Communications Research (2009)
3. Habermas, J.: The Theory of Communicative Action. In: Lifeworld and System: A Critique of Functionalist Reason, vol. 2. Beacon Press, Boston (1987)
4. Habermas, J.: Between Facts and Norms: Contributions to a Discourse Theory of Law and Democracy. MIT Press, Cambridge (1996)
5. Dryzek, J.S.: Deliberative Democracy and Beyond: Liberals, Critics, Contestations. Oxford University Press, Oxford (2000)
6. Young, I.M.: Communication and the Other: Beyond Deliberative Democracy. In: Benhabib, S. (ed.) Democracy and Difference, pp. 120–137. Princeton University Press, Princeton (1996)
7. Basu, S.: Dialogic Ethics and the Virtue of Humor. J. Pol. Phil. 7, 378–403 (1999)
8. O'Neill, J.: The Rhetoric of Deliberation: Some Problems in Kantian Theories of Deliberative Democracy. Res. Publica. 8, 249–268 (2002)
9. Winkler, R.: Europeans Have a Say: Online Debates and Consultations in the EU. The Austrian Federal Ministry for Education, Vienna (2005)
10. Graham, T.: Needles in a Haystack: A New Approach for Identifying and Assessing Political Talk in Nonpolitical Discussion Forums. Javnost - The Public 15, 17–36 (2008)
11. De Nooy, W., Mrvar, A., Batagelj, V.: Exploratory Social Network Analysis with Pajek. Cambridge University Press, Cambridge (2005)
12. Koller, M.R.: Humor and Society: Explorations in the Sociology of Humor. Cap and Gown Press, Houston (1988)
13. Shibles, W.: Humor Reference Guide: A Comprehensive Classification and Analysis. Southern Illinois University Press, Carbondale (1997)
14. Shaver, P., Schwartz, J., Kirson, D., O'Connor, C.: Emotion Knowledge: Further Exploration of a Prototype Approach. In: Parrott, G.W. (ed.) Emotions in Social Psychology: Essential Readings, pp. 26–56. Psychology Press, Philadelphia (2001)
15. Albrecht, S.: Whose Voice is Heard in Online Deliberation? A Study of Participation and Representation in Political Debates on the Internet. Info., Com. & Soc. 9, 62–82 (2006)
16. Dahlberg, L.: Extending the Public Sphere through Cyberspace: The Case of Minnesota E-democracy. First Monday: Peer-Reviewed Journal on the Internet 6 (2001)
17. Jankowski, N.W., Van Os, R.: Internet-based Political Discourse: A Case Study of Electronic Democracy in Hoogeveen. In: Shane, P. (ed.) Democracy Online: The Prospects for Democratic Renewal through the Internet, pp. 181–194. Taylor & Francis, New York (2004)
18. Jensen, J.L.: Public Spheres on the Internet: Anarchic or Government-Sponsored - A Comparison. Scand. Pol. Studies 26, 349–374 (2003)
19. Wilhelm, A.G.: Virtual Sounding Boards: How Deliberative is Online Political Discussion? In: Hague, B.N., Loader, B.D. (eds.) Digital Democracy, pp. 154–178. Routledge, New York (1999)
20. Wright, S., Street, J.: Democracy, Deliberation and Design: The Case of Online Discussion Forums. New Media & Soc. 9, 849–869 (2007)
21. Brants, K.: Politics is E-verywhere. Communications: The European J. Com. Res. 27, 1 71–188 (2002)

22. Beierle, T.C.: Engaging the Public through Online Policy Dialogues. In: Shane, P. (ed.) Democracy Online: The Prospects for Democratic Renewal through the Internet, pp. 155–166. Taylor & Francis, New York (2004)
23. Strandberg, K.: Public Deliberation Goes On-line? An Analysis of Citizens' Political Discussions on the Internet Prior to the Finnish Parliamentary Elections in 2007. Javnost - The Public 15, 71–90 (2008)
24. Stromer-Galley, J.: Diversity of Political Conversation on the Internet: Users' Perspectives. Journal of Computer-Mediated Communication 8 (2003)
25. Barnes, M., Knops, A., Newman, J., Sullivan, H.: The Micro-Politics of Deliberation: Case Studies in Public Participation. Contemporary Politics 10, 93–110 (2004)
26. Graham, T., Harju, A.: Reality TV as a Trigger of Everyday Political Talk in the Net-based Public Sphere. European Journal of Communication 26 (Forthcoming)
27. Van Zoonen, L.: Audience Reactions to Hollywood Politics. Media Culture & Soc. 29, 531–547 (2007)
28. Wojcieszak, M.E., Mutz, D.C.: Online Groups and Political Discourse: Do Online Discussion Spaces Facilitate Exposure to Political Disagreement. J. of Com. 59, 40–56 (2009)

ICT's for Democracy in Latin America?*

Yanina Welp

Center for Research on Direct Democracy
yanina.welp@zda.uzh.ch

Abstract. Should Latin American governments concentrate their efforts in improving efficiency, transparency and accountability or should they also aim to increase the participation of citizens in decision-making? Is there a risk of reinforcing inequality through the promotion of ICT's for democracy in countries with a considerable digital divide? Is there a risk of reinforcing populism, clientelism and concentration of power leaving the promotion of ICT's in hands of strong presidents of the sort that prevail in many Latin American countries today? Based on previous research on Latin America focused on (i) goals and conditions to promote e-democracy; (ii) e-government developments; and (iii) e-democracy initiatives promoted by governments and civil society organizations, the paper explores e-democracy developments and trends and suggests a landscape for further research.

Keywords: e-democracy, e-participation, Latin America, ICT's, Transparency.

1 Introduction

In the eighties and nineties in Western countries scholars were beginning to comment on a crisis of representative democracy which was becoming evident in a decrease in participation in elections, in the distrust and lack of interest of citizens in politics [1], and in the fall of partisan and union affiliation [2]. In this context of crisis, many initiatives, including those based on information and communication technologies (ICTs from now on), have been developed with the aim of revitalising democracy, increasing transparency in public management and opening up new spaces for political participation [3]. Even if there are some common points, a look at Latin America shows a different picture. In most countries of the region the transition from dictatorship to democracy began in the eighties. In this sense, far from being "frozen" (as Lipset and Rokkan suggested for the political parties affiliations in Western countries [4]), until now political affiliations have been weak in the majority of the Latin American countries which -with a few exceptions (e.g. Uruguay)- are characterized by weak political party system institutionalization, high volatility of voters preferences from one election to the next and a more important role played by charisma than by ideology [5]. Furthermore, although democracy has persevered in most cases, it coexists with recurrent political and economical crises, institutional instability, political polarization and citizen dissatisfaction.

---

* I give thanks to Jonathan Wheatley for his comments and suggestions.

E. Tambouris, A. Macintosh, and O. Glassey (Eds.): ePart 2010, LNCS 6229, pp. 42–53, 2010.

Which role can and should play the ICTs in this scenario? Is there a risk of reinforcing inequality through the promotion of ICT's for democracy in countries with a considerable digital divide? Is there a risk of reinforcing populism and concentration of power leaving the promotion of ICTs in hands of strong presidents of the sort that prevail in many Latin American countries today? To deal with these questions the paper summarize previous research findings to explore (i) the context in which e-democracy is developed, with an overview of indicators of quality of democracy, corruption, transparency, electoral turnout and confidence in institutions of representative democracy; (ii) the digital divide and the policies to develop ICTs by governments; (iii) e-democracy initiatives promoted by governments and civil society organizations considering if they are mainly oriented to reinforce representative democracy or if are mainly oriented to extend a participatory democracy. The paper ends with a conclusion on the trends, risks and potentialities; and some suggestions for future research.

2 The Latin American Democracies

This research is focused on 18 Latin American countries. Among these countries, democracy has worked continuously at least throughout the last fifty years in Costa Rica, Colombia and Venezuela; for between 21 and 31 years in Argentina, Bolivia, Brazil, Ecuador, Dominican Republic, Guatemala, Honduras, Nicaragua, Peru, Uruguay; and for less than twenty years in Chile, El Salvador, Paraguay, Panama, and Mexico. This suggests that there is no correlation between the longevity of democracy and the system's stability given that some of the older democracies are also the most unstable or violent, such as Venezuela and Colombia respectively; and some of the younger democracies can be included in the group of the most consolidated not only in the region but also in the world, such as Uruguay or Brazil. Secondly, a paradox undergone by most Latin American countries is frequently quoted as on the one hand, they have more or less institutionalized a democratic regime as a form of government but, on the other, they face a succession of social and political crises. There are abundant examples of this. Many popular demonstrations have led to early elections and/or the establishment of transition and provisional governments. Thirteen presidents in nine of the seventeen countries analyzed here were unable to complete their mandate[1] and in some cases also democracy was seriously in trouble (with the closing of the congress in Peru by Fujimori, in1992; or with the uprising of Lucio Gutierrez in Ecuador in 2000, only to quote two cases).

The previous commentary lead us to one of the most controversial political sciences issues which is the definition of Democracy. The classical Dahl's work suggests the concept of polyarchy to define a set of institutional arrangements that

---

[1] Abdalá Bucarám (1997), Jamil Mahuad (1999) and Lucio Gutiérrez (2005) in Ecuador; Fernando Color de Mello (1992) in Brazil; Fernando de la Rúa in Argentina (2001); Hernán Silas Suazo (1985), Gonzalo Sánchez de Losada (2003) and Carlos Mesa (2005) in Bolivia; Jorge Serrano Elias (1993) in Guatemala; Raúl Cubas Grau (1999) en Paraguay; Alberto Fujimori (2000) in Peru; Joaquien Balaguer (1994) in Dominican Republic, or Carlos Andres Perez (1993) in Venezuela. In 2009 was interrupted the government of Honduras, although this time was a coup d'etat.

permits public opposition and establishes the right to participate in politics. While democracy is an ideal, polyarchy is a measurable dimension. Its minimum requirements are: freedom to form and join organizations; freedom of expression; the right to vote; eligibility for public office; the right of political leaders to compete for support; alternative sources of information; free and fair elections; institutions for making government policies depend on votes and other expressions of preference [6].

The Freedom House Index [7] allows to consider the strengthens of the Latin American contemporary democracies, showing that nine of the countries studied here were considered as *free democracies* in 2008, being the other eight qualified as a *partly free* (for details on this and the following data see table 1 in the annex). The picture of the corruption and lack of transparency is not better. The Corruption Perceptions Index for 2006 [8] shows that just two countries can be considered *relatively clean* (Uruguay and Chile), while the rest are qualified as *corrupt* or *highly corrupt* (the latest applies for Argentina, Bolivia, Paraguay or Venezuela between others). A third index, the Open Budget Index, concerning to transparency on Budgetary Information [9] shows a similar picture. Among the thirteen Latin American countries analyzed, just Brazil and Peru provide with significant information while none shows an extensive provision, in five the provision is qualified as minimal (Ecuador, El Salvador) or scant (Bolivia, Honduras, Panama) and the rest of the countries provide some information (note that Chile and Uruguay were not included in this sample). The lack of transparency not necessarily means corruption, but goes clearly against public capacity to control the power, and contributes to hide corruption.

Given the lack of transparency and the extent to which corruption is endemic to most Latin American countries, is not surprising to find a high level of citizen distrust in political institutions. Although there are remarkable differences between countries, according with CIMA 2008 [10] in all of them citizens trust more in the Church (the average confidence was 67%) and Television News (52%) than in Justice (30%), Parliament (22%) or Political Parties (15%). In four countries, confidence in Parliament is less than 10% (Ecuador, Panama, Paraguay and Peru) while the highest level of confidence is displayed by Uruguay (55%) and Venezuela (42%). The situation is even worse for political parties, here with the exception of Uruguay (40%) and Guatemala (34%), in all the countries confidence is located below 30% with the lowest figures in Bolivia (8%), Chile and Paraguay (5%), Ecuador and Peru (4%). Despite these bad results, polls show that governments are steadily becoming more popular. However, happens that leaders are increasing their power against institutions of representative democracy, while political parties displays the lowest confidence.

It has to be mentioned the constant reform of institutions observed in the sanction of new constitutions and the introduction of direct democratic mechanisms in several countries [11]. Quite often, in scenarios in which an emergent power confront an elite removed from its hegemonic positions, the top down referendum has become a potent weapon to resolve situations of political impasse (Venezuela 1999, Ecuador 2007, Bolivia 2009, Perú 1993). In these cases the most common reason to call for a referendum is an attempt to resolve a struggle between parliament and the president or the president and the governors or authorities of the opposition. The constitutional reform to extend the president mandate is also included in several of these consultations (Colombia, the Zelaya's attempt previous to the coup d'Etat in

Honduras). In some cases, even if the immediate effect of the referendum is a high social polarization, in the long run it could be a first step towards acceptance of the rules of the democratic game. However, other consequence is the weakness of the equilibrium between powers in favor of the president[2]. [12]

To the analyses of Electoral turnout should be noted that in a good proportion of the Latin American countries voting is compulsory. However countries either do not enforce compulsory voting laws (i.e Bolivia, Costa Rica, Guatemala, Paraguay and Honduras) or the enforcement is weak (Argentina, Brazil, Ecuador, Mexico, Peru and Chile). Thus, despite compulsory voting, it seems that these laws merely states what the citizen's responsibility should be. In any case, the average turnout in the six last elections (parliamentary and presidential) is 67%, with strong differences between the highest turnout -Uruguay with 90,7% (and strict enforcement of compulsory voting)- and the lowest -Colombia with 36,6% and El Salvador with 45% on average. The lowest turnout is registered in the countries in which voting is not compulsory. However, also countries without compulsory voting show low turnout (Guatemala, 48% or Mexico 59%) and countries with compulsory voting shows turnout above the average (as Nicaragua with 70% or Panama 75%)[3].

A surprising finding linked with Dahl's third requirement (the right to vote) emerges from the evolution of the number of the registered voter's over time. By analizing the increase of registered voters from the first election of the eighties until the last (e.g. for Ecuador since the elections of 1984 to the elections in 2006) a huge increase of the voters is observed. In the case of Ecuador the electoral roll increased by 145% during the twenty-two year period while the natural increase of population for the same period was just 51%, meaning that at least 62% of the increase in the registered voters comes from the extension of political rights (probably indigenous and rural population not registered previously). A similar picture emerges for several other countries in which a huge increase in the number of voters cannot be explained by the natural increase in the population. This quantitative extension of political rights also exceed 40% (over and above the natural increase in the population) in Brazil, El Salvador, Guatemala, Honduras, Mexico, Nicaragua, Panama and Peru. Only in Chile and Costa Rica does the opposite apply (a relative fall in the number of registered voters of 14% and 3% respectively). The large anomaly in Chile can be explained by the fact that one is required to vote only if is a registered voter, but is not compulsory to register. This apparent drop in the proportion of the population that is registered to vote could therefore be explained by a failure to register. Again, far from being frozen, Latin American political arena seems to be in constant movement.

To sum up, first of all has to be underlined that the region displays strong differences between countries, with a broad range of outcomes in terms of quality of democracy, electoral turnout, etc. Several countries are characterized by a high level of corruption, increasing distrust in the institutions of representative democracy, increasing political conflict and polarization within the framework of recurrent political crises. These crises mainly stem from inequality and poverty but are

---

[2] Uruguay is an exception to this trend given that direct democracy is in hands of the people (Presidents are not allowed to call a referendum). The mechanism has been used with frequency, becoming a factor of political legitimization and given to the people the power of being a veto player in Tsebelis terms [13].
[3] Data calculated on July 2009.

exacerbated by corruption and/or as a result of the failure of elected governments to comply with their electoral programs. Institutional instability in Latin American countries is reinforced by the fact that elections are the primary mechanism of accountability. Elections are central to democratic life, but are not enough to promote responsible governments. In countries where a significant segment of the public has been excluded from access to public goods and lack institutional mechanisms at their disposal, discontent and spontaneous protest are common. In this context, how are ICTs being used to contribute to reinforce good governance and democracy?

3 The Spread of the Information Society

As several scholars have pointed out, widespread access to the Internet is conditional on wealth [14]. However, even if it has been at different speeds and with different consequences for social organization, Internet diffusion has been remarkable in all the regions of the world. In Latin America is observed a gradual increase of users who could provide sustenance to these new initiatives. Data from the International Telecommunications Union for 2008 [15] shows that the most advanced countries have below 40% of Internet users (Brazil 37%, Uruguay 40%), while in some poorer countries access to the Internet remains near or below 10% (Nicaragua 3%, Honduras 13%, Paraguay 14%). Although figures for Internet access are low in this latter group of countries, with notable exceptions (Nicaragua) they also show a constant growth. In any case, the considerable gap between those who have access and those who not is an important challenge for governments.

The development of e-government is desirable for various reasons that are mainly linked to improving the efficiency of public administration. ICTs could contribute to the streamlining of services, the reduction of costs, the reduction of personnel oriented to bureaucratic jobs and the reduction of waiting times, amongst others [16]. While these are the main argument to reform public administration, the diffusion of ICT's was also accompanied by an emphasis on the potential to improve the quality of democracy. e-democracy has been defined as the use of electronic communication as a means for granting citizens the power to make lawmakers and politicians accountable for their actions in the public sphere by strengthening transparency in the political process, the improvement of the quality of the stages of opinion formation or the increase of citizen participation in the decision-making process [17]. Quite often it is difficult to establish a clear line between what e-government is and what e-democracy is given that, for instance, transparency in the public purchase produce a better democracy and probably a more efficient government avoiding corruption. The same applies for e-voting system, which ha been introduced mainly to replace traditional systems with the intention of guarantee more transparent results. The most spread system in Latin America is the Ballot Box (Urna electrónica) developed and used mainly in Brazil and Venezuela [18] but also Costa Rica, Paraguay, Ecuador and some states of Mexico.

The use of ICTs by Latin American governments is widespread. All of them have developed government portals and have strategic and/or action plans. The lack of studies on the field increases the difficulties to asses it, although could be mentioned that the promotion of ICTs is significant and has gained an increasing weight. The use of ICTs by Latin American governments is widespread; all of them have developed government and legislative portals [19], and e-politics [20] also in the local level [21]. However, differences between actions are huge. e.g. previous research has shown that while some portals are a complicated map of scarcely-accessible information, other are more a propagandistic window of the government while a third group is organized in a more user-friendly manner to satisfy citizens' needs (e.g. by profile, theme and/or key facts) [22]. Here we will explore initiatives oriented to promote transparency in the public access to the information and specially on the legislative process; and in participatory experiences in law-making.

4 Opening Democracy through ICTs

There is a tension in the understanding of what e-democracy should be and whom would be the main promoter. Should Latin American governments concentrate their efforts in improving efficiency, transparency and accountability or should they also aim to increase the participation of citizens in decision-making? The answer to this questions leads to a more general question of what type of democracy is desirable. Dalton [23] defines it as follows: "On one side of the democratic spectrum stands the model of articulating citizen demands through representation. This model often takes the form of party-based parliamentary rule and functions primarily through elected representatives (...) At the other end of the spectrum is the model of direct democracy placing control in the hand of the people themselves".

Sartori [24] stresses that representative democracy is the best system of government in contemporary society because it prevents against the radicalization that direct democratic procedures would lead. In turn, the control and limitation of powers allows civil society to exercise their role controlling governments and granting legitimacy to the system through the established procedures for the election of representatives. Sartori argues that the ways in which citizens access information and the degree to which they are subjugated by the pressures of opinion makers define the scope and limitations of substantive democracy. From this point of view, competence and multiplicity of sources of information are a guarantee of an autonomous public opinion, and conditions for democracy. And that is something allowed for new technologies given that where a strong civil society is claiming for information and exercising public control, governments will be forced to open up; and concentrated and powerful mass media will have new competitors. It means, more information has to be offered by governments and more control exercised by the public.

On the other side, even if no system is becoming a direct democratic system various processes have converged to promote a more participatory system. Citizen participation refers to any voluntary action by citizens more or less directly aimed at influencing public decision making and the management of collective affairs [25]. In this sense, citizen participation could be understood as taking part in those public affairs that affect society as a whole.

4.1 Reinforcing Representative Democracy

Parliaments and governments are increasingly uploading information on the website and has to be stressed the creation of portals to promote the access to the information, e.g. in Costa Rica the Comptroller General's Office has developed a portal that brings together systematic public information to which citizens can access.[4] The Federal Institute for Access to Public Information of Mexico, meanwhile, offers information not only on finances but also on a wide range of information identified as public, specifying the procedure.[5] In any case, all the countries of the region display a growing presence on the website and with different scales, an increasing transparency of their work. However, that is not systematic.

From the side of civil society, features which help to empower civil society are interactivity given that users may communicate on a many-to-many reciprocal basis), free speech and free association, and construction and dissemination of information which is not subject to official review or sanction. Civil Society Organizations are using these tools. Although systematic research is required to analyses its outcomes is possible to quote some innovative developments such as the initiative called Congreso Visible (Visible Parliament)[6], launched by the Universidad de los Andes, in Colombia, that arises with the intent to change the bad perceptions citizens have on parliamentarians and prevent corruption. The objectives of the initiative include, among others, the monitoring and evaluation of legislators and parliamentary coalitions or the training of the organizations involved in promoting the participation of citizens and minorities. The public can check out the legislators agenda, bills promoted and voted and other related activities. Participation is not mandatory for parliamentarians but as soon as the initiative starts to be joined for more politicians there is informal pressure to join. This has an immediate effect to return relevant information easily accessible but also play a role in the long run because it is possible to see what a representative votes over time (to what extent it is consistent), changes in their heritage and their legislative activity (how many and what kind of initiatives introduced, how often attends the meetings?). Projects such this are growing in the region and will need further research to know their effects.[7]

4.2 Participatory Democracy

One of the best known participatory democracy experiences is the participatory budgeting but there are also citizen councils, public audiences and other mechanisms which seeks to address the emergence of a growing gap between citizens and the political system [26]. The local level has been a privileged space for participation because this scale of government, so close to the citizenry, facilitates the dialogue between the actors [27]. But even if individual citizens' commitment to the local agenda is more frequent than to the national one, participatory experiences based on ICT's are also growing in the national level. Relevant political processes such as elections, discussion of certain laws that carry a high degree of polarization or debate, or constitutional reforms aroused the interest of the citizenry. Internet facilitates the access to the proposals and also create a forum for debate. The monitoring of

---

[4] Contraloría General de la República: http://cgrw01.cgr.go.cr/
[5] Instituto Federal de Acceso a la Información: http://www.ifai.org.mx/
[6] http://cvisible.uniandes.edu.co/
[7] http://www.institutoagora.org.br

parliamentary activity allows citizens organized to react and make their voices heard before a bill is passed.[8]

There is a greater difference among actions because, while in some cases the creation of sectorial forums, for example, has been promoted (Mexico, Bolivia) or virtual legislative programs in which citizens may participate have been created (such as the virtual Parliament in Peru and Chile), in other cases, the appeal to citizens is mainly symbolic, as in the case of virtual mailboxes to write to the President (Paraguay) [28]. It is important to differentiate the opening of 'symbolic' spaces of participation from spaces where it is possible to raise and follow-up proposals, and from spaces of citizen interaction designed for the formulation of bills. Most of the latter were developed by the legislative assembly. One such program is Virtual Senator, held in Chile, which allows people to know and discuss bills.[9] The views expressed are referred to committees, so the senators members can consider opinions when voting. Other participatory process with a strong use of ICT was the constitutional convention in Ecuador.[10]

5   A Landscape for Further Research

Undoubtedly, the publication of budgets, the laws on access to information, and the monitoring of legislative activity could help controlling corruption and reducing the gap between citizenry and representatives. Although the change is political, is facilitated by technology. New political actors and respect for the rules of the democratic game are forcing an opening up the system. Latin America needs more and better channels for citizens to make decisions; however, strong political leaderships and the digital divide invite us to be cautious. Latin America needs better institutions for a better democracy. In this sense, there is no doubt about the benefits of an efficient and transparent government. Transparency in government activities has an effect of control on the government, and of learning for citizens, who will be more qualified for decision making. The fight against corruption and access to information of public interest is maybe not revolutionary, but can encourage important changes in a region in constant movement.

The development of participatory initiatives using ICTs is not crystal clear. To develop a systematic research agenda is required to highlight the consequences of the discussion of ICT's for democracy. An in deep study of the initiatives to monitor and participate in Parliament activities could be a good starting point. Two dimensions emerged from the previous: on the one hand the analysis of the transparency in the process of law-making (Information about representatives; budget/expenditure; and an assessment of the transparency of the law making process). The second dimension (citizen participation on the policy making) has to be analyzed including on line and not online mechanisms (forums, initiatives to follow parlamentarian activity and send comments or ask questions; but also commission and direct democracy mechanisms,

---

[8] Brasil www.brasil.gov.br/participacao_popular/forum, Guatemala
 www.congreso.gob.gt/gt/forodiscusion.asp or Peru
 www.congreso.gob.pe
[9] http://senadorvirtual.senado.cl
[10] http://www.asambleanacional.gov.ec

specially the bottom up such as initiative and abrogative referendum). That approach to the parliamentary activity (one of the less valued by the Latin American inhabitants after the political parties) could allow to analyses to what extent ICT's are contributing to reduce the political gap.

References

1. Putnam, R.: Bowling Alone: America's Declining Social Capital (1995)
2. Lipset, S.M.: Algunos requisitos sociales de la democracia: desarrollo económico y legitimidad política. In: Batlle (ed.) Diez textos básicos de Ciencia Política. Ariel, Barcelona (1992)
3. Hague, B., Loader, B.D.: Digital democracy, Discourse and Decision Making in the Information Age. Routledge, Londres (1999)
4. Lipset, M., Rokkan, S.: Cleavage Structures, Party Systems and Voter Alignments: An Introduction. In: Lipset, Rokkan (eds.) Party Systems and Voter Alignments: Cross-National Perspectives. Free Press, New York (1967)
5. Mainwaring, S., Scully, T. (eds.): Building democratic institutions: Party systems in Latin America. Stanford University Press, Stanford (1995)
6. Dahl, R.P.: Participation and Opposition. Yale University Press, New haven (1971)
7. Freedom House, http://www.freedomhouse.org
8. Global Corruption Index- International Transparency, http://www.transparency.org
9. Open Budget Index (2008), http://openbudgetindex.org
10. Barómetro Iberoamericano de Gobernabilidad, http://www.cimaiberoamerica.com
11. Payne, M., Zovatto, D., Mateo Díaz, M.: La política importa. Democracia y desarrollo en América Latina, BID/IIDAE, Washington (2006)
12. Welp, Y., Serdült, U.: Armas de Doble Filo. La participación Ciudadana en la Encrucijada. Prometeo, Buenos Aires (2009)
13. Welp, Y., Serdült, U.: Armas de Doble Filo. La participación Ciudadana en la Encrucijada. Prometeo, Buenos Aires (2009)
14. Hargittai, E.: Weaving the Western Web: explaining differences in Internet connectivity among OECD countries. Telecommunications Policy 23, 701–718 (1999)
15. International Telecommunications Union, http://www.itu.int
16. Fountain, J.: Building the virtual state information technology and institutional change. Brookings Institution Press, Washington (2001)
17. Trechsel, A., Kies, R., Méndez, F., Schmitter, P.: Evaluation of the Use of New Technologies in Order to Facilitate Democracy in Europe. EDemocratizing the Parliaments and Parties of Europe; Research and Documentation Centre on Direct Democracy (C2D), University of Geneva (2003)
18. Thompson, J.: Automatización, informatización y voto electrónico en la experiencia electoral reciente de América Latina. Avances y perspectivas, paper presentado en las jornadas Democracia digital, participación y voto electrónico, organizadas por la Fundación CEPS en Madrid los días 14 y 15 de febrero de (2008)
19. Frick, M.: Parliaments in the Digital Age. Exploring Latin America, e-Working Papers 2005/01. e-DemocracyCentre, http://www.edemocracycentre.ch
20. Finkelievich, Susama (coord.): E-Política y e-Gobierno, Links. En (2005), http://www.links.org.ar/infoteca/E-Gobierno-y-E-Politica-en-LATAM.pdf

21. Coroján, Criado: Las administraciones locales y el desarrollo del Gobierno electrónico en Centroamérica. Una aproximación general. Ponencia presentada en el Grupo de trabajo C-19: Retos y oportunidades para el gobierno electrónico en Iberoamérica: El papel de las instituciones, IV Congreso de la Cibersociedad "Crisis Analógica, Futuro Digital" (2009)

22. Welp, Y.: Democracy and Digital Divide in Latin America", e-Working papers 2007/01, e-DemocracyCentre (2007), http://www.edemocracycentre.ch; Un updated version in Spanish can be consulted at: "América Latina en la era del gobierno electrónico. Análisis de la introducción de nuevas tecnologías para la mejora de la democracia y el gobierno, en Revista del CLAD Reforma y Democracia n°41 (2008)

23. Dalton, R.J., Watenberg, M.P. (eds.): Parties without Partisans. Political Change in Advanced Industrial Democracies. Oxford University Press, Nueva York (2000)

24. Sartori, G.: Teoría de la democracia. Buenos Aires (1990)

25. Verba, S., Schlozman, K.L., Brady, H.E.: Voice and Equality. Civic Voluntarism in American Politics. Harvard University Press, Cambridge (1995)

26. Seele, D., Peruzzotti, E. (eds.): Participatory Innovations and Representative Democracy in Latin America. W. Wilson Press/John Hopkins University Press (2009)

27. Borge, R., Colombo, C., Welp, Y.: Online and offline participation at the local level. A quantitative analysis of the Catalan municipalities. Information, Communication & Society 12(6) (September 2009)

28. Welp, Y.: New and Old ways of exersing power. ICT's for Democracy in Latin America. In: C2D Working paper, vol. 31 (2009), http://www.c2d.ch/files/C2D_WP31.pdf

Appendix: Tables

Table 1. Quality of Democracy, Corruption and Transparency

Country	Freedom and Democracy [1]			Corruption[2]	Open Budget Index[3]
	PR	CL	Status	CPI Scores	
Argentina	2	2	*Free*	2,9 *Highly corrupt*	56 *Some*
Bolivia	3	3	*Partly Free*	2,7*Highly corrupt*	6 *Scant*
Brasil	2	2	*Free*	3,3 *Corrupt*	74 *Significant*
Chile	1	1	*Free*	7,3	na
Colombia	3	4	*Partly Free*	3,9 *Corrupt*	60 *Some*
Costa Rica	1	1	*Free*	4,1 *Corrupt*	45 *Some*
Ecuador	3	3	*Partly Free*	2,3 *Highly corrupt*	38 *Minimal*
El Salvador	2	3	*Free*	4 *Corrupt*	37 *Minimal*
Guatemala	3	4	*Partly Free*	2,6 *Highly corrupt*	45 *Some*
Honduras	3	3	*Partly Free*	2,5 *Highly corrupt*	11 *Scant*
México	2	3	*Free*	3,3 *Corrupt*	54 *Some*
Nicaragua	4	3	*Partly Free*	2,6 *Highly corrupt*	18 *Scant*
Panamá	1	2	*Free*	3,1 *Corrupt*	na
Paraguay	3	3	*Partly Free*	2,6 *Highly corrupt*	na
Perú	2	3	*Free*	3,3 *Corrupt*	66 *Significant*
R.Dominicana	2	2	*Free*	2,8 *Highly corrupt*	11 *Scant*
Uruguay	1	1	*Free*	6,4	na
Venezuela	4	4	*Partly Free*	2,3 *Highly corrupt*	35 *Minimal*

Source: Information based on the history of each country, Freedom House, Transparency International and Open Budget Index.

(1) The **Freedomon House** index is built around political rights (PR) questions (grouped into three subcategories: Electoral Process, Political Pluralism and Participation, and Functioning of Government) and civil liberties (CL) questions (grouped into Freedom of Expression and Belief, Associational and Organizational Rights, Rule of Law, and Personal Autonomy and Individual Rights). Even if is one of the most accurate should be taken only as a reference because some cases appeared as a problematic (e.g. Peru –after a year of strong social conflicts-- qualified as free) 1 represents the most free and 7 the least free for 2008 (Free: 1.0 to 2.5, Partly Free: 3.0 to 5.0; Not Free: 5.5 to 7.0. (See Methodology Summary www.freedomhouse.org)

(2) *Corruption Perception Index* 2006. Transparency International. CPI Score' relates to perceptions of the degree of corruption as seen by business people and country analyst and ranged between 10 (highly clean) and 0 (highly corrupt)

(3) *Open Budget Index* 2008. The Survey collect a comparative dataset into: 1) the dissemination of budget information, 2) the executive's annual budget proposal to the legislature and other information to analysis policies and practices, and 3) the budget process. The countries that scored between 81-100 are placed in the performance category *Provides Extensive Information* , those with scores 61-80 % in *Provides Significant Information*, those with scores 41-60 % in *Provides Some Information*, those with scores 21-40 % in *Provides Minimal Information*, and those with scores 0-20 % in Provides *Scant or No Information.*.

Table 2. Increase of Registered Voters, Turnout Average and Internet Users

Country	% increase reg. voters[1]	% increase population	% increase non natural	Turnout average	Internet Users 2008[2]
Argentina	45.6	37.06	6	74.4	28.1
Bolivia	83.2	71.46	7	76	10.8
Brasil	113.7	48.13	44	78.6	37.5
Chile	8.8	25.85	-14	87.8	32.5
Colombia	93.8	53.78	26	36.6	38.5
Costa Rica	71	76.8	-3	66.5	32.3
Ecuador	145.8	51.28	62	63.9	28.8
El Salvador	137.6	41.4	68	45.0	10.6
Guatemala	154.2	72.75	47	48.5	14.3
Honduras	223.3	101.94	60	62.9	13.1
México	126.4	47.24	54	59.8	21.7
Nicaragua	136.2	52.73	55	70.4	3.3
Panamá	117.9	49.08	46	75.2	27.5
Paraguay	152.7	100.92	26	69.8	14.3
Perú	154.3	63.75	55	84	24.7
R.Dominicana	13.2	10.44	3	90.7	21.6
Uruguay	83.5	60.86	14	53.9	40
Venezuela	109.5	56.8	34,4	67	25.5

(1) Owner calculation based on IDEA (http://www.idea.int/vt/) for registered voters and turnout; and on World Development Indicators database and CIA World Factbook for population. In order to calculate the increase in the registered electors was considered the number of people allowed to vote in the first parliamentary election of the eighties and the number of allowed voters in the last parliamentary election (the research was done in April 2009).

(2) International Telecommunications Union 2008.

eParticipation Initiatives in Europe: Learning from Practitioners

Eleni Panopoulou, Efthimios Tambouris, and Konstantinos Tarabanis

University of Macedonia, Egnatia 156,
54006 Thessaloniki, Greece
{epanopou,tambouris,kat}@uom.gr

Abstract. The main objective of this paper is to investigate the use of Information and Communication Technologies (ICT) and derive the success factors of eParticipation initiatives according to the practitioners' view. For this purpose, a European survey took place using questionnaires. The results suggest that the tools and technologies currently employed are mainly general purpose and not specifically designed for eParticipation. The results further suggest that success factors can be grouped together in seven categories, namely commitment by the government; usability; combining online with offline channels; a thorough communication and promotion plan; security and privacy; organisational issues; and topics' complexity and quality of participation. A comparison with published success factors of eGovernment initiatives suggests there are similarities but also significant differences. We anticipate that the results will be of interest to practitioners as they distil others experience in a usable form. We further anticipate that this work will be of interest to researchers as it will enable validating eParticipation evaluation models.

Keywords: eParticipation Initiatives, Evaluation, Good Practice.

1 Introduction

Electronic participation (eParticipation) can be defined as "the use of Information and Communication Technologies (ICT) to broaden and deepen political participation by enabling citizens to connect with one another and with their elected representatives" [1]. eParticipation is currently promoted by relevant policies and initiatives at all levels; for example, "Strengthening Participation and Democratic Decision-Making in Europe" is one of the actions that the European Commission has launched within the i2010 eGovernment Action Plan "Accelerating eGovernment in Europe for the Benefit of All" [2].

The potential for ICT to increase political participation and to address the growing democratic deficit across Europe has long been the subject of academic debate [3]. However, only relatively recently there has been sufficient practical design and application of eParticipation suggesting that this potential could be considered within a real-world context [4]. This arrival of more sophisticated information systems has produced a growing community of research and practice that is investigating

E. Tambouris, A. Macintosh, and O. Glassey (Eds.): ePart 2010, LNCS 6229, pp. 54–65, 2010.

eParticipation. Current investigation includes among others understanding the role of technology in public participation and learning from the experience of others.

Work of academics includes frameworks and approaches to better understand eParticipation as an academic domain. At the same time however there is a lack of field studies, thus a lack of the practitioners' view.

The main objective of this paper is to investigate the use of ICT and derive the success factors of eParticipation initiatives according to the practitioners' view. For this purpose, a survey of eParticipation initiatives across Europe and at different levels (from local to international) was carried out. We anticipate that the results will be of interest to practitioners as it will distil others experience in a usable form. We further anticipate that this work will be of interest to researchers as it will enable validating theoretical models and academic frameworks based on real data.

The rest of this paper is organised as follows. In section 2 we outline relevant work. In section 3 we present the methodological approach used for this study. In section 4 we present the main results while in section 5 the main conclusions are discussed. Finally, appendix A provides a list of the European eParticipation initiatives investigated in this study.

2   eParticipation Evaluation Frameworks

During the last few years, a number of frameworks and models have been proposed in scientific literature attempting to analyse the eParticipation domain. These include a characterisation framework by Macintosh [5], a domain model by Kalampokis et al [6] and the eParticipation analytical framework [7]. More recently, the need for specific eParticipation evaluation frameworks has been identified. For example, Aichholzer and Allhutter [8] suggest there is an "evaluation gap" as resources, such as time, money and effort, are not being taken into consideration in eParticipation frameworks. In the rest of this section a number of frameworks for evaluating eParticipation are presented.

In 2000, Rowe and Frewer presented a framework for evaluating public participation methods [9]. Although it was not proposed for eParticipation, this framework specified a number of theoretical criteria that are essential for effective public participation and divided them in two types: acceptance criteria and process criteria. Acceptance criteria, namely representativeness, independence, early involvement, influence, and transparency, offer a measure of acceptability by the wider public, while process criteria, namely resource accessibility, task definition, structured decision making, and cost-effectiveness, offer a measure of effectiveness.

An attempt to produce a framework for assessing not only eParticipation projects but also eParticipation tools has been made by Tambouris et al [10]. The proposed framework suggests there are three main layers of analysis that need to be addressed: participation areas, tools utilised and technologies used. A template has been produced based on these three levels in order to document and assess eParticipation projects.

An evaluation framework for eParticipation has been suggested by Macintosh and Whyte [11]. The proposed evaluation criteria cover three different perspectives of an eParticipation initiative, namely the democratic, project and socio-technical perspective. The democratic perspective considers the overarching democratic criteria that the eParticipation initiative is addressing, while the project perspective examines in detail the specific aims and objectives of the eParticipation initiative. Finally, the socio-technical perspective considers to what extent the design of the ICTs used directly affects the outcomes. Under each evaluation perspective a number of criteria have been identified as follows (a) Democratic Criteria: Representation; Engagement; Transparency; Conflict and consensus; Political equality; and Community control, (b) Project Criteria: Engaging with a wider audience; Obtaining better informed opinions; Enabling more in-depth consultation; Cost effective analysis of contributions; and Providing feedback to citizens, (c) Socio-technical Criteria: Social acceptability; Usefulness; and Usability.

The above framework proposed by Macintosh and Whyte has been adapted and expanded within DEMO-net [12]. Specifically, the DEMO-net approach keeps the same three perspectives, most of the criteria, and introduces sub-criteria as follows: (a) Project perspective: Engaging with a wider audience; Obtaining better-informed opinions; Scope of deliberation; Effectiveness; Feedback; Process quality; and Sustainability, (b) Socio-technical perspective: Social acceptability; Usefulness; and Usability, (c) Democratic perspective: Representation; Engagement; Transparency; Conflict and consensus; Political equality; and Community control.

3 Methodological Approach

To achieve our objectives we conducted a European survey. More specifically, we employed a three-step methodological approach as follows.

1. We identified eParticipation initiatives from across Europe by employing three different methods: desktop research[1], databases of websites and award nominations[2], and our network of experts and key actors in the field. Overall, we identified 255 initiatives from 23 European countries and were able to collect contact data for 230 of them. An extensive analysis of these cases is presented elsewhere [13] [14].
2. We drafted a questionnaire to be filled in by the owners of the initiatives. The questions were selected based on a preliminary literature review of eParticipation evaluation frameworks (outlined in section 2) as well as of good practice criteria definitions in different contexts, mostly focused in eGovernment good practice and relevant awards for eGovernment initiatives.
3. We contacted the owners of the 230 gathered initiatives and kindly requested their participation in our questionnaire survey. This phase lasted 3 to 4 months as we had to repetitively request participation and ensure adequate time to owners to draft their answers. As a result, we gathered completed

---

[1] For example, initiatives mentioned in the literature as well as initiatives identified through web surfing and the help of search engines. Especially for the European level, extensive desktop research was conducted within the numerous EU institutions, the College of Commissioners, the EU policy documents as well as political parties and civil societies.
[2] For example, epractice.eu, e-participation.net, eEurope Awards for eGovernment, UK e-Government National Awards, Stockholm Challenge awards, etc.

questionnaires from 40 different eParticipation initiatives originating from 12 different European countries and addressing all different levels of participation: international, European, national, regional and local audiences. Although the response rate is low (17.4%) we believe that it is sufficient for the purposes of this study. It should also be noted that this percentage would be higher if a screening of initiatives was performed, e.g. if we excluded initiatives that were officially terminated etc.

An important limitation of the study is the language of communication. Although a large number of languages were employed for identifying eParticipation initiatives in our first methodological step, the next two steps were performed only in English. So, the questionnaire was in English and all communication with initiatives' owners was also performed in English. This might also explain to an extent the low response rate.

4 Results

The results of our survey are provided in this section. The analysis commences with information on the profile of the gathered initiatives and continues with details relevant to their participatory activities (areas and focus of participation as well as stakeholders involved), the ICT used (channels, tools and technologies) and finally an analysis of the lessons learnt.

4.1 Initiatives Profile

Our research sample draws experience from initiatives originating from 12 different countries across Europe; these are: Denmark, Estonia, Finland, Germany, Greece, Italy, The Netherlands, Portugal, Slovenia, Spain, Switzerland and the United Kingdom. Most of the gathered initiatives originate from Germany (10) and the United Kingdom (6).

With regard to the level of participation, the initiatives in our sample are active at all different levels; we have one international initiative and 9 initiatives referring to the European level. The rest 30 initiatives refer to specific European countries either at the national (14), regional (4) or local (12) level. Furthermore, the majority of the initiatives are reported to be driven by the public sector but other ownership types are also represented; 80% of the initiatives are initiated and owned by public authorities, bodies and organisations, while the rest 20% is owned by NGOs, private or independent institutions, Universities, or political parties.

4.2 Use of ICT

Another interesting feature of our sample is the presence of one or more channels supporting the participation process (Fig. 1). All of the initiatives support of course the typical internet channels, while one third of them report that they also use non electronic channels for participation. Interesting is also the usage of mobile channels (usually to involve young people), kiosks (usually to involve people without internet access) and access through other intermediaries (usually to involve people without much experience in ICT). Our survey also revealed interesting details on the ICT tools and technologies used (Fig. 2 and Fig. 3).

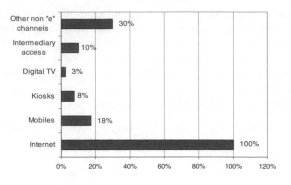

Fig. 1. Use of communication channels

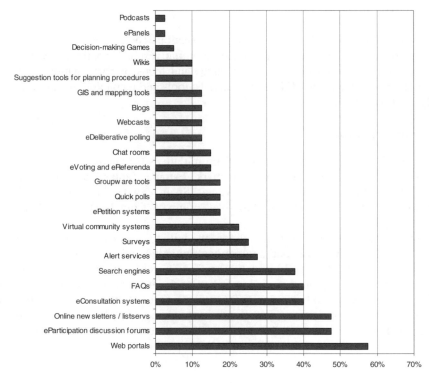

Fig. 2. Use of ICT tools

4.3 Success Factors

The survey questionnaire included specific questions on the problems encountered, the critical success factors and the lessons learnt. The analysis of the results reported under these questions provided an understanding that there is a certain set of issues of importance that come up in most of the reported initiatives. Clearly, one issue may be

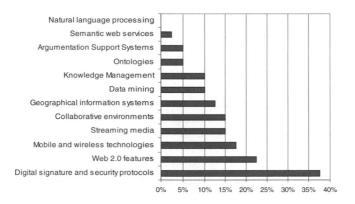

Fig. 3. Use of technologies

a problem for one initiative or a lesson learnt for another depending on a number of factors. This may depend, for example, on the design of the initiative processes, the available budget, the readiness of the different stakeholders, or simply on whether it was anticipated and thus respective proactive measures had been taken beforehand or not. In every case, the gathered bottom-up results indicated that there are essentially seven factor categories to be taken under consideration which might make an actual difference between a successful and a mediocre eParticipation initiative. This section presents the gathered feedback on each factor category and provides the relevant implications as reported by the practitioners in the field.

Commitment by the government. The actual involvement of governmental bodies and agencies not only as owners but throughout the whole participation process has been highlighted by most of the reported initiatives as a critical success factor. In specific, involvement as well as actual commitment of the government has been reported as essential in the following settings:

- *Drive to set up and support the initiative.* Successful initiatives set up by governmental bodies reported that there is an absolute need for champions from within the organisation to embrace and promote internally the project backed up by an actual willingness of the organisation to hold a government-citizen dialogue.
- *Support of the participatory process.* Supporting the initiative from its design to its operation and evolvement is needed from all parts of the organisation; from the officials and management down to the secretariat of every operational unit. The support may be manifested through the business integration of the relevant units/roles to the participatory process but also through means more apparent to the users, such as through actual participation of officials/appointed civil servants in the initiative (virtual presence) and physical presence in related events, meetings, etc.
- *Feedback and integration of results.* Participants of the initiatives reported systematically their fear that "the whole process might lead to nothing" and thus demand a clear commitment for integrating the results of the initiative

into the political process or at least for getting feedback on the overall results of the participation and how these will be used in the future. Unfortunately, this fear is validated by experience so far; there have been otherwise remarkable initiatives which reported that indeed the involved government bodies did not provide feedback to the issues and questions raised or that they provided answers either too generic or too selective (probably only to the "easy" issues raised). Evidently, this issue is of particular importance when trying to create a climate of transparency, trust and creative interaction in the government-citizen relationship.

Usability. A lot has been already published on the importance of usability and user-friendliness for all kinds of eParticipation (and eGovernment) initiatives. And indeed our empirical analysis found that it is one of the most frequent and important success factors. Experience gathered from the owners suggests that any kind of eParticipation initiative should be really easy and intuitive for all kinds of users, from internet savvy ones to those with limited ICT skills. For this reason, it has been reported that special attention should be put into the user interface with the option of dynamic development of technical features whenever it is considered essential. Furthermore, the aims of the initiative as well as the usage rules should be clearly defined and explicitly described online for the users' convenience. Moreover, the provision of help-desk facilities was reported as a positive lesson learnt as users may request assistance with things that may at first seem trivial and straightforward. For example, in one of the initiatives it was discovered that about 5% of the people that accessed the electronic consultations portal did not finally cast their opinion due to problems with the software used. However, the need for simplicity and usability should not become a barrier for enhanced functionality; it has also been reported that users expect from such initiatives to keep in pace with technological developments and to incorporate new features used in different settings, such as more interactivity and social networking.

Combining different channels, both online and offline ones. The channels mix is an important strategic decision for any eParticipation initiative. As mentioned previously, our survey showed that eParticipation initiatives rely heavily on traditional internet access through personal PCs and laptops. However, there is a 43% of eParticipation initiatives surveyed that utilise at least one additional online or offline channel, while one third reported that they combine online with offline channels. However, the channels mix came up also as a success factor of the reported initiatives, mostly as a means to facilitate inclusiveness. Owners' experience showed that multiple channels increase the participation figures; this has been clearly measured in initiatives performing any kind of voting either official national voting or municipal and small scale voting. There are a number of citizens that cast their votes online but there are also citizens who prefer mobile voting or casting their votes in the dedicated kiosks. So, in order to raise the overall turnout experience showed that a combination of channels is needed. Another usual example of increased citizens' participation is through combining online consultation/deliberation tools with offline meetings and workshops. In overall, there has been positive feedback from the owners that did utilise a combination of channels, while others reported their plans to expand their activities to more channels apart from the typical internet access.

A thorough communication and promotion plan. Owners in the survey referred a lot to problems and lessons regarding the need for a thorough communications plan and directly linked promotion with the actual success of the initiative. It has been reported that there is an absolute need for a detailed, professional and intensive communications strategy as well as for the will and the resources to back it up until the end. It is also important for each initiative to develop an appropriate branding including a distinct and easily recognised name and logo, but also to pay special attention to the key message that gets across to citizens (and of course live up to that message). It has been additionally proposed that there should be one dedicated resource with the aim to promote the initiative, to be in constant communication with all kinds of stakeholders and to engage in getting users on board. Of course, many different ways and channels for communication have also been proposed by owners, including advertisements in online and offline media, presence in events and workshops, even demonstrations at the road. Evidently, the right marketing mix is to be decided by each initiative after considering its own specificities.

Security and privacy. Security and privacy of users is one of the concerns that each eParticipation initiative has to face. The absolute need for security is self-evidently manifested in all initiatives that implement any kind of voting mechanisms. All such initiatives have reported that they utilise security mechanisms of different kinds and no security breaches were reported among these. However, when it comes to privacy and the degree of anonymity allowed not all owners seem to agree on a unique and ideal solution. On the one side, it has been reported in most of the initiatives that participation has been deliberately designed to be anonymous in order not to intimidate users who are concerned whether their personal information will be available online to the rest of the participants. On the other hand, it has been also reported that the fact that the contributing users are posting under their full name brings integrity to their opinions as well as an overall trust towards the whole initiative and the produced outcomes. Obviously, the ideal approach to privacy concerns depends also on the actual circumstances of each initiative, the kind of users it targets, the prestige the owner brings to the effort, etc. Nevertheless, it is a feature to be thoroughly debated and decided at the design phase.

Organisational issues. Different organisational concerns have been highlighted by the owners as success factors; these can be summarised in three broad categories: management related, process related, and moderation related.

- *Management.* There is consensus that strong project management is an essential component for success; a senior person should be preferably appointed as a dedicated resource responsible for the whole project's operation. Moreover, it is important to establish an effective and sustainable management process with short tasks and checkpoints and defined communication channels among the team members. Finally, the need for generous timescales and contingency planning has been also highlighted; managers should allow sufficient time for planning and implementation and should try to exploit previous experience in the field (i.e. lessons learnt, replication of tested methods and tools, etc.)

- *Processes*. Processes are of particular importance in eParticipation as the whole initiative should offer an end-to-end effective, satisfying and timely experience. Processes planning starts from the initial conceptualising phase when certain considerations and decisions have to be made. For example, owners stressed the importance of taking into consideration the particular needs and circumstances of the targeted audience (i.e. with regards to internet usage patterns, ICT skills, cultural and political specificities, etc.) and devising a tailor-made participation methodology to fit the purposes of the initiative at hand. Clearly, the ultimate intention is to achieve inclusiveness (i.e. by ensuring that relevant special audiences and minority groups are also considered) and a balanced participation and user engagement to the best possible degree. Moreover, experience showed that active two-way communication between operators and users of the initiatives is a must; it is proposed that tools for users' comments and contact are kept as simple as possible and that users are involved in the development/enhancement process. Finally, clear and realistic business processes are need to be put in place for ensuring that all different roles/departments provide relevant content/feedback in due time and according to the promises made to the participants.
- *Moderation*. All reported initiatives agree on the need for a heavy, active and timely moderation. Moderators need adequate training in order to be able to support and promote open, serious, and high quality participation while they should also possess sufficient awareness of participation principles and practices in order to identify and tackle inevitable difficulties such as the conscious or unconscious domination of the discussion by some extremely active users. In overall, moderation plays an important role in keeping up the commitment and enthusiasm of users.

Topics complexity and quality of participation. Finally, it was reported that the technocratic and legislative complexity as well as the limited knowledge and expertise of users prevented a deep deliberation on the issues at hand limiting thus participation at a superficial and trivial level. Moreover, the fact that many participants did not appear ready to be involved in productive dialogue and they rather preferred to generally express opinions, personal view points or convictions, which were rarely supported by informed arguments, deteriorated the situation. It was therefore suggested that a preliminary processing of the data under discussion to make it understandable by non-experts would be a solution to the aforementioned issue.

5 Discussion and Conclusions

Electronic Participation has recently evolved to re-engage people with the democratic processes by exploiting the potential of ICT. At the academic level, a number of frameworks and models have been proposed for understanding eParticipation including evaluating relevant initiatives. At the practical level, a large number of eParticipation initiatives have been launched at all levels, some with success while others without.

In this paper, we investigate the use of ICTs and the main success factors of eParticipation initiatives according to the practitioners' perspective. For that purpose, we conducted an extensive European study and obtained information using a questionnaire that was developed for this purpose based on the relevant literature.

A first observation of this study is the low response rate of returned questionnaires. This may be due to the fact that some initiatives have officially ended, due to the significant length of the questionnaire or due to the language of communication (English). On the other hand, the different media used by the research team (e.g. email, telephone, fax) for a long period of time and the nature of the initiatives (eParticipation) allowed us to hope for better response at the beginning of our study.

With regards to the communication channel employed, the Internet is the dominant medium (100%) while a significant percentage of initiatives (30%) employs non electronic channels in combination with electronic ones. In terms of ICT tools, portals, plain discussion forums, online newsletters and eConsultation systems are the prominent players. This suggests that eParticipation initiatives mainly use existing, general-purpose ICT tools (which are sometimes tailored) and not eParticipation-specific tools. In terms of technologies, security seems a clear concern while general-purpose developed technologies (such as Web 2.0, mobile and wireless technologies, and streaming media) dominate the field with eParticipation-specific technologies lagging behind.

The results of this study also indicated seven main success factor categories according to the practitioners' perspective. These are commitment by the government; usability; combining online with offline channels; a thorough communication and promotion plan; security and privacy; organisational issues; and topics complexity and quality of participation. In the relevant literature, academics have recently attempted to identify success factors and barriers in the context of electronic Government (eGovernment). Summarising existing work, Gilbert and Balestrini suggest benefits which include: avoid personal interaction, control over service delivery, convenience, cost, personalization and time, while barriers for adoption include confidentiality, easy to use, enjoyable, reliable, safe and visual appearance [15]. Similarly, Ebrahim and Irani [16] suggest eGovernment barriers which include IT infrastructure, security and privacy, IT skills, organisational (e.g. unclear vision, lack of communication between departments etc) and operational cost. In a first attempt to put our results in the context of relevant eGovernment work, we note that there are certain factors which are common, such as usability, security and privacy. On the other hand, it should be noted that there are certain factors deemed particularly important for eParticipation practitioners, which do not seem to deserve particular attention in eGovernment. These include combining online with offline channels, having a thorough communication and promotion plan as well as topics complexity and quality of participation. In addition, organisational aspects in eParticipation have somehow a different orientation as besides project management they also include participatory processes and moderation which are unique to eParticipation. In depth investigation of similarities and differences between eGovernment and eParticipation success factors is outside the scope of this paper and is left for future work as our initial results indicate there might be considerable differences.

Acknowledgments. Work presented in this paper has been partially funded by the EU through the European eParticipation study (http://islab.uom.gr/eP/).

References

1. Macintosh, A.: eParticipation in policy-making: the research and the challenges. In: Exploiting the Knowledge Economy: Issues, Applications. Case Studies. IOS Press, Amsterdam (2006) ISBN 1-58603-682-3
2. Communication from the Commission to the Council, the European Parliament, the European Economic and Social Committee and the Committee of the Regions: i2010 eGovernment Action Plan: Accelerating eGovernment in Europe for the Benefit of All. Commission of the European Communities, Brussels (2006)
3. Barber, B.: Strong democracy: Participatory politics for a new age. University of California Press, Berkeley (1984)
4. Coleman, S., Gøtze, J.: Bowling Together: Online Public Engagement in Policy Deliberation. Hansard Society, London (2001),
   http://bowlingtogether.net/bowlingtogether.pdf
   (accessed March 30, 2010)
5. Macintosh, A.: Characterizing E-Participation in Policy-Making. In: 37th International Conference on System Science, Hawaii (2004)
6. Kalampokis, E., Tambouris, E., Tarabanis, K.: A Domain Model for eParticipation. In: Third International Conference on Internet and Web Application and Services, Athens (2008)
7. Smith, S., Macintosh, A., Millard, J.: eParticipation Analytical Framework. European eParticipation Study deliverable (2008),
   http://www.european-eparticipation.eu (accessed March 30, 2010)
8. Aichholzer, G., Allhutter, D.: Evaluation Perspectives and Key Criteria in eParticipation. In: 6th International Eastern European eGov Days: Results and Trends (2008)
9. Rowe, G., Frewer, L.: Public Participation Methods: A Framework for Evaluation. Science, Technology and Human Values 25(1), 3–29 (2000)
10. Tambouris, E., Liotas, N., Tarabanis, K.: A framework for Assessing eParticipation Projects and Tools. In: 40th Hawaii International Conference on System Sciences, Hawaii (2007)
11. Macintosh, A., Whyte, A.: Towards an Evaluation Framework for eParticipation. Transforming Government: People, Process & Policy 2(1) (2008)
12. DEMO-net Consortium: D13.3 DEMO-net booklet: eParticipation Evaluation and Impact (2008), http://www.demo-net.org (accessed March 30, 2010)
13. Panopoulou, E., Tambouris, E., Tarabanis, K.: eParticipation good practice cases and diffusion. European eParticipation Study deliverable (2008),
   http://www.european-eparticipation.eu (accessed March 30, 2010)
14. Panopoulou, E., Tambouris, E., Tarabanis, K.: eParticipation initiatives: How is Europe progressing? European Journal of ePractice (2008),
   http://www.epracticejournal.eu (accessed March 30, 2010)
15. Gilbert, D., Balestrini, P.: Barriers and benefits in the adoption of e-government. The International Journal of Public Sector Management 17(4), 286–301 (2004)
16. Ebrahim, Z., Irani, Z.: E-government adoption: architecture and barriers. Business Process Management Journal 11(5), 589–611 (2005)

Appendix

This appendix provides the list of eParticipation initiatives included in this research. It should be noted that the names of five initiatives do not appear in the table below because the owners have wished for their feedback to remain anonymous. However, the feedback gathered by these initiatives has been included in the analysis.

eParticipation initiative		Scope
Aarhus Clearinghouse for Environmental Democracy	World	International
Debate Europe	EU	European
European Citizens' Consultations	EU	European
European Ombudsman	EU	European
Fundamental Rights Agency	EU	European
Website of Commissioner Almunia	EU	European
Portal for the involvement of civil society in the Slovenian presidency of the EU	Slovenia	European
Rostra	Denmark	National
Internet Voting in Estonia	Estonia	National
Osale.ee	Estonia	National
Environmental Information Portal PortalU	Germany	National
Kommunalforum.de - City administration network	Germany	National
Online Consultation "Citizen's Portal Draft Bill"	Germany	National
e-pnyka.gr	Greece	National
Virtual Cities	Netherlands	National
The Citizen's Forum	Slovenia	National
Geneva Internet Voting Application	Switzerland	National
iVote.ch	Switzerland	National
e-consultant	UK	National
Food Standards Agency Blog	UK	National
eParticipation for the Regional Land Use Plan Frankfurt/Rhine-Main	Germany	Regional
Senso@Iternato	Italy	Regional
kNOWing	Portugal	Regional
Bus Stop 34	UK	Regional
Living Bridge	Germany	Local
Metropole Hamburg - Growing City	Germany	Local
Participatory Budgeting Freiburg	Germany	Local
Participatory Budgeting Hamburg	Germany	Local
Re-design of the Domplatz	Germany	Local
e-dialogos	Greece	Local
Turin Multimedia Channel	Italy	Local
Madrid-p	Spain	Local
21st Century Voting in Sheffield	UK	Local
Kingston Upon Thames ePetitions	UK	Local
Swindon Electoral Modernisation Programme	UK	Local

Tracking and Explaining E-Participation in India

Rajeev Gowda[1] and Hemangini Gupta[2]

[1] Economics and Social Sciences, Indian Institute of Management Bangalore,
Bannerghatta Road, Bangalore 560076, India
gowda@iimb.ernet.in
[2] Women's Studies Department, Emory University,
550 Asbury Circle, Candler Library Suite 128, Atlanta, GA 30322, USA
hemanginig@gmail.com

Abstract. India has recently witnessed various initiatives that harness information and communication technologies (ICTs) to promote electoral reform and political mobilization. These efforts have been initiated mainly by non governmental organizations drawn from India's urban, English-speaking, upper and middle classes. These efforts have been focused on non-partisan process improvements or short-lived political mobilization with limited success. We analyze these initiatives against the backdrop of modern India's political evolution which has seen the marginalization of upper and middle classes in politics. We see technology as central to the re-engagement of ICT-savvy upper and middle classes with the political sphere. We suggest that political neutrality may be an effective and appropriate strategy for India's upper and middle classes in the pursuit of their policy agendas.

Keywords: India, Political Mobilization, Registration, Reform, Middle and Upper Class E-Participation.

1 Introduction

In many countries including India, Information and Communication Technologies (ICTs) are being utilized by citizens, organizations and governments to engage with political processes. Norris (2003) has articulated how ICTs can improve direct democracy (through, e.g., electronic voting on referenda), representative democracy (through improving the quality of representation and helping elected representatives perform more efficiently), and pluralist democracy (through facilitating the mobilization of multiple interests to influence the political process, including through the formation of new political parties). In this chapter we focus on the Indian experience with regard to how ICTs have been harnessed by citizens and civil society groups to enhance the quality of representative democracy.

In the following sections, we describe the e-initiatives and online mobilizations, which have sought to address issues of political reform, engagement and mobilization in India. In the next section, we examine these efforts and classify them along three dimensions: 1) issues related to voting and electoral rolls 2) dissemination of candidate and voting information 3) agenda setting and policy framing. In the section

E. Tambouris, A. Macintosh, and O. Glassey (Eds.): ePart 2010, LNCS 6229, pp. 66–81, 2010.

that follows, we seek to examine the ways in which e-initiatives have had explicitly political purposes, such as the mobilization of voters, the launch of new political parties or to trigger public responses to controversial political developments. In the section after, we lay out the larger Indian political context so as to better comprehend the nature of voter engagement and the larger implications of Internet access and a well-established IT industry. In our final section, we frame the initiatives discussed in the initial sections against the backdrop of the Indian context and attempt to analyze India's fast-evolving e-landscape and those who take advantage of it for political purposes.

2 Civil Society E-Democracy Initiatives in India

2.1 Voting and Electoral Rolls

The responsibility for conducting elections in India rests with the Election Commission of India (ECI). It is an independent, constitutionally-sanctioned authority responsible for conducting free and fair elections as well as ensuring voter-registration. The standard procedure for voter registration involves physical verification of the voters' claimed place of residence by ECI representatives (Gowda, 2007); however, recently, the ECI has experimented with online voter registration, subject to physical verification. The ECI also uses the web to put into the public domain all the information that the candidate is obliged to share such as his/her educational accomplishments, assets and liabilities and criminal records, if any. Judicial references and election laws are also available online. The website has been fairly popular in terms of the hits it has received, and the ECI has been widely appreciated for its move towards enhancing transparency and user-friendliness.

However, in spite of the ECI's attempts to register India's millions of voters, there remain substantial gaps in electoral rolls. Omissions are rife in urban areas, where people tend to remain unregistered because of migration, or not being present at home when ECI verification is conducted (Ramanathan, 2008). In recent years, urban residents, particularly the educated middle and upper classes, have complained that the process of registering to vote itself is cumbersome (requiring people to demonstrate proof of residence at particular election centers at particular times on certain dates). This dissatisfaction with the enrolment process has been identified as the key barrier to participation by the educated middle and upper classes. In order to redress this problem, a private sector corporation came together with a non-governmental organization and embarked on a campaign to make the voter registration process smoother for the electorate by using ICTs. This campaign is described below:

2.1.1 Jaago Re
Jaago Re (literally translated to "Wake up" in Hindi) was a campaign targeted at overcoming voter apathy ahead of the 2009 General Election. *Jaago Re* has been the tag line used in advertisements by Tata Tea to promote its products, starting in 2007. In 2008 the company decided to address the issue of voter apathy. Working together with the independent non-governmental organization (NGO) Janaagraha, the *Jaago*

Re campaign was an all-India effort primarily conducted online through the website (www.jaagore.com). It provided voters with the information necessary for them to enroll as voters. Although essentially aimed at first time voters and youth, it billed itself as a movement for change via 'active participation in the democratic process.' Once registered, members received information regarding the status of their voter registration and news about the elections and candidates.

Tata Tea treated Jaago Re as a component of its marketing strategy and not as a corporate social responsibility initiative. It engaged the services of a leading advertising agency and put out television and print advertisements. The Jaago Re One Billion Votes campaign managed to secure or assist in over 600,000 voter registrations all over India. Its website received over 16 million visitors and 5 million registrations; thus the campaign can be termed a success in terms of its overall impact and presence (Pinglay, 2009).

2.2 Voting Choices and Information

2.2.1 Association for Democratic Reforms

The next step in the process of voter-mobilization is provision of access to information about political candidates and parties. Given that India's party system is increasingly characterized by fragmentation and multiparty coalitions (Gowda and Sridharan, 2007), it has become difficult for voters to obtain detailed information about candidates and party manifestos. Despite the media's role in disseminating information, lack of adequate information on candidates has raised concerns regarding the quality of representatives in legislatures. For instance, over the last decade, many political parties have chosen to field candidates with criminal records. Further, corruption has increased across the board and voters are hard pressed to sift through candidates who might have amassed wealth through illegitimate means during their term in office.

If voters are to make an informed choice, it is necessary that they be provided with more information about candidates' antecedents and also about parties' manifestoes and track records. Recognition of this point led an independent organization called the Association for Democratic Reforms (ADR) to file a Public Interest Litigation (PIL) in the Supreme Court of India. This effort is a prominent example of citizen activism that resulted in policy change and improvement in the quality of India's democracy (Sastry, 2004). In its own words, the ADR "continues to works towards strengthening democracy and governance in India by focusing on fair and transparent electoral and political processes."

After a long drawn-out battle lasting four years, the Court ruled in favor of disclosure, and declared that candidates must release complete information on their financial, educational and criminal background (if any). Following this verdict and its enactment into law by parliament, the ADR has spearheaded a national 'Election Watch' campaign (detailed below), which has a significant online component. It works with 1200 NGOs across India in an effort toward improving the electoral process in India. The ADR and its partners have also been instrumental in obtaining a ruling from the Central Information Commission in 2008 to the effect that income tax returns of political parties will be made available in the public domain.

2.2.2 National Election Watch

The National Election Watch campaign operates both online (www.nationalelectionwatch.org) and offline and aims to provide voters with: (i) Information on candidates' finances, education and criminal records, based on their sworn affidavits; (ii) Feedback from the public about the work done by their elected representatives; (iii) Data on the state of a constituency measured on human development index parameters; (iv) Ratings of various representatives based on peoples' comments and the demonstrable improvements in their constituencies during their tenure, etc. and (v) A channel to provide feedback to elected representatives, so that they are better informed about constituents' priorities and concerns.

Apart from maintaining a constant vigil on the activities of the elected representatives, the Election Watch campaign seeks to facilitate an online dialogue between the representative and his constituents, enabling the public to evaluate the performance of elected representatives. The Election Watch campaign gets its information mainly from the affidavits of the candidates or by means of petitioning the Election Commission and the government under the Right to Information (RTI) Act which makes it mandatory for the Government to provide relevant information to applicants.

Although its impact on voters is hard to measure, the Election Watch has arguably played a pivotal role in recent improvements in the quality of political representation. For instance, the state of Bihar, for the first time in decades, has no criminally tainted minister in the council. This is because the Chief Minister refused to include anyone with a criminal record in the cabinet and the ready availability of such information in the public domain allowed the press and the public to check on whether he had indeed lived up to his assurance. In Gujarat state, an Election Watch report spurred the Election Commission into investigating candidate's affidavits and initiating proceedings against those who had supplied false information. The number of candidates with serious offenses in the Karnataka state elections came down from 217 in 2004 to 93 in 2008. Above all, major political parties such as the Indian National Congress (Congress) and the Bharatiya Janata Party (BJP) have started examining the records of applicants before nominating them as party candidates.

The internet has been the main medium through which ADR and National Election Watch have communicated the information they receive and the measures they take to the public. It has also been instrumental in stirring up public support for programs and initiatives. Election Watch information is now regularly being used by mainstream media as they profile (usually) "big players" fighting the elections in constituencies that would interest their readers/viewers. Details of financial information are highlighted in mainstream press articles, which garner significant attention, especially if it appears that the financial information provided seems unlikely or dubious, e.g., an understatement of assets by candidates publicly regarded as particularly wealthy.

2.2.3 Liberty Institute's Empower India initiative

Even in smaller towns across India, local media are picking up the information about candidates available online and using it to increase awareness amongst voters. Barun Mitra at the Liberty Institute, which conducts research and advocacy on policy issues including democracy and governance (online at www.EmpowerIndia.org) makes an interesting observation in this regard. During the 2007 State Assembly elections, he found that a number of local media collectives and the *panchayats* (local governments) had used the candidate-background information available on Empower India's website. According to Mitra, it is the poor who sustain democracy, and resources such as these played a very important role in helping them assess the integrity and honesty of elected representatives. He noted that there was more eagerness for candidate information from slum-dwellers in Delhi rather than from a more affluent audience in Kerala. The Kerala audience was privy to the same information, but only saw the service being provided as a website, not as a handle to enhance democratic functioning (Bawa, 2009).

2.2.4 Smart Vote

Another civil society initiative that emerged during the 2009 parliamentary election is 'Smart Vote,' a campaign aimed at using the medium of the internet to enhance the quality of democracy in India by giving voters the means to make a more informed choice. It states as its vision the need to improve the quality of elected representatives. It identifies the parochial mindset of the typical voter as the major impediment to choosing accountable elected officials. Voting choices are made in favor of a party irrespective of the record of the candidate or simply in order to punish the incumbent government. The campaign primarily uses its website and other online media to get across its message. It offers information on the constituency as well as the candidates contesting from it, including past statements and current interviews.

The site also informs citizens about their representatives, their records in parliament, salary and allowances along with other pertinent data. While it is difficult to gauge the site's impact on voters' electoral choices, Smart Vote, in alliance with a television channel, pioneered live, interactive debates between political candidates for the first time in India during the 2009 parliament election. As these debates provided an interface for live interaction of candidates and voters this Smart Vote initiative significantly enhanced candidates' availability and accessibility.

2.3 Policy Analysis and Priority Setting

2.3.1 Parliamentary Research Service

Parliament sessions are filmed and broadcast on a State-run TV channel. Yet, detailed information about bills being considered by parliament is not easy for the public to access. Neither is analysis of the bills easily available to the public. Analysis in the mass media can suffer from lack of sufficient depth, or can represent partisan viewpoints. This problem is shared by other key stakeholders including members of parliament and the media. Because of the use of the party "whip" which mandates that members must vote in line with the party, and the hurried passage of many bills in parliament (Madhukar, 2008) even members of parliament sometimes have little information about what they are voting for or against (Yadav, 2008).

In order to address this problem, a civil society initiative led to the establishment of the Parliamentary Research Service (PRS, online at http://www.prsindia.org/), modeled on the lines of the non-partisan Congressional Research Service in the United States of America. PRS is an independent body that has taken on the challenge of decoding and simplifying bills into 3-4 page briefs which are then circulated to all Members of Parliament, media houses, the top 500 Indian corporations, and also displayed on the PRS website. The website aims to make it easy for the press and the public to understand the nature and implications of bills under consideration in Parliament. Comments from stakeholders are also directed to the relevant Minister.

Members of Parliament, across party lines have welcomed the information generated by PRS and credited it with helping them perform their legislative roles better (Srivastava, 2007). Further, the information provided by PRS has enabled greater transparency about the performance of Members of Parliament. Media coverage of PRS's detailed reports on the actual attendance and participation of Members of Parliament also puts pressure on members of parliament to maintain accountability to voter constituencies.

2.3.2 Praja

ICTs have also been used to help determine what issues and priorities are of concern to voters. This contrasts with the traditional top-down process whereby the candidate offers a platform and the voters' role is limited to a yes/no choice for or against that candidate. The group, *Praja* (meaning 'citizen') conducts online activities to link citizens with each other. It provides a common online platform (a moderated, discussion board) to discuss governance issues. *Praja* conducted a survey on the eve of the 2009 parliament election which allowed voters to identify issues that they considered crucial in this election at both the State as well as national levels. Candidates were later interviewed by representatives of the website on these topics, and the interviews were made public on the website. *Praja* has allowed citizens within communities to access information through a process of mutual sharing and has enabled collective action by uniting people with common concerns.

2.3.3 Resurgent India

Another NGO called Resurgent India, recruited youth over the internet to participate in a Youth Manifesto workshop prior to the 2009 parliament election. Given that India is a predominantly young country with over 70 percent of its population below the age of 35, the theme of this workshop was to assess the platforms of the major political parties from the perspective of youth. The workshop generated an alternative set of agendas—The Youth Manifesto—focused on the needs of youth. The Youth Manifesto was presented to a parliament candidate from the ruling Congress party and to a national executive member of the Bharatiya Janata Party (BJP), India's main opposition party (Gupta, 2009).

3 ICTs and Political Activity

3.1 Political Competition and the Use of the Internet

In India, although a major political party such as the BJP was using ICTs in their most basic form (text messaging, phone calls and a basic Internet presence) as early as 2003, it was not until recently that ICT usage gained prominence within election campaigns (see `https://digitalcommons.georgetown.edu/blogs/isdyahoofellow/tag/rahul-gandhi/`). Limited access and low levels of usage have traditionally been the impediments to using the internet as a campaign tool.

The BJP's 2004 "India Shining" campaign was a path breaker in this regard. The BJP allocated as much as 5% of its total campaign funds to online campaigns, which mainly targeted urban ICT- savvy voters. It revamped its campaign website, aggressively sent out text messages, pre-recorded voice clips and emails to over 20 million people. Although the campaign ended with the party being routed at the polls, the nature and mode of its campaign in 2004 set the tone for the 2009 parliamentary elections   (see: `https://digitalcommons.georgetown.edu/blogs/ msfs-556-spring2009/how-internet-and-mobile-technologies- are-transforming-election-campaigning-in-india/` and Mehra, 2009).

Most political parties expected Internet-based campaigning to have more impact in 2009. This is because a third of India's voters are now under the age of 25. The weightage of the urban voter in the electoral process has also increased 2-3 fold after the recent redistricting exercise (termed Delimitation in India) as well as due to growing   Internet penetration (from 16 million in 2004 to 80 million in 2009; for information about redistricting see www.delimitation-india.com). In fact, the success of Barack Obama's Internet campaign in terms of gaining supporters and raising funds has been seen as a model for future political campaigns in other countries too (Mosk, 2008).

In India the pro-BJP camp was in the forefront on the Internet in terms of content as well as sheer presence and reach. While the BJP's own website consisted mainly of its manifesto, that of its prime ministerial candidate, L K Advani had many interactive features including an active forum and a blog (www.lkadvani.in). The task set out by the BJP camp for its online initiative was to "to contact and mobilize young voters in thousands of college campuses across the country" and build a volunteer movement. There were also links to the L.K. Advani Facebook page, the Advani for PM Orkut (a social networking site) page and the BJP supporters group on Orkut had nearly 30,000 members.

The Friends of the BJP website (http://friendsofbjp.org) is run by volunteers with no formal affiliation to the party. It generated ideas for the BJP to act on, and conducted outreach efforts aimed at enabling the party to win more urban seats. Several BJP leaders   including   Gujarat   Chief   Minister   Narendra   Modi   (online   at www.narendramodi.in) and Madhya Pradesh Chief Minister Shivraj Singh Chouhan (www.shivrajsinghchouhan.in) also have their own websites. The BJP also ran an extensive online advertisement campaign, primarily on Google, with search advertisements across 200,000 keywords (including keywords related to Congress leaders), placement advertisements across 50,000 websites, and banner advertisements across 2,000 websites. With almost a billion searches every month, the BJP's campaign was expected to influence up to 75% of India's Internet users (Sapre, 2009).

The Congress also has a website, which is mainly an online version of its manifesto. Some Congress candidates for parliament including former United Nations Under Secretary Shashi Tharoor and other Congress leaders like the late Andhra Pradesh Chief Minister Y.S.Rajasekhar Reddy have made attempts to leverage the Internet in order to get in touch with voters. One of the authors of this paper is also a co-founder and blogger on www.hamaracongress.com, an independent online forum supportive of the Congress party. This blog enables debate and constructive criticism about national policy and politics and provides a Congress-oriented online counter thrust against other political parties.

Other parties like the Communist Party of India (Marxist) and the Samajwadi party have also tried to use these new media tools to their advantage. The latter party's use of the Internet is ironic because it promised to ban computers in its manifesto! These Internet based campaigns are not expected to have large-scale impact currently due to inadequate penetration and lack of access in rural and small town India, but they do represent attempts by political parties to engage the voter more directly and convey their message in an undiluted manner.

3.2 Activism and Political Mobilization Using ICTs

3.2.1 Citizens Initiative

In 2006, a pioneering attempt to harness ICTs to mobilize voters was initiated by a neutral, non-partisan platform called Citizens Initiative, with which one of the authors was actively involved (Gowda, 2007). Its aim was to enrol graduates to register as voters for an election to Karnataka state's bicameral legislature from the Bangalore Graduates constituency, whose unique feature is an electorate restricted to graduates. Because registration was a cumbersome process involving provision of proof of graduation to the election authorities, less than five percent of potentially eligible voters participated in these elections historically. Citizens Initiative launched an online voter enrolment campaign called "End the Apathy" and targeted graduate voters in ICT companies located in Bangalore that employ hundreds of thousands of graduates. The campaign involved these companies' chief executive officers (CEOs) sending an email to their entire staff exhorting them to enrol and vote and offering the assistance of the companies' human resource development departments where needed. Citizens Initiative's website also provided more information about the election and e-enabled the registration process. Voters who enrolled through this process were also assured of information about candidates at the time of the election.

However, Citizens Initiative was limited in its impact, and it managed to register only around 4000 voters, a fraction of the numbers enrolled by political parties using offline methods. One reason for this failure is graduates' general ignorance of the constituency itself (Shile, 2006). Gowda (2007) analyzes the campaign's failure thus: "[T]he "End the Apathy" campaign of Citizens Initiative contained a general, "do-good, be-an-active-citizen" type of message. But this was a message without a messenger, in the sense that there was no candidate for the potential voter to identify with. Hence, voters did not generally put in the effort to register, even though the process was made as simple as was feasible. In contrast, regular parties enrolled voters on behalf of known candidates and that led to a certain focused commitment from their target voters." Citizens Initiative had been constrained to be neutral and non-partisan by CEOs who were only willing to enable and promote an online voter registration process in their companies on that basis. This neutrality may have ensured its failure at mobilizing graduate voters in a constituency explicitly available to them.

3.2.2 Youth for Equality

In India, the use of ICTs in a significant manner for political mobilization can be dated to begin with a campaign called Youth for Equality in 2006. This campaign was organized to rally students opposed to the Indian Government's extension of the reservation system (similar to affirmative action but involving quotas) to elite

government-run institutions of higher and professional education (online at
http://www.youthforequality.com/). A small group of volunteers,
distributed across various cities, coordinated a series of protests and demonstrations
against the government's move using the website as a platform. Youth for Equality
rapidly generated online branches across India and in many parts of the world where
Indians, particularly students and computer-related professionals, have migrated.
Some members of the organization even contested local body elections in Mumbai,
albeit unsuccessfully. However, when the Supreme Court ruled in favor of the
government's reservation policy (with the proviso that it should be available only to
people below a threshold level of income), Youth for Equality fizzled out and has not
been able to sustain its initial momentum.

3.2.3 Lok Paritran

In 2005-2006, a group of young professionals mainly educated at the elite Indian
Institutes of Technology formed a political party called Lok Paritran that emphasized
meritocracy (http://www.lok-paritran.org/). They mobilized membership
and funding through the Internet and spawned support groups on various social
networking sites. They followed the unique strategy of plunging into the electoral fray
wherever elections were being held with the hope that the excitement associated with
elections would draw volunteers and supporters. When Lok Paritran contested the
election for the legislature in the state of Tamil Nadu, they were able to draw enough
votes in two constituencies to cause the defeat of powerful politicians from mainstream
parties (Gowda, 2007). Since the agenda of Lok Paritran favored the middle class, IT-
savvy demographic segment, their use of the Internet allowed them substantial gains in
Mylapore, one of the urban Chennai constituencies they contested (Muthalaly, 2006).
However, while the party did grow and establish a network of branches across the
country, it was unable to sustain itself. It has since split into many splinter groups and
has been unable to build constructively on its initial electoral forays.

3.2.4 Bengaluru Unites

More recently, young people in Bangalore were mobilized in simultaneous protests
across Bangalore city by 'Bengaluru Unites' - an initiative spear-headed by one of the
authors of this paper. Over the months of February and March, 2009, a series of
attacks against women in the name of 'culture' and 'tradition' took place in some parts
of Karnataka state, followed by seven attacks on women in Bangalore city, its capital.
Sensing the anger, disgust and fear among the people of Bangalore, the campaign
utilized the Internet and mass media to successfully organize a series of simultaneous,
geographically dispersed protests across Bangalore city against 'moral policing.' The
organizing platform was a blog site: www.bengaluru-unites.blogspot.
com. A cell phone number was provided to those who wished to join in: upon texting
the name of a locality to this number, a reply text would inform them of the nearest
protest site. Thousands of college students and working professionals, including many
who had never indulged in political action ever, participated in the protests (Srinivas,
2009). The overwhelming numbers of young people participating in the protests
(between the ages of 18-35) suggest that ICTs are a particularly powerful medium to
mobilize India's youth.

3.2.5 The Pink Chaddi Campaign

Perhaps the most significant and widespread recent use of the online medium in mobilizing real-time political engagement took place in February 2009, with the launch of the 'Pink Chaddi' campaign. Initially set up as a Facebook group, 'The Consortium of Pub-Going, Loose and Forward Women' countered 'moral policing' by the Sri Rama Sene, the same extreme right-wing group that Bengaluru Unites protested against. Its membership rapidly shot to 58,000 and it commenced activities offline as well. In face of widespread protests, and media attention and activism, the extreme right-wing group, the Sri Rama Sene, was forced to back down from its proposed plan of 'forcibly marrying off men and women seen together on Valentine's Day' (Gupta, 2009).

4 The Indian Political Context

4.1 The Evolution of the Indian Polity

India is the world's largest democracy characterized by periodic polls, universal suffrage and multiparty competition. India also meets the broader definition of an ideal democracy: political and civil freedom, popular sovereignty and political equality (Diamond and Morlino, 2004). Varshney (2000) points out that India's 'deep' democracy satisfies two key criteria of democratic theory: contestation and participation. Contestation is satisfied because elections in India are truly competitive and incumbents are routinely challenged and defeated. Participation is satisfied because all sections of India's population vote or engage with the political process, and historically excluded sections are also finding greater access and representation. Arguably, India has successfully overcome the lack of democracy-enabling conditions such as industrialization, urbanization, mass literacy and a minimum standard of living, as well as serious obstacles to democracy such as religious, linguistic, and ethnic heterogeneity, inequality, and extreme poverty (Gowda and Sridharan, 2007).

Yadav (1999) describes India's electoral system as having gone through three phases since the first democratic election in 1952. The first electoral phase lasted from 1952-67 and was dominated by the Congress party. Its leadership was drawn significantly from the educated, upper castes who had led the movement for independence. This period was marked by low electoral participation and an insignificant and fractured Opposition. In the second phase, which lasted till the 1990s, as per Yadav, the Congress party retained this core position in the electoral system, even as a democratic upsurge brought many new entrants from the middle and "backward" (referring to groups that were historically on the lower rungs of the social status, economic, and educational ladders) classes into 'electoral politics'. The 1990s mark Yadav's Third Phase, a period often described as characterized by intense factionalisation of political space, coupled with excessive political corruption, non-governance, disorder and instability.

This third phase witnessed decline in the quality of democracy, rise of 'election fatigue,' and disinterest and cynicism with regard to politics among the educated, upper and middle classes (Gowda and Sridharan, 2007). Yadav (1999), however, reads the churning of the 1990s as the signs of a new social order, witnessing the ascent to leadership of increasing numbers of citizens from the lower rungs of the social hierarchy--the Other Backward Castes (OBCs) and Dalits. Noting the decline in political involvement of the upper castes and middle classes, Yadav asserts that India defies the textbook rule of political participation whereby the rich and powerful are more likely to vote in elections.   In India, an urban, educated, upper-caste citizen is far more likely to refrain from voting when compared to his counterpart amongst rural, uneducated, lower caste voters.

Varshney (2000) agrees that the social base of participation has distinctly shifted downwards – towards the countryside and the lower castes: "If there is any apathy towards voting, it is in India's larger cities and in their more affluent parts." Political theorists have pointed out that India's early politicians had definite Oxbridge backgrounds and they have gradually been replaced by leaders drawn from the lower castes, beginning with the relatively peaceful Dalit revolution in South India (Varshney, 2000). The rise of Dalit and OBC parties in the 1990s led to a reversal of the traditional patterns of political domination as as lower castes increasingly challenged the hegemony of the upper class upper caste English-speaking politician. Jaffrelot (2008) points out that this displacement by OBC and Dalit parties might account for the withdrawal of the middle and upper classes from occupying centre-stage in Indian politics.

Another explanation for the withdrawal of the middle and upper classes perhaps lies in India's 'parallel' approaches to governance. India has a complex system of patronage politics where voters consider caste and ethnic ties while voting, and patrons, in turn, respond with personal favors and interventions in bureaucratic functioning to help their supporters identified along lines of caste, language or ethnicity (Chandra, 2004). The rise of lower-caste and Dalit politicians means that upper and middle class voters do not share the same identity-based rapport with their representatives. However, upper-caste, affluent citizens can afford to secede from this form of political engagement by relying on strategies such as bribes, employing a middle man to navigate bureaucratic labyrinths or by using the private sector to meet desired ends –choices that are possibly unavailable to those less privileged.

We argue that the churning associated with the Third Electoral Phase might have unwittingly given rise to a 'Fourth Electoral Phase': marked by a tentative return to political engagement by a rising number of middle classes. Election campaigns in the recently concluded parliament election keenly targeted this traditionally apathetic class. In addition, recent media editorial commentary has suggested that India's urban elite regard the rise of lower caste parties as "disturbing" and unsettling (Mustafa, 2009). We suggest that this discomfort can translate into increased political engagement by the upper castes in an attempt to regain some measure of control over a changing political sphere increasingly dominated by backward caste and class groupings.

Our 'Fourth Electoral Phase' coincides with the Election Commission's redistricting of parliament constituencies to take into account population movements from rural to urban areas. This has increased electoral representation in favor of urban areas. Urban areas have more middle and upper classes when compared with rural areas. The Fifteenth General Election in 2009 is the first parliament election using these newly redrawn constituencies. Its results, surprisingly, indicate that the original figure of the well-educated, foreign-returned, upper class and caste politician might be making a comeback. The election of a large number of foreign-educated, well-heeled politicians might partly be because of the return of the middle class voter (though many such politicians have been elected from rural constituencies).

The final feature of the Fourth Phase is its coincidence with India's economic "liberalization." This period, commencing from 1991, has been marked by a lowering of bureaucratic barriers such as licensing requirements for industry, and is credited with unleashing entrepreneurial energies across India. It has been marked by a significant expansion in the numbers of the urban upper and middle classes (Jaffrelot and van der Veer, 2008). This period is also marked by increased ICT-fluency and literacy, with estimates suggesting that by 2020, approximately 60% of India's population will be IT-enabled (Internet usage figures from www.internetworldstats.com). It is the combination of India's urban upper and middle classes re-engaging with government and utilizing ICTs that enables us to explain the range of ICT-enabled reform and political initiatives that we described in earlier sections of this chapter.

5   Analysis and Conclusion

ICTs and the ease with which the middle and upper classes can access and use them may have played a central role in enabling the re-engagement of these classes with the political process (in contrast with the "digital divide" that prevents many poor Indians from engaging with ICTs (Keniston, 2004)). This is in line with Castells' (1998) thesis that electronic communication offers the possibility of enhancing political participation in a wider sphere. Castells (1998) points out that 'online information access and computer mediated communication facilitate the diffusion and retrieval of information, and can enable interaction and debate in an autonomous, electronic forum, bypassing the control of the mainstream media'. He articulates how citizen initiatives can take the lead in this regard: 'More importantly, citizens can form, and are forming, their own political and ideological constellations, circumventing established political structures, thus creating a flexible, adaptable political field' (Castells, 1998, p 350).

However, as India's middle and upper classes begin to harness ICTs in e-democratic initiatives, what stands out is their substantial emphasis on "neutral" reforms and non-partisan interventions. This may be partly influenced by their wariness of being "tainted" through association with mainstream political parties (and sections of the bureaucracy) that are popularly considered to be corrupt. Alternatively, it may reflect a desire on the part of the upper and middle classes to be able to achieve their goals regardless of which political formation is in office. But, as in the case of the Citizens' Initiative drive to register graduate voters, this neutrality can carry within it the seeds of its own destruction. Because there was no candidate who they could identify with and whose agenda they could support passionately, large numbers of potential voters ignored the voter registration drive even when this effort focused on a constituency that consisted only of graduate voters.

Another feature that stands out as common to many of the initiatives we describe (e.g., ADR, PRS, Liberty Institute, etc.) is their focus on information access. This approach limits reform to the provision of information in a non-partisan manner. Once that is accomplished, people are left to make their own judgments and choices. These

NGOs do not go beyond information provision to lead campaigns that bring about transformative change by pushing political parties to nominate better candidates. Such behavior on the part of these NGOs perhaps reflects a mindset and "business ethic" that privileges a certain clockwork efficiency (Lefebvre, 2008) rather than the messiness of political engagement. (In the case of ADR, however, the emphasis on information provision arose because it considered that to be the only achievable policy goal in the politico-judicial context wherein the reform campaign was conducted (Sastry, 2004)).

Where possible, the upper and middle classes have bypassed the democratic process in their pursuit of efficiency in governance. This is particularly evident in the efforts of the Bangalore Agenda Task Force (BATF), a body constituted by the Government of Karnataka during 1999-2004 to improve the performance of various civic agencies in the city of Bangalore. The members of the BATF included captains of India's information technology industry and BATF was able to effect change because it had the active support of the state's chief minister. It was able to set targets and change the behavior of government agencies without any official authority. This has led to critics raising questions about its legitimacy and its lack of concern for issues affecting the poor (Ghosh Rao, 2005). When the government and chief minister changed, BATF faded away. Of particular interest to our analysis, however, is the fact that one of the key members of the BATF also funded the establishment of the e-Governments Foundation. The e-Governments Foundation's stated goal was to utilize ICTs and geographic information systems to enhance the ability of municipal governments to levy taxes more effectively. Many municipal governments across India have utilized products and services from e-Governments Foundation (e.g., online grievance redressal systems) to enhance the effectiveness of governance and public service delivery.

In analyzing the engagement of elites with politics, Yadav (1999) points to a "Bhasha-English" divide, where "Bhasha" represents the rhetoric of social justice and democratic rights and English refers to the logic of globalization-friendly macroeconomic and bureaucratic management. Yadav argues that the success of the lower castes in the electoral sphere was a mere "consolation" that did not translate into an ability to guide policies. This is because the process of economic liberalization (pushed through by "stealth" (Jenkins, 2004)) had ensured that "most significant economic decisions were removed from the political agenda." Thus, while the lower classes "had the consolation of winning the elections, the other could continue to rule" (Yadav, 1999 p. 2398).

Given that the middle and upper classes are able to substantially achieve their policy goals without going through the rigors of the electoral process, it is not surprising then to see that there is very little attention to active political mobilization that sustains itself over elections and over time. The one example of a party with a middle-class-oriented agenda that utilized ICTs to organize nationwide is Lok Paritran, which we described above. While Lok Paritran gained substantial attention online and in the English language mass media, it did not succeed electorally, and has since split into many splinter groups.

There is only one example of middle class political mobilization, partly using ICTs, that has resulted in the formation of a political party that has won at least one seat in a state assembly election. This is the Lok Satta party in Andhra Pradesh whose founder, Jayaprakash Narayan, was recently elected to the state legislature. But Lok Satta explicitly began as a neutral, reform-oriented NGO, built a base of supporters mostly through extensive grassroots activity, and only converted itself into a political party about two years ago. As an NGO it participated actively in Election Watch and used its website to promote electoral reforms. More than ICTs, it is offline mobilization that has been central to its success. A key factor that enabled Lok Satta's only victory was Narayan's choice of Kukatpally constituency, which includes a large number of ICT professionals. Narayan's class background, reformist and non-mainstream-party-driven agenda, and ICT-enabled methods all found favor among such an electorate.

ICTs have clearly been the preferred technology of choice when the upper and middle classes needed to mobilize quickly to respond to particular policy and political developments that ran counter to their class interest or commonly-held values. As described above, Youth for Equality, Bengaluru Unites, and the Pink Chaddi campaign all turned to ICTs as the media of choice for their efforts towards mobilization and advocacy. Upadhya (2007) argues that the Internet and ICTs are natural choice of interface for the middle and upper classes, whose homogenous identity itself was largely constituted through the expansion of the information technology sector. Based on our explorations of ICT use by upper and middle classes, we can conclude that their future political mobilization efforts will centrally involve ICTs. However, as they proceed with their efforts, India's upper and middle classes will need to imagine new forms of inclusive citizen engagement based on ICTs and e-tools that are accessible and useful to all sections of Indian society and that bring about genuine reform. Only such inclusive efforts will help them overcome what Castells terms the current "legitimacy crisis" of the State (1998, p. 342).

Acknowledgments

The authors thank Rahul De, Karthik Shashidhar, Tanmay Belavadi, Aditya Sridhar and Simantini Mukherjee for their contributions to earlier drafts of this chapter and thank the anonymous reviewers whose suggestions substantially transformed this chapter.

References

1. Norris, P.: Deepening Democracy via E-governance. World Public Sector report. United Nations (2004)
2. Gowda, R.: Early Indian Initiatives in E-Democracy. International J. Electronic Governance 1(2), 174–189 (2007)
3. Ramanathan, R.: Fuzzy Electoral Math. Mint (May 22, 2008), http://www.livemint.com/2008/05/22003058/Fuzzy-electoral-math.html (retrieved July 22, 2009)
4. Pinglay, P.: The websites of India's e-election. BBC Worldwide (May 3, 2009), http://news.bbc.co.uk/2/hi/south_asia/8020522.stm (retrieved May 14, 2009)

5. Gowda, R., Sridharan, E.: The Consolidation of India's Democracy: The Role of Parties and The Party System, 1947 – 2006. In: Diamond, L., Ganguly, S., Plattner, M.F. (eds.) The State of India's Democracy, pp. 3–26. JHU, Baltimore (2007)
6. Sastry, T.: Electoral Reforms and Citizens' Initiatives. Economic and Political Weekly 39(13) (2004)
7. Bawa, Z.: Transparency and Politics: Politically Aware and Participatory Citizenry. Centre for Internet and Society (2009),
   http://www.cis-india.org/research/cis-raw/
   histories-of-the-internet/transparency-and-politics/
   2009/05/05/internet-politics-and-transparency-2 (retrieved May 11, 2009)
8. Madhukar, C.V.: 46-Day Report Card, The Indian Express (December 24, 2008)
9. Yadav, Y.: The Paradox of Political Representation. Seminar 586 (2008)
10. Srivastava, M., Madhukar, C.V.: His work on bills makes it easy for MPs to take part in debates Mint (May 21, 2007)
11. Gupta, H.: Youth Present Their Ideas to Political Leaders. Citizen Matters (April 22, 2009),
    http://bangalore.citizenmatters.in/articles/view/
    1033-bengaluru-youth-manifesto-elections (retrieved May 9, 2009)
12. Mehra, P.: Mediums and the Message. Mint (March 19, 2009)
13. Mosk, M.: Obama Rewriting Rules For raising Campaign Money Online. The Huffington Post, pp. A06 (March 28, 2008)
14. Sapre, O.: BJP Goes For The Kill, The Economic Times (March 13, 2009),
    http://economictimes.indiatimes.com/PoliticsNation/
    Advani-for-PM-ads-invade-the-net/articleshow/4258123.cms
    (retrieved May 14, 2009)
15. Gowda, R.: Early Indian Initiatives in E-Democracy. International J. Electronic Governance 1(2), 174–189 (2007)
16. Muthalaly, S.: Lok Paritran Pleased With Its Performance. The Hindu (May 13, 2006),
    http://www.hinduonnet.com/2006/05/13/stories/
    2006051322570300.htm (retrieved May 11, 2009)
17. Srinivas, S.: Bengaluru Unite. In: a Protest Campaign Citizen Matters (February 13, 2009),
    http://bangalore.citizenmatters.in/articles/view/
    813-bengaluru-unites-protest-campaign (retrieved May 11, 2009)
18. Gupta, H.: Moral Panic in the Media Infochange India (2009),
    http://infochangeindia.org/Media/Related-Features/
    Moral-panic-in-the-media.html (retrieved May 10, 2009)
19. Diamond, L., Morlino, L.: The Quality of Democracy, pp. 1–37. CDDRL Publication (2004)
20. Varshney, A.: Deeper but Unfinished. Seminar 485 (2000)
21. Yadav, Y.: Electoral Politics. In: The Time Of Change – India's Third Electoral System 1989- 1999. Economic and Political Weekly, vol. 34, pp. 2393–2399 (1999)
22. Jaffrelot, C.: 'Why Should We Vote?'. In: Jaffrelot, C., van der Veer, P. (eds.) Patterns of Middle Class Consumption in India and China, pp. 39–43. SAGE, New Delhi (2008)
23. Chandra, K.: Why Ethnic Parties Succeed: Patronage and Ethnic Head Counts in India. Cambridge University Press, Cambridge (2004)
24. Mustafa, K.: Mayawati: A Dalit's Daughter Strides Towards Delhi. India Together (May 18, 2009),
    http://www.indiatogether.org/2009/may/soc-mayawati.htm
    (retrieved May 8, 2009)

25. Jaffrelot, C., van der Veer, P.: Introduction. In: Jaffrelot, C., van der Veer, P. (eds.) Patterns of Middle Class Consumption in India and China, p. 19. SAGE, New Delhi (2008)
26. Keniston, K.: Introduction: The Four Digital Divides. In: Keniston, K., Kumar, D. (eds.) IT Experience in India: Bridging the Digital Divide, pp. 11–36. SAGE, New Delhi (2004)
27. Castells, M.: The Power of Identity. Blackwell Publishers, Oxford (1998)
28. Lefebvre, B.: The Indian Corporate Hospitals: Touching Middle Class Lives. In: Jaffrelot, C., van der Veer, P. (eds.) Patterns of Middle Class Consumption in India and China, pp. 88–109. SAGE, New Delhi (2008)
29. Ghosh Rao, A.: Public-Private or a Private Public? Promised Partnership of the Bangalore Agenda Task Force. Economic and Political Weekly Special Articles (November 19, 2005)
30. Jenkins, R.: Labour Policy and Second-Generation of Economic Reforms in India. In: Jenkins, R., Khilnani, S. (eds.) The Politics of India's Next Generation of Economic Reforms, Special Issue of India Review, Washington, DC, November 2004, vol. 3(2) (2004)
31. Upadhya, C.: Employment, Exclusion and 'Merit' in the Indian IT Industry. Economic and Political Weekly 42(20), 1863–1868 (2007)

e-Participation Experiences and Local Government in Catalonia: An Explanatory Analysis

Clelia Colombo

Researcher, Autonomous University of Barcelona, Av. Diagonal 409,
08008 Barcelona, Spain
ccolombo@gencat.cat

Abstract. This research analyzes the main explanatory factors in the impulse of citizen participation experiences in public decision-making, both online and offline, looking for differences and similarities regarding Internet use for participation. It focuses the analysis in Catalonia, one of the Spanish and European Union geographical areas that have headed the impulse of participatory experiences. It focuses on the local level of government, a prolific space for these activities. Anyway, their impulse among different municipalities has been very heterogeneous and data has not been collected in a systematic way. In general terms the analyses show that political variables such as the political party of the mayor or electoral abstention rate would be explanatory for promotion of e-Participatory experiences, as well as variables relating to the participative context of the municipality or population size.

Keywords: e-Participation, citizen participation, Internet.

1 Introduction

The end of the 20th century and the beginning of 21st have been marked by the revolution of information and communication technologies (from here on ICT), which burst onto the industrial era causing a change of paradigm toward the network society [10]. In this same period of time the old representative democratic system has fallen victim to a situation of democratic disaffection, meaning a lack of citizen confidence and participation in its institutions [29]. In this context, new participative practices are arising with the aim of approaching political representatives and citizens. We are talking about citizen participation understood as citizen participation experiences in public decision-making.

Incorporation of ICT in politics has introduced fundamental changes in democratic political systems [11][13][27]. Depending on the model of political management in which they are incorporated, we find models of e-Administration, e-Government or e-Governance (where e-Participation experiences are included). ICT are facilitating these practices with more extensive and direct information and greater communication between political representatives and citizens. Even so, we find important differences in the impulse and development of electronic participatory experiences (e-Participation). Thus, several questions arise: What fosters promotion of e-Participatory experiences? Which factors determine its development?

E. Tambouris, A. Macintosh, and O. Glassey (Eds.): ePart 2010, LNCS 6229, pp. 82–94, 2010.

Literature related to the study of incorporation of ICT in politics has been focused mainly on e-Government [32][35][36]. However, there are fewer studies related to ICT incorporation in democratic innovation mechanisms such as citizen participation [25][18].

Literature on citizen e-Participation has been based mainly on case studies of concrete experiences [14][3][16] and comparative empirical studies are scarce and incipient [28][24]. Moreover, existing research is mostly descriptive and evaluative, leaving out of the analysis the study of a varied set of explanatory factors of the e-Participation experiences. This paper analyzes the main explanatory factors in the generation of institutionalized citizen participation experiences that do or do not incorporate ICT in their development, focusing analysis on variables that have been little studied by e-Participation literature such as political, sociological or contextual variables.

2 The State of the Art in ICT and Citizen Participation

2.1 Democratic Deficit and Citizen Participation

The beginning of the new millennium has been marked by a political legitimacy crisis. This phenomenon -democratic disaffection [29]-, involves loss of citizens' confidence in their political representatives and the crisis of state institutions and parties.

Even so, in the same space of time, there has been a revitalization of civil society and citizens have adopted a more critical and reflective role requiring a greater degree of cooperation and interaction with the State. Thus, we find new forms of citizen participation. In this context there has been a change in the traditional conception of doing politics, introducing some transition experiences form traditional government to a new form of relational government which incorporates complexity elements, as well as all stakeholders' participation –governance-. It fosters increased citizen participation in public decision-making [9].

Citizen participation in the public sphere is diverse and includes different forms and intensity, drawing on a wide variety of situations from institutionalized participation promoted by public administrations, to participation in social movements or civic networks. This research focuses on the study of innovative citizen participation experiences promoted by local public administrations, where participatory experiences have had a better reception due to the greater proximity between citizens and representatives [5][31][19].

2.2 Incorporation of ICT in Citizen Participation

Incorporation of ICT in politics has introduced fundamental changes in politics and has meant new relationship possibilities between citizens and political representatives. Depending on the public management model to which they are incorporated they constitute models of e-Administration, e-Government or e-Governance, in which e-Participation experiences are encompassed [21][20][4][22].

ICT introduce strong technical improvements which can lead to the improvement of information, communication, consulting, deliberation and decision channels, making them more immediate, simple and effective [12]. ICT facilitate closer and more personalized communication [10] and allow taking part more directly and collectively in the political system. ICT also allow minimizing time and distance problems, reduce the costs of organization and enable communication without technological limits.

Thus, the network would make it possible to advance toward new forms of politics and citizen participation. Even so, there are some limits such as the digital divide [34][2]. Therefore, ICT have to be used as a complement of traditional analogous political practices [20].

e-Participation experiences turned up at the end of the eighties and the nineties, with the incorporation of technologies such as telephone, television or more recently Internet, into democratic innovation mechanisms. In recent years e-Participation experiences have developed immensely. Even so, there are difficulties in achieving radical changes in political systems through technological mechanisms [27][16] and we find important differences in the impulse of e-Participation experiences.

3   The Case of Catalonia

The study object is delimited as initiatives in the area of Catalonia where numerous participative experiences have been carried out and that is one of the leading European regions in terms of participatory experiences. Since the eighties it has enjoyed important support for participatory experiences promoted by local governments [7], heading the impulse of citizen participation in the Spanish case [15]. There are numerous participatory initiatives, cooperation and exchange networks, a common general strategy for participation defined by the Catalan Government, financial resources, consortiums and resources for Information and Communication Society development, and basic political consensus for maintaining participatory initiatives.

In the eighties, the city of Barcelona played an important international leadership role in citizen participation. Later on, the Regional Government of Barcelona gave its impulse through a specialized service working transversally in all areas of local government. A set of public and private institutions -such as universities or think tanks- have offered strong support and collaboration networks to interested city councils [19]. In 2004, Directorate General for Citizen Participation of the Catalan Government was created devoted to citizen participation promotion in Catalonia.

4   Methodology

4.1   Research Question and Hypothesis

The research aims to contribute relevant information to the following initial research questions: 'Which are the main explanatory factors in the generation of citizen participation experiences promoted by local governments in Catalonia?' and 'Are there specific explanatory factors of e-Participation experiences impulse at the local level in Catalonia?'

The existing literature on e-Government and e-Governance at the local level, has studied traditionally variables of socioeconomic and technological context and population size. The intention is to explore the importance that political variables may have in the generation of participatory experiences and electronic experiences. This research sets out the following hypotheses:

- The political party in charge of the city council influences participatory experiences. Thus, political parties on the left would promote more experiences [15][6][31].
- Political electoral participation influences participatory experiences. So, the higher the abstention rate, the greater the probability of finding participatory experiences [6].
- Participatory context influences in participatory experiences. Thus, the stronger the participatory context, the higher citizen participation experiences promotion [23].
- Technological context would influence the impulse of e-Participation experiences, so the more technological the municipality, the higher e-Participation experiences promotion.
- The greater the population size, the higher the citizen participation experiences promotion [30][17][6][8].

4.2 Dependent Variable

This research aims to explain the following dependent variables:

- Citizen participation experiences in public policy development, both online and offline, such as: participatory experiences in urban plans, municipality's budget, or other public policies.
- Participatory websites' functionalities such as: mailboxes, e-mails, complaints and suggestions mailbox, forums, blogs, surveys, consultations or documents.

Citizen participation refers to any voluntary action by citizens more or less directly aimed at influencing the management of collective affairs and public decision-making [33]. Following the Arnstein ladder of participation [1], we consider as participatory initiatives those that include a level of interaction and influence in the decision-making process -from elemental to more in-depth participation levels: information, communication, consultation, deliberation and decision-making-. These experiences can be continuous or limited in time, so we can have punctual experiences, processes and permanent experiences.

4.3 Explanatory Variables

This paper aims to analyze the explanatory variables of citizen participation experiences and channels at the local level with the aim of contrasting and further analyzing previous research and literature [15][30][17][6][8][31]. It studies political, sociological, economic and technological explanatory variables, which have been grouped into different analytical categories:

- Political context: local government's political color, electoral abstention rate.
- Participatory context: e-Participation platforms, legal regulation of citizen participation, citizen participation department and number of consultative boards.

- Socioeconomic context: Gross Domestic Product per inhabitant, average age of the population and population with Spanish nationality.
- Technological context: through the proxy of Internet bandwidth percentage of the municipality's population[i].
- Municipality size: number of inhabitants in the municipality.

4.4 Study Object and Sample

We analyze citizen participatory experiences promoted by Catalan local governments between January 2007 and June 2009. Catalonia has 946 municipalities distributed as shown by table 1. Even though more than 50% of municipalities have less than 1000 inhabitants, 89.27% of the population is concentrated in municipalities with more than 5000 inhabitants and 54.52% in municipalities of more than 50000. Previous studies [30][17][8], show that population size is a determining factor for the development of web sites, online services and channels of interaction. Other studies show that in Catalonia medium-size and large municipalities have led development of citizen participatory experiences [23][7]. Taking all this into consideration, the paper analyzes a sample of 199 Catalan municipalities: all Catalan municipalities with more than 5000 inhabitants[ii].

Table 1. Distribution of Catalan municipalities by population

Population sections	Number of municipalities	% Population	% Municipalities
Less than 1000	490	2.61	51.8
1000 to 5000	256	8.12	27.1
5001 to 20000	139	18.45	14.7
20001 to 50000	38	16.30	4.0
More than 50000	23	54.52	2.4
Total	946	100	100

4.5 Research Methods

A quantitative approach was adopted. In the moment of elaborating this research any public administration, private company or university has carried out an exhaustive collection of e-Participation experiences in the Catalan area. Therefore, a database was set up by the author that collected the distribution of the dependent variable and the explanatory variables in each municipality of the sample. It was constructed between June and October 2009, gathering data from different sources: the analysis of several existing non-exhaustive databases on participatory experiences[iii], the observation of e-Participation experiences web sites, the study of municipalities' web sites, the use of aggregated databases on economic, socio-demographic and technological characteristics of municipalities, or public information on municipality's resources and its legal and political framework. The information was completed through direct contact with city councils, when necessary. The construction of this database allows bringing up a quantitative analysis of the main explanatory factors of the generation of these experiences. With this objective, multivariate explanatory statistical analyses are carried out, relating the dependent variable with the different proposed explanatory ones.

5 Analysis and Findings

The study object is structured in different ways regarding Internet use, time sustainability and the participatory level achieved. Thus, we have the following dependent variables: online and offline participatory experiences, e-Participation experiences, offline participation experiences, total of e-Participation, total of participation, e-Participation index and participation index. Table 2 presents the main statistical sample measures for each one of the analysis' variables.

Table 2. Sample values of variables analysis

	Variables	N	Min.	Max.	Mean	Std. Dev.
Dep. variables	Online & offline participatory experiences	199	0	6	1.29	1.54
	e-Participation experiences	199	0	6	0.77	1.21
	Offline participation experiences	199	0	5	0.52	0.92
	Total of e-Participation[iv]	199	0	15	5.65	2.67
	Total of participation[v]	199	0	15	6.18	2.95
	e-Participation index[vi]	197	1	7	2.81	1.66
	Participation index[vii]	197	1	3	1.75	0.75
Explanatory variables	Ln_population07thousands	199	1.62	5.53	2.67	0.89
	Population07thousands	199	5.06	251.85	24.29	36.28
	% Electoral abstention[viii]	199	29.44	50.47	38.66	4.32
	% Bandwidth connection	199	8.4	29.4	17.88	3.50
	GDP per inhabitant	169	4.10	81.10	20.48	10.83
	Average age	199	33.54	45.26	38.83	1.87
	% Spanish nationality	199	53.15	97.92	87.63	7.50
	Mayor of PSC[ix] & locals	199	0.00	1.00	0.50	0.50
	Mayor of ERC[x] & Locals	199	0.00	1.00	0.10	0.31
	Mayor of ICV[xi] & locals	199	0.00	1.00	0.01	0.12
	Mayor of PP[xii]	199	0.00	1.00	0.005	0.07
	Mayor of local & indep. lists	199	0.00	1.00	0.07	0.26
	Participation formalization factor[xiii]	190	-0.99	3.35	0.00	1.00
	e-Participation Platform	199	0	1	0.22	0.42
	% Post-compulsory education	199	16.13	60.71	31.63	7.90
	Participatory web functionalities	199	0	10	4.87	1.92

Table 3. Regression analysis coefficients

Model	Number of experiences						Total of e-Participation				e-Participation index			
	Online & offline experiences		Online experiences		Offline experiences		Total e-Participation		Total Participation		e-Participation index		Participation index	
	Coeff.	Std. error	Coeff.	Std. error	Coeff.	Std. error	Coeff.	Std. error	Coeff.	Std. error	Coeff.	Std. error	Coeff.	Std. error
Ln Population	0.433**	0.179	0.288**	0.143	0.143	0.130	0.627**	0.288	0.785**	0.314	0.309*	0.181	0.208**	0.094
Mayor of ICV & loc	1.394	0.933	1.878**	0.748	0.032	0.677	1.723	1.512	1.734	1.647	0.770	0.948	-0.469	0.495
Mayor of PSC & loc	-0.193	0.237	0.007	0.190	-0.199	0.172	0.139	0.385	-0.053	0.419	0.059	0.241	-0.100	0.126
Mayor of ERC & locals	-0.118	0.345	0.005	0.277	-0.138	0.250	-0.365	0.559	-0.502	0.609	0.120	0.351	0.001	0.183
Mayor of PP	0.791	1.263	-0.283	1.013	1.041	0.916	-0.509	2.049	0.550	2.232	0.980	1.285	0.688	0.671
Mayor of local & ind. lists	0.226	0.402	0.084	0.322	0.141	0.291	0.651	0.649	0.806	0.707	0.634	0.407	0.182	0.213
Part. Formaliza tion factor	0.396**	0.123	0.112	0.099	0.273**	0.089	0.411**	0.198	0.705***	0.216	0.299**	0.124	0.220***	0.065
e-Participati on platform	1.335***	0.268	1.404***	0.214	-0.044	0.194	3.183***	0.401	3.168***	0.437	2.063***	0.252	0.457***	0.131
% Electoral abstention	-0.021	0.032	-0.049*	0.026	0.025	0.023	-0.088*	0.052	-0.063	0.057	-0.035*	0.033	-0.003	0.017
GDP per inhabitant	-0.005	0.010	-0.004	0.008	-0.002	0.007	0.006	0.017	0.005	0.018	0.007	0.010	0.002	0.005
% Bandwidth connection	0.045	0.038	0.024	0.030	0.022	0.027	0.042	0.061	0.065	0.067	0.038	0.039	0.022	0.020
Average age	0.003	0.063	-0.087*	0.050	0.085*	0.045	-0.074	0.102	0.013	0.111	-0.040	0.064	0.020	0.033
% Spanish nationality	0.012	0.014	0.004	0.011	0.008	0.010	-0.011	0.023	-0.003	0.025	0.000	0.014	0.000	0.007
% Post-compulso ry educ.	-0.009	0.017	-0.002	0.013	-0.007	0.012	0.009	0.027	0.002	0.029	0.007	0.017	-0.003	0.009
Part. web functional ities	0.081	0.060	0.049	0.048	0.028	0.044	-	-	-	-	-	-	-	-
Constant	-1.268	3.759	4.110	3.014	-4.948*	2.726	9.309	6.078	4.294	6.622	3.251	3.812	0.204	1.990
N Adjuste d R²	169[xiv] 0.426		169 0.419		169 0.124		169 0.460		169 0.479		169 0.461		169 0.279	

*p < 0.1 **p < 0.05 ***p < 0.001 Source: own elaboration

In order to analyze the association between citizen participation experiences and the explanatory variables, controlling by the factors that might affect them, we performed seven multiple linear regression analyses. As can be observed in table 3, there are some differences and similarities in the multiple linear regression analyses that were carried out.

5.1 e-Participation Experiences

To study the explanation of Internet incorporation in citizen participation experiences, we compared multiple regression models for online experiences, total of e-Participation and e-Participation index. The first variable measures the number of e-Participation experiences promoted; the second measures all electronic experiences, adding to the previous ones the participatory website functionalities; lastly, e-Participation index measures the experiences' degree, considering together their number, participation level and time sustainability.

The analyses show that explanatory variables are very similar in the three cases, even though we observe differences in some variables. As table 3 shows, Internet use for citizen participation would be explained in the three models by the population size, the existence of an e-Participation platform and the electoral abstention rate. Thus, there would be a greater electronic participation in larger municipalities, with an e-Participation platform and with lower electoral abstention.

On the other hand, we find some differences, worth pointing out. The variable of participation formalization factor is not significant in the explanation of the online experiences' number, while it is explanatory for the total of e-Participation and for the e-Participation index. We also find differences in the model of the number of e-Participation experiences promotion, where having a mayor from ICV (a party on the left) and a low average population age would be explanatory, while they would not in the other two models.So, we could think that when we deal with more stable e-Participation structures -as in the cases of e-Participation index or the total of e-Participation- having a strong participation formalization would be a key factor in the use of Internet for citizen participation. Instead, when we only study the number of experiences, having a mayor from ICV or a young population, would be explanatory of their impulse. This could be showing that Internet incorporation in participatory experiences would be more favorable in municipalities with these characteristics, even though these characteristics would not be explanatory of the level or sustainability of these experiences.

5.2 Offline Participatory Experiences

Secondly, we dealt with the explanatory factors of offline participation, analyzing the variables offline experiences and participation index. The analyses show that there is only one common variable explanatory for both offline models: the participation formalization factor, which would explain the number of experiences promoted, their participative level and their time sustainability. On the other hand, we find differences in the significance of other variables such as 'average population age', which would explain the number of experiences promoted while not explaining their degree in terms of level and sustainability. It is worth mentioning that although in the explanation of the number of e-Participation experiences age had a negative coefficient, in this case its coefficient is positive. Finally, the variables of population size and electronic platform for citizen participation are explanatory for the degree of offline experiences, while they are not for the number of experiences promoted by municipalities.

5.3 Online and Offline Citizen Participation

Finally, this section studies jointly citizen participation experiences carried out offline and using the Internet. Thus, we analyze variables of offline and online experiences, and total of participation.

The developed analyses show that for both models, variables of population size, electronic platform for citizen participation and the participation formalization factor are explanatory. Even though the values of the coefficients are quite different, it is worth pointing out that their signs are equal, being all positive.

Thus, it could be stated that even in the explanation of the number of participatory experiences (online and offline) and in the explanation of these experiences, taking also into account the web site participatory functionalities, the population size would be explanatory. So, the greater the number of inhabitants, the higher the number of experiences promoted, even though its effect would be greater in the case of 'total of participation'. Likewise, municipalities with electronic citizen participation platforms would promote more experiences than municipalities without such a platform. Thus, it could be stated that this variable -although having a positive effect in both dependent variables- would have a stronger effect when it comes to explaining experiences and web site functionalities, than if only experiences are explained. This could mean that the use of e-Participation platforms could be related to the opening of participatory functionalities in municipal web sites and could be indicative of a stronger participatory culture in the municipality, which would also have effects on the offline participatory experiences. Finally, municipalities with a higher participation formalization factor would promote more participatory experiences. Again, the coefficient of the variable is higher in the case of the explanation of the experiences plus web site functionalities than in the case of the explanation of the experiences.

6 Conclusions and Discussion

This paper has analyzed the possible explanatory factors of citizen participatory experiences promoted at the local level in Catalonia, both online and offline. It has analyzed the most relevant variables considered by the literature: political, technological and socioeconomic variables, and the size of the municipality. We have studied their influence in the number of experiences promoted and in their degree of participatory level and time sustainability reached. We also conducted analyses in order to evaluate whether the explanatory factors for offline participation can also be explanatory for e-Participation experiences.

Regarding the hypotheses, the analyses show that political variables would be explanatory for e-Participation experiences in Catalonia, as suspected, but they won't be for the offline ones. This may indicate a greater generalization of offline experiences, so their development would not be any longer explained by a left political color, as previous research indicated [15][6][31] or by the electoral abstention rate [6][7].

Electoral abstention rate would be explanatory for e-Participation in the sense that the lower the abstention rate, the higher the e-Participation. This would be contrary to previous research [6], even though previous research analyzed offline experiences. This may indicate that e-Participation experiences would still be pioneer and innovative, and would need a more participatory environment to be promoted. So, political variables would be explanatory for them, but not for offline experiences, which would be currently more widespread than in previous years.

On the participatory context, in general terms we found empirical evidence in all the models but the online experiences, that the higher the formalization of citizen participation in the municipality, the greater the citizen participatory experiences. So, there would be a positive relation between promoting participatory experiences and having formal participation councils, legal regulation and a special department in the city council. This would be in line with our hypothesis and with previous research [23].

Unfortunately the data used does not allow us to find significance in the technological variables collected. Nonetheless, it worth mentioning that having an e-Participation platform is significant in all the models but the offline experiences one. This could be due to a possible relation between having an e-Participation platform and being a more participatory oriented municipality.

Regarding population size, it could be said that the greater the population size, the greater the citizen participation, both online and offline, as we had expected and in line with previous research [30][17][6][8]. Even though, in the case of offline experiences, the non-significance of this coefficient may be showing a generalization of those experiences in all the municipalities.

Finally, with the exception of the age, none of the socioeconomic variables explains online or offline participation. So, we could conclude that promotion of participatory experiences would be tied to political context and participatory will variables, not to differential population characteristics of the municipality. This would be derived from the non-significance of the analyzed socioeconomic variables, as well as from the significance of the age variable in the number of experiences explanation, which would favor e-Participation in young populations and offline participation in older ones. Thus, participatory experiences would be related to the political context of the municipality and strategies and tools that reflect the interest in developing them. So, we could conclude that in this moment, e-Participation would not be yet a generalized tool, but it would already represents the democratic innovation arrow.

References

1. Arnstein, S.R.: A ladder of citizen participation. Journal of the American Institute of Planners 35(4), 216–224 (1969)
2. Barber, B.: To what extent are new telecommunication technologies democratic? IDP. Internet, Derecho y Política, 3 (2006), http://www.uoc.edu/idp

3. Barrat, J., Reniu, J.M.: Democracia electrónica y participación ciudadana. Informe sociológico y jurídico de la consulta ciudadana Madrid Participa. Ayuntamiento de Madrid / Scytl / Accenture, Madrid (2004)
4. Bellamy, C.: Modelling electronic democracy: towards democratic discourses for an information age. In: Hoff, J., Horrocks, I., Tops, P. (eds.) Democratic Governance and New Technology. Routledge, London (2000)
5. Blanco, I., Gomà, R.: Gobiernos locales y redes participativas. Ariel, Barcelona (2002)
6. Blanco, I., Font, J.: La participación local: factores estructurales, ideológicos e instrumentales. In: Working Papers Online Series, Universidad Autónoma de Madrid (2005), http://www.uam.es/centros/derecho/cpoliticapapers.htm
7. Borge, R., Colombo, C., Welp, Y.: Online and offline participation at the local level. Information, Communication & Society 12(6), 899–928 (2009)
8. Brown, M., Schelin, S.: American Local Governments: Confronting the E-government Challenge. In: Drüke, H. (ed.) Local Electronic Government: A Comparative Study. Routledge, New York (2005)
9. Brugué, Q., Gomà, R.: Gobierno local y políticas públicas. Ariel, Barcelona (1998)
10. Castells, M.: La era de la Información, La sociedad red, vol. I. Alianza, Madrid (2000)
11. Ciulla, E., Nye, J.S. (eds.): Governance.com: Democracy in the Information Age. Brookings Institution Press, Washington (2002)
12. Clift, S.: The E-democracy E-book, Publicus.net (2000), http://www.publicus.net
13. Clift, S.: E-Democracy, E-governance and Public Net-Work, Publicus.net (2003), http://www.publicus.net
14. Coleman, S., Gøtze, J.: Bowling Together: Online Public Engagement in Policy Deliberation. BT & Hansard Society, London (2001)
15. Colino, C., Del Pino, E.: Un fantasma recorre Europa: Renovación democrática mediante iniciativas de promoción participativa en los gobiernos locales. II Jornadas de Sociología Política, UNED, Madrid (September 11-12, 2003)
16. Colombo, C.: e-Participació: la incorporació d'Internet en la presa de decisions públiques. El cas de Consensus, ciutadans en xarxa' in Revista Catalana de Sociología (2007)
17. Criado, J.I.: Construyendo la e-Administración Local. EuroGestión Pública, Madrid (2004)
18. Finquelievich, S., Baumann, P., Jara, A.: Nuevos paradigmas de participación ciudadana a través de las tecnologías de la información y la comunicación (2001), http://www.links.org.ar
19. Font, J., Galais, C.: Experiències de democràcia participativa a Catalunya: un mapa analític, Generalitat de Catalunya. Direcció General de Participació Ciutadana, Barcelona (2009)
20. Hacker, K., Van Dijk, J.: Digital Democracy. Issues of Theory & Practice. Sage Publications, London (2000)
21. Hagen, M.: A Typology of Electronic Democracy (1997), http://www.uni-giessen.de/fb03/vinci/labore/netz/hag_en.htm
22. Hoff, J., Horrocks, I., Tops, P. (eds.): Democratic Governance and New Technology. Routledge, Londres (2000)
23. IGOP: La participació ciutadana als petits municipis (2005), http://www10.gencat.cat/drep
24. Jensen, M., Danzinger, J., Venkatesh, A.: Civil Society and Cyber Society: The Role of the Internet in Community Associations and Democratic Politics. The Information Society 23, 39–50 (2007)

25. Macintosh, A., Whyte, A.: Evaluating how e-Participation changes local democracy. In: Irani, Z., Ghoneim, A. (eds.) Proceedings of the e-Government Workshop, eGov'06. Brunel University, London (2006)
26. Norris, P. (ed.): Critical citizens. Oxford University Press, Oxford (1999)
27. Norris, P.: Building knowledge societies: the renewal of democratic practices in knowledge societies. UNESCO World Report (2004), http://www.pippanorris.com
28. Pratchett, L.: Making local e-democracy work? In: Virapatirin, M., Peixoto, T. (eds.) e-AGORA, Le Livre Blanc de la e-démocratie locale: Réflexions et Perspectives. Ville d'Issy-les-Moulineaux, Paris (2006)
29. Putnam, R., Goss, K.: El declive del capital social. Un estudio internacional sobre las sociedades y el sentido comunitario. Circulo de lectores. Galaxia Gutenberg, Barcelona (2003)
30. Salvador, M., CortéS, R., Sánchez, R., Ferrer, L.L.: Els ajuntaments de Catalunya a Internet. Estudis de Ciències Polítiques i Gestió Pública. UPF, Barcelona (2004), http://www.upf.edu/cpgp/
31. Schneider, C.: La participación ciudadana en el gobierno de Buenos Aires (1996-2004): El contexto político como explicación. In: CIDOB Working papers, CIDOB (2007)
32. United Nations, UN Global e-Government Survey. United Nations online Network in Public Administration and Finance, UNPAN, New York (2004)
33. Verba, S., Schlozman, K.L., Bredy, H.E.: Voice and Equality. Civic Voluntarism in American Politics. Harvard University Press, Cambridge (1995)
34. Warshauer, M.: Technology and social inclusion: Rethinking digital divide. Massachusetts Institute of Technology, Massachusetts (2003)
35. West, D.: E-Government and the transformation of service delivery and citizen attitudes. Public Administration Review 64 (2004)
36. Wong, W., Welch: Does e-government promote accountability? A comparative analysis of website openness and government accountability. Governance 17 (2004)

Notes:

[i] Internet bandwidth percentage of the municipality's population is the only ICT variable disintegrated and representative at the municipal level in Catalonia.

[ii] The city of Barcelona is not included in the sample due to several reasons. Its complex administrative structure, the city council's high participatory activity and the lack of systematization and information centralization of the participatory experiences promoted entail a lack of exhaustive and systematic information on all the experiences promoted. Moreover, Barcelona city council tried to gather all this information through several research projects, which were rejected due to the great amount of resources required.

[iii] Databases used to collect data are: Democratic Innovation program and Local Government of Catalonia; the Catalonia's Public Administration School Database; the Participatory Democracy Local Observatory; the Participatory Democracy International Observatory; the Pi Sunyer Foundation good practices bank; database of the Directorate General for Citizen Participation; as well as information coming from other municipal studies or web sites.

[iv] The total of e-Participation is the sum of the number of e-Participation experiences and the participatory website functionalities.

[v] The total of participation is an addition of eParticipation experiences, plus offline participation experiences, plus participatory website functionalities.

^{vi} Measures eParticipaiton taking into account the number of eParticipatory experiences, its participatory level (information, communication, consultation, deliberation, decision) and its temporal sustainability (process, punctual or permanent). It also measures participatory website functionalities and their participatory level. This index is constructed through a weight average of these variables, weighting last two variables 0'5 (participatory website functionalities are important for eParticipation but do not consitute complete eParticipation experiences themselves). High values make reference to municipalities with high eParticipation (big number, of high participatory level and time lasting experiences).

^{vii} Measures citizen participation taking into account the number of offline participatory experiences, its participatory level and its temporal sustainability. The same weight is assigned to each one of those variables.

^{viii} This variable measures the average electoral abstention rate in each municipalitiy taking into account the last electoral participation rates (general elections 2008, regional elections 2006 and local elections 2007).

^{ix} Partit dels Socialistes de Catalunya (PSC) is a centre-left party that has led Catalan government since 2003.

^x Esquerra Republicana de Catalunya (ERC) is a left-leaning party that strives for independence of Catalonia. It is the 4th or 3rd political force, depending on the elections.

^{xi} Iniciativa per Catalunya- Els Verds (ICV) is a small left-leaning party, concentrated in larger cities, which strongly defends the carrying out of participatory initiatives.

^{xii} Partit Popular (PP) is a right-Spanish party, which has little presence throughout Catalonia.

^{xiii} This factor arose from a factorial analysis of the following variables: citizen participation legal regulation in the municipality, citizen participation consultative boards, citizen participation department in the city council.

^{xiv} The difference between N=199 as basis for the analysis and N=169 in Table 2 is due to missing values in 30 municipalities for GDP per inhabitant variable.

The AUGMENT Project: Co-constructive Mapping and Support of Accessibility and Participation

Annelie Ekelin[1], Peter Anderberg[1], and Kishore Reddy[2]

[1] Blekinge Institute of Technology, School of Computing, School of Health,
SE-37179 Karlskrona, Sweden
{Annelie Ekelin,Peter Anderberg}@bth.se
[2] Indian Institute of Technology in Madras (IIT-M),
Dept.of Computer Science, India
enigma2006.kishore@gmail.com

Abstract. This paper presents an ongoing multi-disciplinary research-and development project in which we are exploring emerging methods and practices for participatory design of tools and content of accessibility information in India and Sweden, based on user created content. The initial development of the AUGMENT-Project also includes the production of a prototype for sharing information. The joint set up and unfolding of public digital spaces and co-operative creation of processes and infrastructure for user-driven accessibility information is making use of existing handheld mobile phones which offer the possibility to upload pictures and comments via an application with a map-based interface. The research initiative is exploring and comparing cross-cultural participatory methods for cultivation of shared transformational spaces. The paper discusses both the notion of user-driven content and co-creation of tools and methods, drawing upon the tradition of Scandinavian Systems Design, explicitly arguing for direct user-representation in systems development.

Keywords: eParticipation, user-driven content, participatory design, map-based interfaces, disability, social media.

1 Introduction

Recent Swedish research on rehabilitation engineering [1] has shown that disability is dependent on the situation, not primarily on the individuals. This means that problems are possible to jointly minimize or solve to a greater extent than the mainstream understanding of disability problems has previously assumed. Accessibility, thus, should be seen as an act of co-construction, not something which has to be provided for someone else. Accessibility information needs to be constantly re-formulated and customized, depending on the individual's circumstances and current location in space and time, rather than simply and statically presented as one-size-fits-all and relying on individuals learning generalized strategies of how to use "off-the shelf information". New solutions providing access for disabled groups are frequently

E. Tambouris, A. Macintosh, and O. Glassey (Eds.): ePart 2010, LNCS 6229, pp. 95–103, 2010.

developed -this is not an issue any longer-the issue is rather: how are these new solutions communicated among those who need the information and in which way are their personalized interpretations contributing to the understanding of accessibility? How can shared spaces be opened and cultivated for co-construction of accessibility?

1.1 Reconfiguring Accessibility

The AUGMENT project aims to work with groups and individuals who have experience of accessibility problems and who are not satisfied with current accessibility solutions, which have primarily concentrated on regarding accessibility as a stabilized artifact [11] rather than a situation which is dependent on reinterpretation. The organization of physical places affects disabled people's possibilities of participation. The physical environment in Sweden to some extent lacks relevant customization and there are also gaps in accessibility for groups of people with various disability problems. But the picture is not one-sided. In relation to rebuilding of physical environment, a number of accessibility problems are solved over time. The issue is rather how these changes and reinforcements are communicated to the affected groups and individuals who are dependent on such information. A repeatedly formulated wish from representatives of these groups is the possibility to describe environments with the help of images and other examples of "rich pictures", where the user her/himself can decide about and evaluate the offered accessibility. In a recent charting of different EU-initiatives, HANDISAM, the Swedish Agency for Disability Policy Coordination, point out that the aim of steering development and research towards more inclusive projects and solutions has been based on the i2010 strategy, the guiding framework for accessibility issues. There are ongoing discussions about legislation of eAccessibility within EU and the European Commission highlights the importance of prioritizing a coherent, mutual and effective strategy for eAccessibility, or web accessibility, in order to boost the development of the eSociety in line with a new social agenda. [3, p12]

This is not, however, the main priority today. There is also great demand for flexibility and mobility, and a new generation of mobile web tools has been developed, contributing to supporting and enhancing this mobility and flexibility. Interactive features make it possible for individuals to contribute on various levels by posting experience based information on the web site. Providing accessibility is not simply about providing information, but also about providing means of co-construction of the expressions of accessibility as well as form and content – providing space for exploring a multitude of experiences of variations of disability in relation to accessibility issues. The visualization possibilities of for instance policy development by the introduction of map-based interfaces for a better representation of content, as for instance described in Renton & Macintosh [16], is one way of making use of computer-supported argument visualization (CSAV) tools in support of public participation in for instance public e-consultations. [15] However, there is also another perspective which takes its starting point in proactive participation orchestrated mainly by the active citizens themselves, namely the creation of both content and platforms as offered by the tools of social media. The practices of supporting and utilizing User Created Content is developing fast also entering the arena of eGovernment, going far beyond the original personal or entertainment purposes of social media, contributing also to information sharing.[18]

The research reported in this paper describes ongoing work, which takes its starting-point in regarding disability issues as a fundamental part of the discussion of participation, rather than regarding disability as a specific condition in need of specialized participatory solutions based on seemingly more accessible versions of applications or tools. However, the core factor of the research is not solely disabilities; rather the main focus is the scope of participation. Similar research could be made in cooperation with non-disabled users and the information could also be represented by an interface not using georeferenced data, but since the research is closely related to regional development the project is firmly based in identified local needs.

Secondly, the aim with the paper is also to contribute to the ongoing development of theories and methods for eParticipation, thus it is discussing the essence of participation for design, through the strivings of including marginalized groups and citizens' in contributing to both prototype development and content generation. At the same time the paper also problematizes the issue of designing for participation, by putting the spotlight on the fact that what we might have taken for granted as a starting point for inclusive design – adapted web tools and web interfaces – might not be the best way forward, since it is based on presumptions about disability as a non-flexible condition which has been deprived all possibilities of self-representation.

1.2 The Research Approach

The research approach we have chosen concentrates on case studies, small-scale action-oriented R&D projects with a base in using qualitative ethnographic studies coupled with engineering development work. The basis for this approach is the Scandinavian tradition of workplace democracy [4] [5] [6] [9] with a deliberate use of multiple perspectives through iterative negotiation processes in ICT development. One aim is to achieve conceptualization based on the interplay of practice and theory with a focus on participatory design processes.

We acknowledge that there need to be more research studies concentrating on developing more inclusive methods for participation. We also base our approach on the strivings from people who are experiencing disability in various forms and work towards a flexible and situation-dependent re-conceptualization of the notions and practices of accessibility, disability and participation. Additionally we wish to collect material for development of a new agenda for the Scandinavian approach to systems design-also including what has been labeled PD in the Wild, [7] [8]

1.3 The Theoretical Basis

In order to decompose the predefined and somewhat sealed category of participation, we make use of Hannah Arendt's theory of action [2] which once was considered a defense of participatory politics in the 1960's. Arendt's thoughts about civic humanism, morals and politics have in some sense been re-established during the late 1990's are useful as a conceptual tool when scrutinizing the reintroduction of participatory values in the current decade, when user-generated content and user participation have become the latest writing on the wall. Arendt understands human beings as creatures who act, in the sense of starting things, and who set off chains of events. Her writings on actions in *The Human Condition* [2] were a powerful account of the human capacity for action, celebrating human creativity, stating that people have the capacity to act even in unlikely situations and under limited circumstances. In the introduction to the second edition of the book Canovan explains the basics of Arendt's theory [2, pVii-xx]. Arendt emphasized that politics takes place among plural beings, and understood activity in three forms, where action is distinguished from labor and work. Labor corresponds in her interpretation to the bodily activities of a human being, while work in her interpretation was equivalent to the artificial world of objects that human beings build on earth. Action corresponds to our plurality as distinct individuals, or our possibilities to make new beginnings and start new processes. The political features of human beings are plural, and the capability for new perspectives and actions will not fit into a predictable model unless these capacities for action are drastically curtailed. These three forms could also be used as a tool to open up the black-boxed category of participation, since participation also contains nuances and variations as well as human actions. The form labor could in the context of full-scaled user-involvement be equivalent to *automatic participation*, the second form could be labeled *dutiful or instructed participation* and the third category *proactive* participation.

2   The Project

The local development has consisted of constructing a suitable interface, a user-generated database, and a wiki-solution for handling and maintaining data as well as a mobile interface together with users. The task is mainly charting of "inaccessible" places and the aim here is working with various groups of users and cases, for instance hospitals, public places, and common recreation places. The main issue is to offer possibilities for direct participation by those affected. There is also a sister project running in Tamil Nadu, India called *The Walk-on-Water project* [13] [14], which has a different focus, but which we are using for trans-cultural comparison of evolving practices of user-driven and participatory design of public e-services based on co-construction among multiple local stakeholders of databases containing current, meaningful local information.

In order to be able to concentrate on design of an easy-to-use solution with the user as co-constructer, the development process in the pilot project is focused on a specific modification (or module) of an existing and established application. An example of a basic similar solution is Google maps Street View (http://maps.google.com/) where you can walk around on the streets virtually and examine pictures and surroundings by assessing information on the map. In real life, use of GPS-based technology with positioning makes it possible to contribute to the map content with personal photos and comments.

The locally developed prototype contains a set-up of a user-driven accessibility database combined with a wiki solution in order to handle different versions of information (the information could be exemplified by possibility of scaling a specific environment, individual evaluations, and location of for instance toilets and so on). The aim of the project is to find new methods for continuous up-dating and ways to secure accurate, up-dated and high quality of status of accessibility in the local area. The content generation has hitherto concentrated on upload of pictures and comments. The use of the content is made searchable by issue name and also includes a rating possibility which draws upon socially responsible enactment of citizenship by individuals. Some of the basic functionalities developed so far are the possibility to place oneself on the map and plan a journey and also to identify any possible obstructions in the way. The project benefits for the involved group of stakeholders are primarily practical: to jointly develop new ways of working around co-constructive provision of accessibility information. It is also a way to gain goodwill for local authorities by the introduction of a user-driven accessibility database which makes use of the implementation of a Wiki-solution in order to handle information. This is in line with recent development of new methods for accessible update of information and visions of creating good governance as well as shared responsibility for the quality of accessibility information. For the region, the suggested project is a way to offer improved accessibility for citizens at the same time as the affected groups are given a possibility of greater influence on the content of accessibility data as well as the presentation form and management of the data.

On the political level, the issue of inclusion of all citizens is crucial, and the establishment of more well informed and democratic decision-making concerning accessibility issues is in line with visions of good governance. For the involved researchers, the project is expected to contribute to the development of more inclusive methods for participation, and a re-conceptualization of notions of accessibility and disability, as well as providing material for development of a new agenda for the Scandinavian approach to systems design with an even broader scope of direct participation than previously. We are also exploring differences between the related research traditions of end-user innovation and participatory design, and what we can learn from these differences, concerning how to provide useful feedback efficiently and effectively to software providers, software engineers and interaction designers, and thus support the development of sustainable infrastructures for inclusive design-in-use (Dittrich et al, 2002; Dittrich et al, 2009). Steinman, Krek and Blaschke [17] examined in a previous paper whether online map-based applications can contribute to improvement of citizen participation or not and found that the users in 12 projects, mainly from the United States of America and Germany, had little or no possibility to contribute actively in any part of the planning process. The applications lacked two-way communication and real-time statements from the users. This is also in line with experiences of previous work with the Komindu-project [10] for spatial planning in southeast of Sweden and the development of a national support-system for local planners in Sweden, the Planning Portal of which the latter had a distinct top-down perspective and the first one was more open to those discussions, but at the time being, not yet ready to make the switch and let through user-driven development.

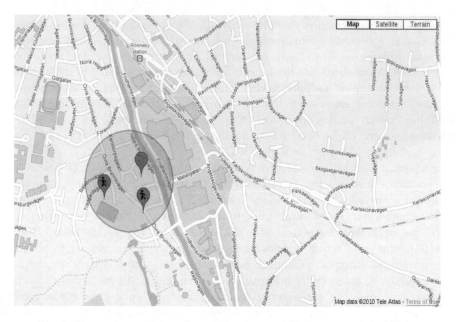

Fig. 1. Obstructions within a given radius for a specific category of disabilities

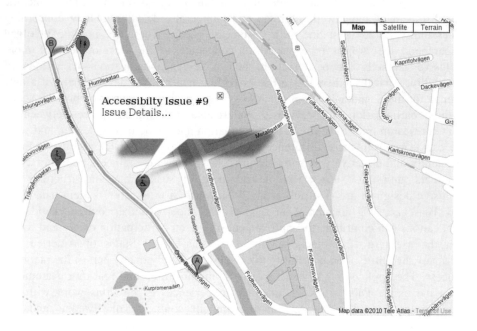

Fig. 2. Obstructions for getting from A to B for a specific category of disabilities

3 Discussion and Conclusion

The discussions and workshops in the AUGMENT project have hitherto circulated around three basic issues:

1) The need of a pro-active approach among the involved user-groups of disabled people. Simply, they need to be able to judge in beforehand whether this is a viable road to travel, if the path is too steep or the stairway is too long – but not based solely on facts and measurements but also on experiences of finding out local workarounds by people in the same situation. The best way to do this is by judging several opinions from people who have experienced similar situations and preconditions and solved them in creative ways. The need for a collective accessibility memory has therefore to be visualized and represented besides the suggestions on possible choice of road to travel and the actual hindrances to overcome. Technically this could be achieved by calculations based on frequency of suggested solutions as well as spaces for visualization of others creative mode-thinking and possibility to compare this to own planning.

2) To what extent is user-driven content co-constructed or built on the pre-described understanding of in what way users are supposed to drive or present their descriptions and statements? Is it possible to redefine user-driven content based on how the users' wants to define the tools for achieving this?

3) Finally, the instrument of rating is not the best tool in order to assure timeliness and credibility since it is easily manipulated and relies on the principle that "everyone wants to contribute" in a user-driven context. However, being pro-active, active and even passive is also part of a socially responsible citizenship, as interpreted by an individual.

Those variations are acknowledge as subject of interest in a project like AUGMENT where we aims to put more effort on individual, local action and whatever comes out of it rather than trying to apply a pre-defined model of participation. In that respect, projects which put emphasis on supporting user-driven content creation can come closer to what Arendt emphasized as creative action, but there is also a risk of it becoming a new variation of dutiful and instructed participation, since it tries to capture the very essence of individual creativity and formalize this as a prescribing method. Several ways of creating and representing a collective opinion as for example in the rating system must be developed and visualized in order to give the full nuances of what user-driven content might look like-from the perspective of those who are supposed to be driving it.

Trials of direct participation in co-construction of accessibility creation are thus a possible way to test the connection between proactive citizenship and effective local agency, as well as these trials of participation are a way to test the democratic basis of these initiatives. The provision of a tool for co-creation of accessibility information is also an opportunity for people to experience their own effective agency. Such an approach emphasizes the learning aspects, specifically learning how to act in order to keep control over an initiative that takes place outside the boundaries of the pre-defined and categorical activities of participation such as given the tools of a map-based system but not the possibility to redraw the maps or jointly judge not only the accuracy of the displayed information, but also the accuracy of user-driveness; as automatic participation, i.e. in the form of handing in and displaying information, or as in the second form, dutiful or instructed participation as taking part in a rating system, which easily could be manipulated by those who want to lobby actively for a specific solution, or as in proactive participation where all participants are not only negotiating the accuracy of the provided information but also actively re-constructing the problem into a possibility based on individual place-based and timely understanding.

However, there are many more layers which are not visible within the given frames for how a user-driven approach or a socially responsible citizenship is supposed to be performed. In that respect this project comes closer to what Arendt once emphasized as creative action, but it is also close to becoming a new variation of dutiful and instructed participation, when formulating what user-driven content might look like compared to traditional accessibility information. Issues raised during the initial work in this project, which only recently begun, has hitherto raised the following critical issue: how is it possible to create this link between individual, creative performance and "one and a half centimeters of basic accessibility information" which always is needed, as one of the workshop participants expressed it during the work of defining the limits of individualization and self-representation in relation to accessibility information?

Acknowledgment

We are very grateful for the support and constructive comments from professor Sara Eriksén, Blekinge Institute of Technology and professor Timothy A Gonzalves, IIT Madras (IIT-M) and IIT Mandi.

References

1. Anderberg, P.: FACE-Disabled people, Technology and Internet Doctoral dissertation (2006), http://www.certec.lth.se/doc/face/
2. Arendt, H.: The Human Condition, 2nd edn. The Univeristy of Chicago Press, Chicago (1998)
3. von Axelson, H.: kartläggning over initativ för eInkludering I EU och Sverige. Delrapport: Regeringsuppdrag N2008/5985/ITP (2008)
4. Bjerknes, G., Bratteteig, T.: User participation and democracy: A discussion of Scandinavian research on system development. Scandinavian Journal of Information Systems 7(1), 73–98 (1995)
5. Blomberg, J., Giacomi, J., Mosher, A., Swenton-Wall, P.: Ethnographic Field Methods and Their Relation to Design. In: Schuler, D., Namioka, A. (eds.) Participatory Design: Perspectives on Systems Design, Lawrence Erlbaum, Hillsdale (1993)
6. Blomberg, J., Burrell, M., Guest: An Ethnographic Approach to Design. in Handbook of Human-Computer Interaction. In: Jacko, J., Sears, A. (eds.) Interactive Systems, Lawrence Erlbaum Associates,Inc., New Jersey (2002)

7. Dittrich, Y., Eriksén, S., Hansson, C.P.: PD in the Wild; Evolving Practices of Design in Use. In: Binder, T., Gregory, J., Wagner, I. (eds.) PDC 2002 Proceedings of the Participatory Design Conference, Malmö, Sweden, June 2002, pp. 124–134 (2002)
8. Dittrich, Y., Ekelin, A., Elovaara, P., Eriksén, S., Hansson, C.: Making e-government happen: Everyday co-development of services, citizenship and technology. In: Sprague Jr., R.H. (ed.) Proceedings of the 36th annual Hawaii International Conference on System Sciences HICSS'36, January 6-9 2003. IEEE Computer Society, Los Alamitos (2003)
9. Ehn, P.: Scandinavian design: On participation and skill. In: Schuler, Namioka (eds.) Participatory design, Principles and Practices. Participatory Design: Perspectives on Systems Design. Lawrence Erlbaum, Hillsdale (1993)
10. Ekelin, A., et al.: Komindu-A Small Project About Big Issues. In: I PDC04 Proceedings of the Participatory Design Conference. Artful Integration: Interweaving Media, Materials and Practices, Toronto, Canada, July 27-31, vol. 2, pp. 28–31 (2004)
11. Ekelin, A.: The Work to Make eParticipation Work, Dissertation No. 2007:11, Blekinge Institute of Technology (2007)
12. Ekelin, A.: Situating eParticipation. In: Avdic, A., Hedström, K., Rose, J., Grönlund, Å. (eds.) Understanding eParticipation. Contemporary PhD eParticipation Research in Europe. Örebro University, Department of Business, Economics, Statistics and Informatics (2007)
13. Eriksén, S., Kawlra, A., Jhunjhunwala, A., Ekelin, A.: Planning beyond the Urban-Rural Divide: Participatory design of ICT for sustainable development in India and Sweden. In: Bengs, C. (ed.) INSTEC book to be published autumn (2010) (in press)
14. Eriksén, S., Ekelin, A.: Beyond the Buzz: Participatory, sustainable, convergent and high quality public e-services -developing methods and practices in India and Sweden. In: Proceedings of the 31st Information Systems Research Seminar in Scandinavia IRIS (2008)
15. Macintosh, A.: eParticipation in Policy-Making: The research and the challenges. In: Cunningham, P., Cunningham, M. (eds.) Exploiting the Knowledge Economy: Issues, Applications and Case Studies, pp. 364–369. IOS press, Amsterdam (2006)
16. Renton, A., Macintosh, A.: Computer supported argument maps as a policy memory. Information Society Journal 23(2), 125–133 (2007)
17. Steinman, R., Krek, A., Blaschke, T.: Can Online Map-Based Applications Improve Citizen Participation? In: Böhlen, M.H., Gamper, J., Polasek, W., Wimmer, M.A. (eds.) TCGOV 2005. LNCS (LNAI), vol. 3416, pp. 25–35. Springer, Heidelberg (2005)
18. User-Created-Content: Supporting a Participative Information Society. SMART 2007/2008. Final Report. Consultancy Firms IDATE, TNO, IViR (2008)

Genres of Participation in Social Networking Systems: A Study of the 2009 Norwegian Parliamentary Election

Marius Johannessen

University of Agder, Department of Information Systems
Service box 422, NO-4604 Kristiansand, Norway

Abstract. In the Norwegian context, eParticipation in the form of online campaigning has been on the agenda since 2001. After Obama's successful presidential campaign in 2008, expectations about the use of SNS in the Norwegian parliamentary election were high.

This study explores genres of participation in the early stages of the 2009 Norwegian parliamentary election campaign. The main finding is that the political parties have seen the need for a presence in SNS', and that a genre repertoire for political communication through SNS is beginning to evolve. However, there is little agreement between citizens and politicians about how the different genres should be enacted. Further work with genres is presented as a possible solution to lessening this communication gap.

Keywords: eParticipation, Social Networking Systems, Genre theory, Genre Repertoire, election campaign.

1 Introduction

Online campaigning has been on the agenda in Norway since the parliamentary election in 2001. Back then the Internet played a marginal role, but it was expected that this would change in coming election campaigns [1]. Barack Obama's successful online campaign in 2008 created expectations that the political parties in Norway would use social networking systems (SNS) with a similar degree of success [2].

The Norwegian research project *power and democracy*[1] conducted a study of the state of democracy in Norway between 1998 and 2003. One of the main conclusions of the study was that representative democracy is in decline. The loyalty to political parties and the broad social movements that characterized the period following World War II is replaced by an electorate that moves from one party to the next, more or less guided by the current headlines in the media. Single issues have become more important than party politics. This means that power is slowly moving from the parliament towards lobbying and non-governmental organizations (NGO's) [3].

As a research field, eParticipation examines how to include citizens in the public discourse. Online campaigning and participation in the decision-making process are typical eParticipation activities [4]. There is an increasing belief in several countries

---

[1] For information in English, see
http://www.sv.uio.no/mutr/english/index.html

E. Tambouris, A. Macintosh, and O. Glassey (Eds.): ePart 2010, LNCS 6229, pp. 104–114, 2010.
© IFIP International Federation for Information Processing 2010

that eParticipation can be an important factor for strengthening democracy [4, 5], and in Norway, politicians are signaling that they want more citizen dialogue and user-involvement in the political process [6].

Many eParticipation projects fail to get a "representative sample of the population" to participate [7]. In contrast, SNS' have a large user base as well as functionality that could help foster participation. The massive interest for SNS use in the Norwegian election, and Obama's success with SNS, makes this an interesting area for eParticipation research. The purpose of this paper is to examine the SNS communicative strategies of Norwegian political parties in the 2009 parliamentary election, and to examine whether there is evidence of an emerging genre repertoire of political communication in SNS. Genre theory is used as theoretical lens for the study.

The rest of the paper is structured as follows: Chapter two provides a brief literature review of social networks in eParticipation and election campaigns as a form of eParticipation. Chapters three and four present the research method and findings of the study, and Chapter five provides a summary of the paper with some possible directions for future research.

2 Background and Prior Research

A functioning democracy requires good communication between citizens and their elected representatives [8]. Communication is hindered by the fact that traditional political engagement through parties is in decline, being replaced by engagement in single issues and various interest groups [3]. To improve communication, political parties have begun experimenting with information and communication technologies (ICTs), as this has proven effective in the delivery of online services [9]. There is as yet little evidence of success in eParticipation projects. Several case studies point out potential benefits [10], but there are some challenges involved. Many politicians are reluctant, because they feel that eParticipation goes against the values of representative democracy, or because they are uncertain about technology use [11]. There is also disagreement about the outcome of dialogue in eParticipation projects. Politicians mainly want to inform, while citizens want to influence the decision-making process [12]. To shorten the gap between citizen and politician, Päivärinta & Sæbø [13] have developed four different models of democracy, ranging from partisan and liberal democracy (where politicians set the agenda) to deliberative and direct democracy (where citizens set the agenda). Democracy models could be used to create an explicit agreement on the outcome of eParticipation projects.

Another challenge to eParticipation is that many projects have few users and fail to get a "representative sample of the population" to participate [7]. Despite this, citizens are active users of the Internet in other areas. We share information and content, participate in online networks and even exchange political ideas in various SNSs [6]. An increasing number of private companies are using SNSs to communicate with clients and customers[14], and customers are beginning to expect this type of dialogue [15]. Media use is becoming ever more fragmented. In the past you would reach everyone through TV or printed newspapers. Today people access news in a number of different sources, making it difficult to reach out to everyone. By using SNS, it becomes easier to utilize the "long tail", the many small internet-based services where different groups of people go for information [16-18].

2.1 Social Networking Services

Web 2.0, social networks, social media and new media. There are many labels attached to the new phenomena we observe in digital media today. The concept of web 2.0 first emerged in 2005, when O'Reilly Publishing examined the companies that survived the burst of the "dot com bubble". These companies had something in common; Their services got more useful as the user base grew, utilized "collective intelligence" through tags and recommendations, and relied heavily on user-generated content [16]. User-generated content and user-involvement have been put forth as the most important elements of web 2.0 [17, 19]. Because of the study's focus on online campaigning, this paper will use the concept of social networks/social networking services (SNS), and examine how these were used by political parties to communicate with citizens. SNSs are web-based services where users can 1) create and maintain a public or private profile. 2) create a list of other users they are connected to, and 3) see their own and others' contact lists [20]. The most popular SNSs are those that focus on user-generated content, participation, openness and network effects [21].

Social networking is not mainly about technology, but about covering people's needs for access to and sharing of information, collaboration and the creation of identity and self. As such, SNS should be treated more as a cultural than technological phenomenon [22]. To reap the benefits of SNS, owners of information needs to open their data, think in terms of collaborative production of ideas and content, and to share ideas with others in order to create better information[15].

2.2 Election Campaigns and Social Networks

Campaigning is all about getting the message out to the public, and convincing the public that your party has the best policy. The election campaign has a very big influence on the outcome of the parliamentary election. More than 40 % of Norwegian voters wait until the final weeks of the campaign before deciding who gets their vote, and many change their mind several times during the campaign [23]. Younger voters are more likely to cast their vote differently from one election to the next [24]. When the Norwegian newspapers became politically independent, political parties lost the power to decide what should be on the public agenda [3]. The media has taken over this role, and are trying to write about the things they believe voters are concerned about [3, 24]. Web statistics site alexa.com shows that younger age groups are still a majority in social networking sites such as Twitter and Facebook, and SNSs are among the most visited web sites in the world. Politicians wishing to influence the public should therefore have a presence in SNS, a presence that could help in taking back some of the agenda-setting power that the media currently possess.

Norwegian political parties have used the Internet in election campaigns for years, but SNS was first introduced in 2007. Inspired by Barack Obama, the 2009 election was the first time Norwegian parties were expected to really go in for SNS as a campaign tool [25]. Norwegian parties started using the Internet during the election campaign in 2001. This first attempt mainly produced digital copies of party documents and brochures, but even so the number of visitors to these sites increased a lot during the campaign [1]. At the 2005 parliamentary election, all the major parties had good web sites, and the Internet was seen as a natural part of the campaign.

However, users still preferred other media, with only 13 % of voters accessing the web sites of political parties [26]. In the 2007 local and regional elections parties had begun experimenting with SNS, publishing videos to Youtube, creating profiles on Facebook and writing blogs [27]. Facebook provided an outlet for the party grass-roots and sympathizers to some extent [27], but there was little evidence of a real dialogue between politicians and citizens [28].

3   Method

The study was conducted using a qualitative, interpretive approach. Data was collected through semi-structured interviews with representatives from the seven political parties that were represented in the parliament before the election (Socialist Left, Labor, Center Party, Liberals, Christian people's party, Conservatives and the Progress Party). Five interviews were made face to face, while two of the parties only had time for e-mail interviews. All of the interview subjects were hired by their respective parties to work with social networking strategies. The Interviews lasted between 40 and 77 minutes, and were taped and transcribed. To create a more complete account of the parties' election campaigns, observation and analysis of content and interaction in the SNSs used by the parties were applied. This made it possible to compare what the information workers said with what their employers, the politicians, were actually doing, and to create an overview of the genre repertoire in SNS political communication. Data was collected between March and May in 2009.

Interview questions and content analysis were guided by genre theory. Genre theory can be applied to study the role of communication in social processes. Genres evolve over time, in the interplay between institutional practice and the people communicating [29]. Genre theory provides us with a lens for detailed understanding of political communication, beyond the scope of democracy models [8] and the observation of technological functionality [30]. Originally, genres were recognized by having similar form and content, where form refers to physical and linguistic features, and content to themes and topics of the genre [29]. Later, when the Internet became more popular, functionality offered by the medium delivering the genre was added as a third construct [31]. A set of genres used by a given community can be seen as a genre repertoire[30]. The genre repertoire of a community can reveal a "rich and varied array of communicative practices" shaped by community members in response to norms, events, time pressure and media capabilities [30]. The genres reported in table 1 are based on the interviews, and the genres in table 2 are discovered by following the framework of Päivärinta et al [32].

4   Findings

The interview guide and guidelines for content analysis were created using the 5W1H method for genre analysis [8, 33]. 5W1H consists of the questions "where, why, when, who, what" and "how". The purpose is to uncover how the genre is enacted, in what situations it is used, who the participants are and why the genre is used. By asking the same questions in interviews and content analysis, the difference between the parties becomes a lot clearer than from interviews only. In addition to 5W1H, interview subjects were asked about their experience of the 2007 election, and what they would do differently this time.

Where - Interview subjects were asked about their party's presence in SNS and the Internet, and why they had chosen these services and not others. All of the parties have their own web site; everyone provides video and photo sharing, have a presence on Facebook and blogs. And with the exception of the Progress Party, everyone used Twitter. In addition, Labor and the Center Party also had a presence in the Norwegian SNS *Origo*. They all had the same explanation for why they had chosen these outlets, that they wanted a presence a) where people already are, and b) in the most relevant services for political participation.

Why – Parties agreed on why they where present in SNS, using words such as engaging citizens, dialogue and communication:

"We want to meet people where they are, be it in the store, at stands or online. That is why it is so important to us to have a presence in social media. Dialogue is the key to good solutions, and social media are a great place for dialogue" (Center Party).

Despite two-way communication being the objective, the parties are aware that this is not an easy task, and that earlier attempts have become one-way information channels: *"Social media needs to be used correctly. Not just as a microphone for press releases, as we and other parties have a tendency of doing, because of a lack of time for dialogue"* (Liberals)

What – Answers were a bit more varied on the question of what types of content the parties wanted to present. The party's policy was most important, and again it was pointed out that SNS could help disseminate this to groups that are difficult to reach through other channels. Labor and the Socialist Left are most explicit about spreading content that can help engage citizens in dialogue, and get party sympathizers to volunteer for "real world" activities: *"To us, the most important thing is that citizens can become active participants in the offline world. We don't want people to just sit in front of their screens, watching videos. We want to inspire, to get people to talk to others, to recruit people, go knocking on doors, get people out of the chair and into the voting booths"* (Labor)"

Who – There is some variation in who from the party that participates in communication through SNS. The common reply to this question was "as many as possible of those politicians who are interested", and the goal was to make party leaders and candidates for parliament to participate. Age was put forth as a barrier to participation, as older candidates were not used to communicating online, and had no wish to learn: *"Some of our older candidates find the whole thing a bit scary and difficult. That is a challenge to us, to teach them that it is actually really simple once you get started."* (Christian People's Party)

Others were less concerned about age, because they experienced that more and more middle-aged people are joining social networks, partially as a consequence of political presence: *"We see statistics that older people are joining as well. Jens' [the prime minister] Facebook profile led to a lot of 40 to 50 year olds joining, because when the prime minister was there, they had to be as well"* (Labor)

Most parties had no explicit strategy about who they wanted to communicate with. Some had no thoughts at all about this; some just said they wanted to engage potential voters, without saying anything about who their potential voters are. The Christian People's party is explicit about wanting to reach younger age groups, as their existing voters are mainly older people. The Liberal party has defined their typical voter as young and urban, and is trying to reach out to this group, but has no strategy about how they can accomplish this.

When – Everyone replied that they did not want to use SNS only during the election campaign. They point out that the use of SNS is not mainly a campaign tool, but part of a bigger strategy to engage in a dialogue with citizens: *"IT goes without saying that the work we put in now will continue...There's a virtual world out there that is just as important to be present in as the real world...You just have to pay attention to what is happening and use the Internet for all it is worth"* (Conservatives)

The Socialist Left party claims that the election campaign is less important than to maintain a constant dialogue and receive input from voters about their policy: *"If you only use this during the election campaign...that is not the time policy is formed, so if you are serious about dialogue it does not make sense to stop after the election"*

The Liberal party voiced some concern about time and resource constraints, and said that this could potentially be an obstruction to continued use: *"These things tend to stop after the election. We don't want it to, but it takes an effort, both from politicians and us employees, and also some financial resources."*

How – Parties were asked about how they wanted to communicate. If they wanted one- or two-way communication, to engage citizens in campaigning, how they wanted to structure communication, and what type of language they used in SNS.

There is broad agreement that content and language must be adapted to the specific medium. Interview subjects were eager to discuss blogs, and the importance of a less formal language and a more personal approach to writing came up several times during many of the interviews: *"Contrary to what politicians are used to, you need to be more open, honest, listening, trying to write so that the audience are moved by the content, be humble"* (Labor)

Contributions from citizens are also wanted, both in terms of policy debates and user-generated content. The Liberals, the Socialist Left and Labor announced competitions via YouTube, Twitter and Facebook, where they asked voters to create their own videos or web applications that the party could use.

Learning experience – 2007 was the first time that political parties experimented with SNS, and all of them provide tales of a steep learning curve. Labor and the Liberals point out that 2007 was an experiment, where the primary objective was to test new channels of communication: *"We tried some things, and got some negative responses. Our objective has been to be first movers, because then you get a lot of coverage in the media. So quality was sometimes lacking"* (Labor). The Center party was not very happy with their own efforts two years ago: *"I am tempted to say that we do everything differently today"*

4.1 Genre Repertoire

In the interviews, dialogue, contributions from citizens and involvement are mentioned as the overarching objective of party presence in SNSs. Table 1 presents these as genres, identified through the 5W1H method. These should be considered genre objectives, as there are many ways of creating dialogue, providing contributions or getting involved.

Table 1. Genres identified in interviews

	Dialogue	Contribution	Involvement
Why	Involve citizens in public debate	Knowledge about citizen concerns	Raise funds. Get people to volunteer
When	Continuous	Election time	Election time
What	Conversation between citizens and politicians/citizens and citizens	Q&A. Voter stories	Competitions, membership forms, information
Who	Politicians, party members, citizens	Politicians, party members, voters	Voters, sympathizers
Where	SNS, web site	SNS, web site	SNS, web site
How	Encourage dialogue. Open and personal language. Citizen-generated content.	Encourage contributions and questions from voters	Competitions, theme sites, cross-publication

To identify the genres that make dialogue, contributions and involvement possible, I conducted a content analysis of the SNSs where the parties were present. Table 2 summarizes the identified genres, following the method created by Päivärinta, Halttunen and Tyrväinen [32]. The producers and users of information are identified to indicate the direction of communication. By mapping the medium the genre is presented through, we can learn something about which medium is suited for which genre. The final column shows which genre objective the genre is related to. When examining the individual Social network sites, we see how the functionality of the medium has great influence on communication. For example, Facebook wall posts and Twitter messages are very similar, but still produce very different outcomes because of the way they are presented.

Table 2. Genres identified through content analysis

Genre	Producer	User	Medium	Related to
Policy comment	Citizen	Citizen, party	Facebook, blog, Origo, Twitter, video	Dialogue, contribution
Call for action	Citizen, party	Citizen	Facebook, Twitter, video	Contribution, involvement
Q&A	Citizen	Party	Facebook, Twitter, blog	Dialogue
Appeal to party	Citizen	Party	Facebook, Twitter, blog	Dialogue, contribution
Greeting	Citizen	Party	Facebook, blog	Dialogue
Personal accounts	Citizen	Party	blog	contribution
Video response	Citizen, party	Citizen, party	YouTube	Contribution

The list presented in table 2 should not be considered complete. These are the genres that were present during the time of observation. Due to the changing nature of SNS, it is more than likely that new genres have been added. The list should be considered as a starting point for a more comprehensive mapping of genres, not as a finalized list.

Policy comments are comments from citizens on party policy. These come in many forms. As Wall or discussion posts on Facebook or Origo, in Twitter messages, blog comments or as video responses. Video responses are rare, but not unheard of. Policy comments can be seen both as contributions to policy development and as part of a dialogue.

Calls for action mainly originate with the party, but are often distributed through citizens supporting the party making the call. This genre incorporates calls for volunteers, competitions and calls for action in specific cases. Several parties have created Facebook groups for parts of their policy. Calls are presented in video, with links to the video posted to Facebook and Twitter.

The Q&A genre is perhaps the genre that citizens are least satisfied with. Many questions on Facebook walls remain unanswered, or are answered unsatisfactorily. Some citizens ask why politicians bother having a presence in SNS when they do not engage in conversations with citizens.

Appeals to the party are similar to policy comments. The difference is that where policy comments reflect directly on the party's political program, appeals are more specific, asking what the party intends to do with this or that matter. There is some frustration among citizens when these are not answered.

Greeting is an interesting genre. At his birthday, Prime Minister Jens Stoltenberg received hundreds of greetings wishing him a happy birthday. In other cases, we see greetings thanking the party for something they have done, or cheering them on to fight for a specific case. This genre, while not directly political, could be seen as narrowing the gap between politician and citizen, creating a sense of personal attachment between the two.

Personal accounts are mainly found in blogs, as response to politicians asking for the stories of individual citizens. The most interesting example is where the minister of health asks for people's stories as input to a major health reform. This initiative generated around a thousand replies from citizens wanting to share their experiences with the Norwegian health system.

Video responses from citizens are rare, but some examples exist. These can be either interviews where citizens respond to something politicians have said, or responses to the competitions where parties ask citizens to contribute. There are also responses between parties, where video is used in a similar manner to newspaper debates, and responses between politicians belonging to the same party.

Even though we see an emerging genre repertoire in political communication through SNS, the content analysis shows that there are some challenges that need to be addressed. The main problem, especially with the policy comment, Q&A and appeal to party genres, is that for some, communication is still mostly one-way. Some parties and politicians are not responding to questions, and comments and appeals are even less likely to receive answers, while others are better at responding. On the other hand, calls for action and policy comments where parties have asked for comments, receives a lot of attention and feedback. This is in line with other research, claiming that political use of SNS is not yet following web 2.0 principles fully, but rather functions as a "web 1.5" [34].

5 Conclusion

Political parties in Norway report that they are serious about using SNS to create dialogue, contributions and involvement from citizens. They want to increase political awareness in the population, get sympathizers to participate in offline activities, and to have citizens influence policy development. They report that this is not just an election time activity, but something they want to continue doing after the election in order to create a better dialogue between party and citizen.

The content analysis shows that while there has in fact been developing a genre repertoire for political communication in SNS, there is little agreement on how some of these genres should be enacted. Genres involving citizen-initiated dialogue are the most problematic, while politician-initiated genres have more success. This could be because politicians still are uncertain about how to communicate in SNS, and what communication through SNS should mean for the political process. It could also be a question of politicians and citizens not understanding the genre, and not understanding the appropriate level of democracy for each individual genre. Further research should address this, and develop a genre repertoire that helps politicians and citizens to reach a mutual understanding of what they are communicating about, as well as what the outcome of communication should be. Genre theory and democracy models have demonstrated the communicative gap between politicians and citizens, and could prove useful in closing this gap.

References

1. Hestvik, H.: Valgkamp2001.no. Partier, velgere og nye medier. Ny kommunikasjon? In: Aardal, B., Krogstad, A., Narud, H.M. (eds.) I valgkampens hete: strategisk kommunikasjon og politisk usikkerhet. Universitetsforlaget, Oslo (2001)
2. Edelman, The Social pulpit. Barack Obama's social media Toolkit (2009)
3. Østerud, Ø., Engelstad, F., Selle, P.: Makten og demokratiet: en sluttbok fra Makt- og demokratiutredningen. Gyldendal akademisk, Oslos (2003)
4. Sæbø, Ø., Rose, J., Skiftenes Flak, L.: The shape of eParticipation: Characterizing an emerging research area. Government Information Quarterly 25(3), 400–428 (2008)
5. Tambouris, E., Liotas, N., Tarabanis, K.: A Framework for Assessing eParticipation Projects and Tools. In: Hawaii International Conference on System Sciences, Hawaii (2007)
6. Brandtzæg, P.B., Lüders, M.: eCitizen 2.0: The Ordinary Citizen as a Supplier of Public Sector Information. Ministry for Government and Administration Reform, Oslo (2008)
7. Dahlberg, L.: The Internet and Democratic Discourse: Exploring The Prospects of Online Deliberative Forums Extending the Public Sphere. Information, Communication & Society 4(4), 615–633 (2001)
8. Sæbø, Ø., Päivârinta, T.: Autopoietic cybergenres for e-Democracy? Genre analysis of a web-based discussion board. In: Hawaii International Conference on System Sciences (2005)

9. Komito, L.: e-Participation and Governance: Widening the net. The Electronic Journal of e-Government 3(1), 39–48 (2005)
10. Sanford, C., Rose, J.: Characterizing eParticipation. International Journal of Information Management 27(6), 406–421 (2007)
11. Ekelin, A.: To be or not to be active: Exploring practices of e-participation. Springer, Berlin (2006)
12. Rose, J., Sæbø, Ø.: Democracy Squared: Designing On-Line Political Communities to Accommodate Conflicting Interests Scandinavian. Journal of Information Systems 17(2) (2005)
13. Päivärinta, T., Sæbø, Ø.: Models of E-democracy. Communications of the Association for Information Systems 17(4) (2006)
14. Bughin, J., Manyika, J., Miller, A.: McKinsey global survey results: Building the web 2.0 enterprise. In: McKinsey Quarterly survey on web 2.0 (July 2008)
15. Tapscott, D., Williams, A.: Wikinomics: How mass collaboration changes everything., 2nd edn. Portfolio/Penguin Group, New York (2008)
16. O'Reilly, T.: What is web 2.0? Design patterns and business models for the next generation of software (2005), http://oreilly.com/web2/archive/what-is-web-20.html (cited September 2, 2010)
17. User centric media: Future and challenges in european Research, European Commission: Information society and media (2007)
18. Enders, A., et al.: The long tail of social networking. Revenue models of social networking sites. European Management Journal 26(3) (2008)
19. OECD, Participative web and User-created Content: Web 2.0, wikis and social networking, OECD (2007)
20. Boyd, d.m., Ellison, N.B.: Social Network Sites: Definition, History, and Scholarship. Journal of Computer-Mediated Communication 13(1), 210–230 (2008)
21. Anderson, P.: What is Web 2.0? Ideas, technologies and implications for education. In: JISC Technology and Standards Watch (2007)
22. Rose, J., et al.: The role of social networking software in eParticipation, in DEMO-net: D14.3. In: Svendsen, S.B. (ed.) DEMO-net: The Democracy Network (2007)
23. Aardal, B., Krogstad, A., Narud, H.M.: I valgkampens hete: strategisk kommunikasjon og politisk usikkerhet, p. 431. Universitetsforl, Oslo (2004)
24. Aardal, B., Holth, I.J.: Norske velgere: en studie av stortingsvalget 2005, p. 381. Damm, Oslo (2007)
25. Fredriksen, A., Alnes, E.: Valgseier med hjelp av Internett, NRK (2009)
26. Karlsen, R.: Den første internettvalgkampen? Velgernes informasjonskilder. In: Aardal, B., Holth, I.J. (eds.) Norske velgere: en studie av stortingsvalget 2005. Damm, Oslo (2007)
27. Kalnes, Ø.: Norwegian Parties and Web 2.0. Journal of Information Technology and Politics 6(3), 251–266 (2009)
28. Andresen, S.: Valgkamp på nett: partiledernes bruk av blogg som politisk kommunikasjonsverktøy i valget 2007. S. Andresen, Oslo (2008)
29. Yates, J., Orlikowski, W.J.: Genres of Organizational Communication: A Structurational Approach to Studying Communication and Media. The Academy of Management Review 17(2), 299–326 (1992)
30. Orlikowski, W.J., Yates, J.: Genre Repertoire: The Structuring of Communicative Practices in Organizations. Administrative Science Quarterly 39(4), 541–574 (1994)

31. Shepherd, M., Watters, C.: The evolution of cybergenres. In: Proceedings of the Thirty-First Hawaii International Conference on System Sciences (1998)
32. Päivärinta, T., Halttunen, V., Tyrväinen, P.: A Genre-Based Method for Information Systems Planning. In: Rossi, M., Siau, K. (eds.) Information Modeling in the New Millenium, pp. 70–93. Idea Group Publishing, Hershey (2001)
33. Yoshioka, T., et al.: Genre taxonomy: A knowledge repository of communicative actions. ACM Trans. Inf. Syst. 19(4), 431–456 (2001)
34. Jackson, N.A., Lilleker, D.G.: Building an Architecture of Participation? Political Parties and Web 2.0 in Britain. Journal of Information Technology and Politics 6(3), 232–250 (2009)

Political Deliberation in the Blogosphere: The Case of the 2009 Portuguese Elections

Rui Pedro Lourenço[1,2]

[1] INESC Coimbra, Rua Antero de Quental, 199,
3000 Coimbra, Portugal
[2] Faculty of Economics, University of Coimbra, Av. Dias da Silva. 165,
3000 Coimbra, Portugal
ruiloure@fe.uc.pt

Abstract. In 2009, a unique Portuguese electoral cycle comprised european, local, and national elections. During the three month non-stop campaign period, more than a hundred experienced bloggers, supporters of the three main political parties, created three non party-sponsored blogs. These blogs were the focal point of the political blogosphere during that period and ceased their activities at the end of the electoral campaign, thus providing a unique opportunity to better understand the political blogosphere. Web mining techniques were used to obtain data concerning the visits to those blogs (from Sitemeter) and the blog's content itself (posts, comments, and links). Data suggests that blog readers don't look for different points of view, blog commentators usually limit themselves to one blog, bloggers do not comment on other blogs other than their own, and relatively few links exist between all three blogs. These results undermine the idea that the political blogosphere can enhance the deliberative character of the public sphere.

Keywords: Political blogosphere; Public sphere; Deliberation.

1 Introduction

Political talk is an essential part of democracy [1]. It can occur in the privacy of our homes, in the inner circle of friends and family, and constitutes the basic public participation tool of common citizens. However, political talk in restricted environments suffers from limitations with respect to the availability of information, the exposition to opposing views and arguments, and the possibility to influence policy formulation and public decision processes.

In order to overcome these limitations it is essential that contemporary democratic societies nurture public arenas where citizens may engage in political talk in a free and autonomous manner. These public arenas relate to the concept of public sphere which is generally used to designate "the social space between the state and civil society" [2] where "something approaching public opinion can be formed" [3] after "exposure to a sufficient amount of information, and also to an appropriately wide and diverse range of options" [4].

E. Tambouris, A. Macintosh, and O. Glassey (Eds.): ePart 2010, LNCS 6229, pp. 115–125, 2010.

In this context, deliberation is a process by which individual preferences and points of view change due solely to the force of the better argument, that is, without coercion [5]. As a social process, deliberation can be viewed as a communicative process which involves the serious consideration of arguments in favor and against a certain proposition [6], and by which participants are willing to change their preferences and points of view [7]. Putting aside some demands for discursive rationalism required by Jürgen Habermas [3] to qualify discussion in the public sphere as deliberation, some authors characterize the deliberative process by its result, "the endogenous change in preferences resulting from communication" [8].

The importance of deliberation in contemporary democratic systems is emphasized by deliberative democrats such as John Dryzek when he states: "the essence of democracy itself is now widely taken to be deliberation, as opposed to voting, interest aggregation, constitutional rights, or even self-government" [7].

The Internet, and particularly the blogosphere, may contribute decisively to the improvement and enlargement of the public sphere, providing the necessary conditions for the development of public deliberative processes, including freedom of speech and association.

The nature of the blogosphere, where a significant part of what is written is devoted to criticize other people's opinion, is considered an indication of its deliberative potential [9]. Also, the structure of blogs sets them apart from the traditional media and suggest that they are an adequate platform to foster political deliberation: readers may create content related to the posts they read and other people's comments; it is possible to create links between posts and comments which express opposing points of view and arguments; blogs maintain a list of other blogs (blogrolls) which usually include blogs from different political areas [9, 10].

Nevertheless, concerns remain about the potential of these digital media to fragment and polarize the public sphere, and that, in reality, political blogs readers and writers tend to isolate themselves from opposing points of view and arguments [4]. American cultural blogs, for instance, seem to follow this pattern [11]. They specialize in a unique form of art and subculture and adopting well defined points of view, thus mimicking some of the most influential political blogs [11].

These concerns are justified by empirical studies that analyzed the content and blogroll of influential American political blogs and concluded that the vast majority of the links connected blogs and bloggers who share the same ideological area [12,13]. This seem to confirm that it is not enough to provide structural conditions for meaningful deliberation: to consider the political blogosphere as truly deliberative it is necessary that blog contributors and readers are willing to be exposed to opposing arguments, to discuss them with others and reflect upon them. Otherwise the blogosphere effect on the public sphere will be mitigated and will limit itself to reproduce what empirical studies reveal about the "real life": citizens prefer to discuss political issues with those who share their values and points of view, trying to avoid conflict situations [14].

So, it is important to the quality of democracy to understand if the Internet, and the blogosphere in particular, can contribute to reduce this natural aversion to confront ideas due, for instance, to the possibility to allow anonymity and avoid face-to-face contact between the participants in a discussion.

The goal of this work is twofold. First, it aims at enhancing the knowledge about the deliberative nature of the political blogosphere. Previous research efforts focused on structural and qualitative content analysis of blog contributions (written posts, comments, and links). This work tries to complement previous research by assessing the behavior of blog readers, those who just observe the debate without contributing to it [14], through quantitative analysis of blog visiting data. Second, it aims at better understanding the Portuguese political blogosphere and assess its deliberative nature.

2 Research Methodology

In 2009, Portugal witnessed a unique political cycle which comprised three, very close, electoral events: the European Parliament election in July, the General election (National Assembly and Government) in September, and the Local Authorities election in October.

Also, at that time the ruling party had an absolute majority in the National Parliament and, because of that, there was some acrimony between opposing political parties. As it would be expected, the existing political climate and the concentration of electoral events fostered very vivid discussions both on traditional media and on the Internet.

During that period of time, supporters from the three main political parties created three non-official party blogs. These blogs were created in the end of July, lasted until the end of September, and were mainly focused on the General Election. They gathered a total of 114 authors, including some of the most prominent political bloggers, and became the reference for the political blogosphere during that period of time.

The coincidence of such political (electoral) events and the creation of these three dedicated blogs provided the ideal opportunity to analyze the Portuguese political blogosphere.

To better understand the data, the process used to collect it, and the analysis made, the following terminology will be used throughout the remaining of the text:

— *Authors* or *Bloggers*: those that created each of the three blogs and therefore have the possibility to write posts and create links in the blog they "belong to". Naturally and author of a specific blog might also create comments in his/her own blog and on any of the other blogs;

— *Visitors* or *Blog readers*: all those that accessed the blogs, including authors from one of the three blogs and commentators.

Web mining techniques were used to collect all data (covering the period when the blogs were active – approximately 2 months) from the 3 blogs including post text, post author, post links, comments text, and comments author (nickname and URL[1]). Additionally, visiting data (IP address and access time) was collected from Sitemeter[2] regarding each blog. Due to technical difficulties only data regarding blog visits in the 15 days prior to the General election were collected and analyzed (during general electoral campaign). Contrary to blog content, which is available for analysis still today, visiting data by Sitemeter has to be collected in a real-time way, as only the last 100 accesses are publicly available at any given moment.

---

[1] Uniform Resource Location.
[2] www.sitemeter.com

Table 1 presents the characterization of the three blogs analyzed, including its name, URL and political affiliation[3].

Table 1. Blog's characterization

Blog name	URL	Party	Political spectrum
SIMPlex	simplex.blogs.sapo.pt	PS	Center-left (ruling party)
Jamais	jamais.blogs.sapo.pt	PSD	Center-right (main opposition party)
Rua Direita	ruadireita.blogs.sapo.pt	CDS-PP	Right-wing

3 Data Collected

Table 2 presents an overview of the number of authors (bloggers) registered on each blog, and the number of posts, comments and links produced.

Table 2. Blogs' content

	Nr authors	Nr posts	Nr comments	Nr links
SIMPlex	41	1285	6638	1990
Jamais	33	1000	2729	1112
Rua Direita	40	908	1142	938
TOTAL	114	3193	10509	4040

This general data is further detailed in the next sections.

3.1 Visiting and Electoral Data

Each blog was associated with one of the three main Portuguese political parties. Table 3 shows the electoral score (number of votes) of each party and the number of corresponding blog visits, as recorded by Sitemeter, during the time the blogs were active. Using just these parties (and blogs) as the universe of total number of votes, it is possible to calculate the percentage of votes and blog visits for each party/blog and compare them.

Table 3. Number of votes (political parties) and number of visits (blogs)

Blog/Party	Votes (party)		Visits (blog)		Dif.
	N^4	$\%^5$	N^6	%	(p.p.)
SIMPlex/PS	2068665	48,0%	187583	51,7%	+3,7
Jamais/PSD	1646097	38,2%	132044	36,3%	-1,8
Rua Direita/CDS-PP	592064	13,8%	43404	12,0%	-1,7
TOTAL	4306826	100,0%	363031	100,0%	

---

[3] Although political party affiliation was explicitly stated in all three blogs, all of them also stated that these were non-official party blogs.

[4] Source: http://aeiou.visao.pt/mapa-dos-resultados-finais=f530790 (30/09/2009)

[5] These values were calculated just considering the number of votes in these three parties.

[6] Source: Sitemeter (30/09/2009). SiteMeter defines a "visit" as a set of page views originating from the same IP address within a 30 minute time interval.

According to this data, the difference (measured in percentage points) between political parties votes and blog visits ranges from -1,8 to + 3,7.

Data collected from Sitemeter regarding each visit of a reader to each blog included the IP address[7] of the computer where the visit was initiated and the time at which that visit was initiated.

The concept of *reading event* was defined to assess how many blogs each visitor read when accessing the blogosphere. For that matter, visits were considered in 30, 60, 90, and 120 minute periods. For instance, visits coming from the same IP address and occurring in less that 120 minutes apart were considered as being part of the same *reading event* by the same reader (visitor).

Table 4 presents the number of reading events considered for each of the time periods considered, and the percentage of those events that involved just one, two, or all three blogs.

Table 4. Number of blogs visited on the same *reading event*

	30 min.	60 min.	90 min.	120 min.
Nr of reading events (total)	73192	65070	59862	56130
Just visiting 1 blog	84%	82%	81%	80%
Visiting 2 blogs	14%	16%	17%	17%
Visiting all 3 blogs	2%	2%	2%	3%

If we consider reading events grouping visits from the same IP address in 120 minutes interval, we can see that, under these conditions, blog readers visited only one blog in 80% of the reading events, they visited two blogs in 17% of the reading events, and they visited all three blogs in only 3% of the reading events.

3.2   Comments Data

One important indicator of a deliberative political blogosphere is *cross commenting*: bloggers (authors) associated with a particular blog write comments in another blog.

Table 5 presents the number of bloggers associated with each blog and the number of them which made comments in other blogs.

Table 5. Blog authors and comments in other blogs

	Nr of authors	Nr of authors who wrote comments on another blog	Nr of authors who wrote comments on both other blogs
SIMPlex	41	11	1
Jamais	33	8	2
Rua Direita	40	4	0
TOTAL	114	23	3
	100%	20%	3%

---

[7] Several limitations exist regarding these data. Those limitations and their impact on analysis will be addressed in section 5.

Data shows that 20% of all the blog authors (114) wrote comments on another blog other than his/her own, and only 3% wrote comments on both the other two blogs.

Another way to analyze cross comments is to consider how many comments were made by bloggers outside their own blog. Table 6 presents the total number of comments written by bloggers of each blog (in all three blogs) and how many of those comments were written in another blog (other than the blogger's own blog).

Table 6. Number of comments written by bloggers of each blog

Bloggers from	Total number of comments written	Comments written in another blog	
		N	%
SIMPlex	1277	65	5%
Jamais	353	21	6%
Rua Direita	287	4	1%

Collected data shows that very few comments were made by authors of a certain blog in another blog. For instance, among the 1277 comments written by "SIMPLex" bloggers only 65 (5%) were made either in "Jamais" or "Rua Direita". As for bloggers from the other blogs the numbers are in the same magnitude.

We can also analyze how many of the comments written in each blog were made by authors (bloggers) of the other blogs. Table 7 shows, for each blog, the origin of its comments.

Table 7. Origin of the comments on each blog

	Number of comments on each blog	Written by bloggers from:			
		SIMPlex	Jamais	Rua Direita	Other
SIMPlex	6638	18,3%	0,3%	0,0%	81,5%
Jamais	2729	2,2%	12,2%	0,1%	85,6%
Rua Direita	1142	0,5%	0,4%	24,8%	74,3%

According to this data, very few comments made on each blog were attributed to bloggers from any of the other two blogs. The vast majority of comments on each blog were either made by their own bloggers or by other visitors (including anonymous ones).

If we consider the entire universe of blog readers (not just bloggers from the three blogs) we might have a complementary perspective. Table 8 presents the number and percentage of blog readers that wrote comments exclusively in one of the blogs, in two of the blogs and in all three of them.

Table 8. Number authors who wrote comments in one, two, or three blogs

Authors of comments	Nr	%
In just one blog	1272	80%
In two blogs	255	16%
In three blogs	56	4%
TOTAL	1583	

This data suggests that the majority of blog readers (80%) wrote comments in just one blog. By contrary, only 4% of all identifiable blog readers (those having the same nickname and URL) wrote comments in all three blogs.

3.3 Links Data

Another useful data to assess the deliberative nature of the political blogosphere is the one related with links made from a particular blog to one of the other blogs, as shown in Table 9.

Table 9. Posts linking to one of the other blogs

	Total number of posts	Posts linking to other blogs N	%
SIMPlex	1285	125	10%
Jamais	1000	117	12%
Rua Direita	908	75	8%

Data shows that between 8% and 12% of posts in one blog had links to one of the other two blogs.

4   Discussion

Using the data collected it is possible to address the questions presented next.

4.1   Can the Blogosphere Be Used to "Predict" Electoral Results?

Some traditional polling techniques rely on fixed phone interviews to collect raw data with which electoral projections are made. But the use of fixed phones is steadily decreasing and rising mobile phone penetration rate makes it more difficult to collect such data. This prompts concerns about electoral projections accuracy and suggests the possibility that other media might be better to collect such data. Among others, the blogosphere, as a forum for political debate, could be considered an alternative way to know citizen's political preferences and predict electoral results.

Data from Table 3 suggests that blog visiting numbers came close to actual electoral results (in percentage of this universe). This does not mean that it would be possible to predict electoral results this way, but it seems to confirm that the blogosphere might indeed provide a barometer to political preferences.

Further research is necessary to develop the procedures to collect and analyze blogosphere data. It is necessary to address issues such as visiting numbers manipulation: it would be very easy to manipulate visiting numbers once it was known that those numbers were being used to make electoral projections. It is also essential to take into account the socio-demographic specifics of political bloggers and blog readers and, more generally, the limitations of Internet access and digital divide. These and other difficulties make it very challenging to create a reliable procedure to produce electoral projections from political blogosphere data.

4.2   How Deliberative Is the Portuguese Political Blogosphere?

In a truly deliberative public sphere, participants seek to confront opposing points of view before forming their own opinion. Structurally, the blogosphere provides a facilitating discussion environment since it allows bloggers to comment each other posts and link to them. By writing comments in another blog, bloggers engage in a discussion with the author of the post they are commenting, and therefore contribute to the exchange of arguments and points of view.

However, data collected suggests that very few bloggers made comments on one of the other blogs (Table 5). Not surprisingly then, very few comments in each blog where made by bloggers from one the other blogs (Tables 6 and 7). It is, of course, possible that some comments were written anonymously (or under a nickname) and were not associated with a particular blogger. However, bloggers from these particular blogs were all well known and identified themselves as authors of their posts, which makes it not very plausible that they would not do the same with their comments.

Instead of commenting on other blogs, authors have the possibility to confront ideas and exchange arguments by linking their posts to posts and comments in the other blogs. Again, data indicates that the number of posts with links to one of the two other blogs ranges between 8% and 12% (Table 9).

Not all references to posts and comments from other blogs are expressed by crossed comments or linking. Sometimes the author of a post merely gives indication on his/her text that he/she is participating in a wider debate. Nevertheless, these last two results seem to indicate that either there is not that much interaction between political bloggers, or that the linking mechanism that blogs make available are not being properly used, thus making it more difficult for a reader to follow the discussion.

Previous work that analyzed the political blogosphere limited their scope to blog structure and content (blogroll, post and comment analysis) and blog writers (post authors) behavior. This work seeks to contribute to a broader perspective by including blog readers' behavior in the analysis.

According to Table 8, 80% of all identifiable visitors who wrote comments in all three blogs just wrote comments on a single blog, 16% wrote comments on two different blogs, and 4% wrote comments on all three blogs.

Finally, this work also tried to assess the behavior of blog readers that don't even write posts or comments using visiting data collected by Sitemeter. Analysis show that if we consider 120 minute intervals between recorded visits, the vast majority of blog visitors (80%) accesses only one of the three blogs. On the opposite side, just 3% visits all three blogs in a 120 minute interval (Table 4).

If we consider these two results together, they indicate that even blog readers do not seek to confront different opinions and points of view. This might be just a similar behavior to the bloggers involved, or it might be a consequence of the lack of structuring (limited use of post links) by post authors (bloggers).

5   Conclusion

The blogosphere is a continuously evolving environment: every day new blogs are created and old ones end. Bloggers cease their collaboration in one blog and start writing in another. Commentators use different nick names and "hide" behind anonymity. Some blog readers simple accompany the discussion without intervening. This makes it very difficult to analyze the political blogosphere and assess its deliberative nature and the impact it has on the public sphere and political life. The ultimate research challenge regarding the political blogosphere is then to evaluate its real impact on the points of view and voting behavior of bloggers, blog commentators, blog readers, and society in general.

The 2009 Portuguese electoral cycle, and the political environment that surrounded it, led to the creation of three non-official blogs affiliated with the three main political parties. This provided a unique opportunity to study the Portuguese political sphere and contribute to assess if indeed it plays a role in enhancing a deliberative public sphere. This study broaden the work done on previous studies by, among others, specifically including in the analysis the behavior of blog commentators and readers using Sitemeter statistics.

Results must be considered cautiously as there were several technical limitations to the process of data collecting and analysis. For instance, blog visiting data from Sitemeter's free version includes only the first 3 octets of the IP address. Firewalls, and NAT[8] mechanisms could mask the real IP address of blog visitors. Analysis of visiting data considered a visiting profile where blog readers would access blogs within 120 minutes interval: a larger interval would perhaps identify visits to more blogs originating in the same IP address but that could be attributed to dynamic IPs or simply to the fact that different users use the same computer. Also, to establish the authorship of different comments by the same visitor, we considered matching nicknames and URL when provided. This means that, although some take great pride in their nickname and use it as "trademark", others simply jump from one nickname to another thus making it very difficult to correctly match comment authors.

Despite all these limitations, this study found no evidence that the potential of the blogosphere structure is being used to promote a truly deliberative arena, thus confirming previous research: there is limited interaction between bloggers from different ideological areas, and, perhaps more importantly, most blog readers and commentators do not seek to expose themselves to different and opposing points of view and arguments: blog readers do not take advantage of the diversity of the blogosphere and are perhaps trying to avoid opposing points of view, or just seeking to confirm their own.

In accordance with the main findings of this study, a simple analysis of political bloggers' posts indicates that they rarely (if ever) changed their points of view (as expressed by their posts) during the course of the electoral period debate, at least not a public manner. On the contrary, discussion seems to have contributed to the radicalization (polarization) of their points of view. This type of analysis is much more difficult to be made when it comes to blog readers (including commentators), since it is very easy to write comments anonymously and under different nicknames which makes it more difficult to analyze the evolution of participation.

---

[8] Network Address Translation.

So, we are still far from understanding the real impact of the political blogosphere on bloggers, commentators, readers and society in general regarding preference formation and voting behavior. This study contributed to advance the knowledge in this area but certainly much more research still needs do be done.

The number of blogs that were analyzed, as much relevant as they were during the electoral period, limit the possibility to reach generalized conclusions. Future research must take into consideration a larger number of blogs, during a larger time framework, and covering also non-electoral periods. Also, further blog content analysis is necessary to ascertain the meaningfulness of posts and comments, in order to identify threads of discussions among blog writers and commentators, and to consider only meaningful posts and comments when analyzing links between blogs.

Tools such as Sitemeter can be used more extensively, but in order to get good quality data it is necessary to get blog administrators to collaborate, raising privacy issues (particularly of blog readers) and perhaps influencing bloggers behavior.

Pre and post discussion surveys could also be used to evaluate the impact of the blogosphere on blog readers. However, apart from practical (logistical) and representativeness issues, such methods would raise questions on how to isolate the specific impact of the blogosphere from the impact of other media and discussion forums (traditional media, discussions with family and friends, campaigning events, …).

The fact that political blogs are getting ever more attention and exposure from the traditional media is a good indicator of their potential impact, but measuring such an impact on "silent" blog readers and society in general is still a challenging research task.

References

1. Barber, B.R.: Strong democracy: Participatory politics for a new age. University of California Press, Berkeley (1984)
2. Brants, K.: Guest Editor's introduction: the Internet and the public sphere. Political Communication 22, 143–146 (2005)
3. Habermas, J.: The Public Sphere: an encyclopedia article. New German Critique 3, 49–55 (1974)
4. Sunstein, C.R.: Republic.com. Princeton University Press, Princeton (2001)
5. Kemp, R.: Planning, public hearings, and the politis of discourse. In: Forrester, J. (ed.) Critical Theory and Public Life, pp. 177–201. The MIT Press, Cambridge (1988)
6. Fearon, J.D.: Deliberation as discussion. In: Elster, J. (ed.) Deliberative Democracy, pp. 44–68. Cambridge University Press, Cambridge (1998)
7. Dryzek, J.S.: Deliberative democracy and beyond: liberals, critics, contestations. Oxford University Press, Oxford (2000)
8. Stokes, S.: Pathologies of deliberation. In: Elster, J. (ed.) Deliberative Democracy, pp. 123–139. Cambridge University Press, Cambridge (1998)
9. Balkin, J.: What I learned about blogging in a year,
   http://balkin.blogspot.com/2004_01_18_balkin_archive.html#10
   7480769112109137
10. Woodly, D.: New competencies in democratic communication? Blogs, agenda setting and political participation. Public Choice 134, 109–123 (2008)

11. Teachout, T.: Culture in the Age of Blogging. Commentary Magazine (2005)
12. Adamic, L., Glance, N.: The political blogosphere and the 2004 U.S. election: divided they blog. In: 3rd International Workshop on Link Discovery (LinkKDD '05). ACM, Chicago (2005)
13. Hargittai, E., Gallo, J., Kane, M.: Cross-ideological discussions among conservative and liberal bloggers. Public Choice 134, 67–86 (2008)
14. Witschge, T.: Online Deliberation: Possibilities of the Internet for Deliberative Democracy. In: Euricom Colloquium Electronic Networks & Democratic Engagement (2002)

On Sustainable eParticipation

Francesco Molinari

University of Siena, Dipartimento di Studi Aziendali e Sociali
Piazza S. Francesco 8, 53100 Siena, Italy
mail@francescomolinari.it

Abstract. Among the various analytical dimensions purporting to an appraisal of the replication potential of eParticipation projects, institutional factors deserve considerably more attention by theorists and practitioners alike. This paper introduces a "process oriented" definition of sustainable eParticipation, based on five key attributes: juridical compliance, legitimacy, social value, efficiency, and productivity. These can be used to assess the level of potential integration of a participatory practice or trial within the legal, political, social and organisational contexts of the public sector institutions involved. We posit that sustainable participation will emerge whenever these five dimensions are not jeopardised, compromised, or are left unaltered, by the introduction of participatory elements into any decision-making process regarding issues of public relevance. Empirical investigation is recommended to assess the impact of specific Preparatory Actions on eParticipation by using the five propositions introduced.

Keywords: Sustainability, Impact, eParticipation, Public Decision-Making, Appraisal.

1 Introduction

Over the last decade, a significant increase in the number, variety and quality of ICT supported political participation (henceforth: eParticipation) trials has become quite notable, particularly in Western and Southern European countries. In retrospect, the impulse of the European Parliament and the financial support by the Commission have had big merits in establishing a pan-European community of practice, made up of academia, governments and solution providers from virtually all countries of the Union[1].

Sound progress has been made since the European Commission started to support this emerging research strand under the 5th and 6th Framework Programmes in the ICT domain. Or since 2005, when the Parliament invited the Commission to launch a Preparatory Action on eParticipation, which is now counting on over 20 multinational projects and a coverage of two thirds of the EU countries [15]. While these initiatives

---

[1] This is mirrored by two specific initiatives sponsored by the European Commission, the PEP-NET Thematic Network of Practitioners (http://pep-net.eu) and the MOMENTUM eParticipation Coordination Action (http://ep-momentum.eu).

E. Tambouris, A. Macintosh, and O. Glassey (Eds.): ePart 2010, LNCS 6229, pp. 126–139, 2010.
© IFIP International Federation for Information Processing 2010

are mostly "owned" by national or local public authorities as prime motors and ultimate addressees of such "top-down" experiments, there is also evidence of a fast growth of "bottom-up" eParticipation, being driven by citizens and private sector blogs and social networks [18]. This whole scenario seems to support the view of ICT enthusiasts that electronic participation can bring a higher number of people back again to the democratic arena, particularly at local level, the dimension where most political and administrative processes actually take place[2].

Though no pan-European collection of cases currently exists, available evidence on the "success stories" of eParticipation is receiving a great deal of attention from both practitioners and researchers in various European countries, as reflected by the many conferences and seminars that are taking place every year and a number of scientific articles and volumes that are being written to analyse this phenomenon. However, on the evaluative side, the results of most projects that have reached a closure apparently stay below the expectations that accompanied their start-up. The most evident limitations are twofold:

- The first one is implied by the number of active participants in the electronic trials, which is typically very low, and in any case not statistically representative, nor amenable to representation, of the underlying target group, not to speak of population as a whole [7];
- The other relates with the relatively poor impact of the (majority of) projects and achievements on the underlying decision-making process of the governmental agency involved. This issue has been usually referred to as the sustainability of eParticipation ([3], [11]).

Both issues are obviously interrelated, as for example, a low interest shown by the public in a given project will most likely reduce its impact, while on the other hand, the experimental nature of most eParticipation projects, which are innovating both on the technological and the methodological viewpoint, seems a compelling argument against the use of merely quantitative criteria to evaluate the impact of the trials completed. However, given the high interest stirred and the encouraging results of most projects in several participation areas, an answer is called for to a key question: is all this just a passing fad or does it evoke a permanent change, driven by ICT, in the C2G (Citizens to Governments) interaction?

In this paper, we contend that a positive answer to the above question largely depends on whether and to which extent the participatory process(es) designed might

---

[2] It's also worth mentioning the political impact of several Resolutions of the Council of Europe's Parliamentary Assembly, from No. 800 of 1983 (*"Democracy atrophies without frequent participation by citizens who should, wherever possible, be consulted on matters closely concerning them, through appropriate mechanisms"*) through No. 980 of 1992 on citizens' participation in politics, up to No. 1121 of 1997 on the instruments of citizen participation in representative democracy. More recently, the Council of Europe's Committee of Ministers has issued several Recommendations to Member States, such as No. 19 of 2001 on the participation of citizens in local public life, No. 11 and 15 of 2004 on e-voting and e-governance, respectively, and the latest (No. 1 of 2009) on eDemocracy itself. http://www.coe.int/t/e/integrated_projects/democracy/02_activi ties/002_e%2Ddemocracy/Recommendation%20CM_Rec_2009_1E_FINAL_P DF.pdf

"embed" into the preexisting system of governance of the public sector institutions involved. A more refined definition of sustainable eParticipation is then provided, which we have developed and tested in the context of one of the aforementioned Preparatory Actions, evolving from previous research done in the area [1, 2, 4, 19]. Use of this definition is invoked as a further dimension, which we call of project appraisal, to the evaluative framework developed by [21, 22] with a main focus on used technologies, adopted methods and tools, and supported C2G interaction areas.

The remainder of this paper goes as follows: Section 2 summarizes the antecedents of using the sustainability concept in the evaluation literature in general, and in the specific domain of eParticipation assessment in particular. Section 3 highlights the role of institutional aspects in the shaping of participation and locates the discourse on sustainability in the framework introduced by previous literature. Section 4 overviews a specific implementation example, making reference to the system of governance in the Italian Region of Tuscany. Section 5 discusses the implications of the above case, in terms of a "process oriented" definition of sustainable eParticipation, based on five attributes: juridical compliance, legitimacy, social value, efficiency, and productivity. Section 6 includes some conclusions and recommendations for future work.

2 Sustainability as an Evaluative Concept

Generally speaking, sustainability is an important criterion to assess the results of any project/programme (P/P). In the evaluation literature[3], sustainability analysis usually focuses on the following six dimensions (see also Figure 1):

1. *Stakeholders' Ownership*: or the actual level of sharing of the objectives and achievements of the P/P by the stakeholders involved;
2. *Institutional Compliance*: or the extent to which the P/P is "embedded" in the organisational/regulatory structures of the community;
3. *Financial Autonomy*: whether the P/P is likely to continue after the end of funding; whether enough funds are available to cover all costs; whether the costs are likely to be borne after the funding ends;
4. *Socio-cultural Integration*: whether the P/P takes into account the local perception of needs and respects participants and beneficiaries cultures and beliefs; whether and how the changes induced by the P/P can be accepted by the stakeholders involved;
5. *Technical Feasibility*: or the extent to which the technology and knowledge provided fit into the existing skills and infrastructure available to participants; whether beneficiaries are likely to operate and maintain the technology acquired without further external assistance;
6. *Continuity Over Time*: or the concrete possibility of extending or replicating successfully the P/P at hand or other similar interventions.

---

[3] Following Elliot Stern (quoted in [20]), by evaluation we intend "*any activity that, throughout the planning and delivery of innovative programmes, enables those involved to learn and make judgments about the starting assumptions, implementation processes and outcomes of the innovation concerned*". Referenced sources of this paper include: [5, 6, 8, 10].

Fig. 1. The six dimensions of sustainability

Not surprisingly, sustainability evaluation looks like a complex task with multi-faceted dimensions; it is also strictly related with impact analysis, as they both deal (among other aspects) with the likely or foreseen effects of the P/P in the medium to long term. These effects are - by definition - going beyond the results produced and/or the benefits induced within the P/P's scheduled life, and this is why they are normally defined *outcomes* rather than outputs.

Impact and sustainability assessment is thus related with the progress of *time*. It wouldn't make sense to try and evaluate these in the same way as we might want to do with relevance, a criterion mostly utilized at the design stage, or with efficiency and effectiveness, which can be best demonstrated after implementation or right at the end of the P/P, using information derived from its internal budget or other accounting evidence.

Finally, sustainability is also extensively mentioned in literature as an evaluation criterion of eParticipation trials. Though it may look tautological, this is mostly seen as an approach to detecting the barriers to continuity or replication over time of a successfully achieved pilot ([2], p. 23). In fact, as the same scholars ([2], p. 11) stated: *"eParticipation in practice can still be characterised as 'experimental' or 'pilot'. Sustainable eParticipation is rarely achieved..."*. Likewise, in their analysis of barriers, challenges and needs of eParticipation research, others ([4], p. 29) noted that: *"We need to move to an environment and culture where there is clear commitment and willingness of political and administrative representatives to engage with eParticipation"*. By a similar vein, ([1], p. 12) locate sustainability among the key aspects to be analysed while evaluating an eParticipation project. Some attributes in focus coincide with the qualifications of sustainability offered in a seminal work by [8]. Likewise, ([19], p. 13) define the process of sustainability assessment as: *"The detection of operational and policy barriers in order to ensure the continuity of a case without creating any disharmony and imbalance in a system"*. Taking inspiration from the Stockholm Challenge Award[4], the same authors qualify and integrate this definition, by adjoining sustainability to the 'future development' concept.

To summarise, we can tentatively map the surveyed pieces of research on the evaluation of eParticipation sustainability to the six conceptual dimensions listed at the beginning of this section, as displayed by the following Table:

---

[4] http://www.stockholmchallenge.se/evaluation-criteria

Table 1. Key dimensions of eParticipation sustainability

Dimension	Source	[2]	[4]	[1]	[19]
Stakeholders' Ownership		√	√	√	√
Institutional Compliance			√		√
Financial Autonomy				√	√
Socio-cultural Integration		√	√	√	
Technical Feasibility		√		√	√
Continuity Over Time		√	√	√	√

As Table 1 shows, sustainability is mostly associated with stakeholders ownership, as well as with continuity over time of the eParticipation trials. However, there is no demonstrated link between these two dimensions, or at least not a stronger one than with any possible alternative displayed.

Furthermore, such a descriptive approach leaves partly unattended what the proper means should be to ensure that the ultimate goal of replication is actually achieved. In other words, it would be appropriate to turn the above instances of the sustainability concept, from evaluation into *appraisal* dimensions: where the notion of appraisal[5] refers to the process of assessing, in a structured way, the case for proceeding any further with a proposed method, channel or tool for electronic Participation.

3   Sustainability as an Appraisal Criterion

Recently, [21, 22] proposed a framework for assessing and scoping eParticipation projects focusing on the technologies used, the methods and tools adopted, and the C2G interaction areas supported. According to its proposers, this framework lends itself to a *twin assessment* of eParticipation, reflecting on the one hand the suitability or appropriateness of ICT introduction into the democratic process, and on the other hand the actual degree of citizens' involvement in public decision-making. While this framework has evolved into various modeling attempts [23, 12] that produced some encouraging applications in the domain of descriptive analysis, its potential for project appraisal may have been overlooked, with particular respect to sustainability assessment. To highlight this latter aspect, we have matched the evaluation criteria presented in Section 2 with a simplified version of the framework, as shown by the following picture.

Proceeding from bottom to top, we observe that technologies, methods and tools, and C2G interaction areas (that [21, 22] specifically call eParticipation areas), all undoubtedly pertain to the domains of P/P design and implementation, in which the principal assessment criteria are the "standard" ones of relevance, efficiency and efficacy. In particular, since we (after [14]) normally refer to eParticipation as the use of ICT to enhance people's activism and citizens' involvement in public affairs, this level of analysis can be further refined by focusing on ICT role to enhance relevance and efficiency, and to the participatory techniques used in the trial as a means towards

---

[5] http://en.wikipedia.org/wiki/Project_appraisal

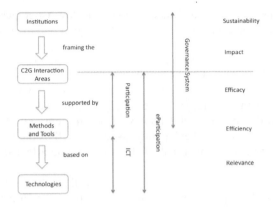

Fig. 2. A framework for eParticipation appraisal

increased efficacy. However, what is important to stress in this perspective is that the institutional dimension (or what we call the governance system) looks like the only appropriate realm for impact and sustainability appraisal.

Put in this way, the message seems quite clear: staying below the dotted line, i.e. at the level of eParticipation (*stricto sensu*, i.e. political participation + ICT usage), we can only evaluate the relevance, efficiency and efficacy (or effectiveness) of a project, or trial thereof. If we want to approach the more challenging task of assessing impact and sustainability, we will have to scale up to the level of the governance system itself. Like any social system, this is made up of *actors* (individuals, such as policy makers, but also collective bodies, like political parties, business associations, trade unions, voluntary organisations and other stakeholders) and *institutions* (e.g. laws, regulations, traditions, cultural and social norms). Notice that democratic processes, as defined by [22], are an integral part of the governance system themselves. Now, the interaction and the reciprocal links among actors are at least framed, and ultimately shaped, by the structure and profile of institutions *en force*[6]. This seems particularly the case of the C2G interaction areas, where both "offline" and "online" participation trials typically materialise (for instance: urban planning, public sector budgeting, climate change policy, and so on).

4   The Tuscany Case

To make an example of how institutions can actually shape participation, it is worth mentioning the case of the Tuscany Region in Italy.

In the last ten years, the Regional Government of Tuscany, under the pressure of national level constitutional reform, has undergone a quite complex transformational pathway, aimed at migrating from traditional consultation and concertation with local

---

[6] Of course, it can also be vice versa, which is not relevant, however, to the flow of our analysis, located in the short-to-medium run where existing institutions may be taken as invariant with respect to the outcomes of C2G interaction.

stakeholders (business associations, trade unions, and lower-tier public authorities) - meant to involve the private and public sector of the Region into the various instances of strategic programming and implementation - towards proper participation of the citizens in the process of legislation, regulation and more generally, public decision-making.

Historically, the Tuscan model of Cooperative Governance, first established by the Regional Law No. 49 of 1999, held several degrees of analogy with the EU Multilevel Decision Making system: a metaphor increasingly used by the academics to highlight the fact that many different levels of authority - from the central to the peripheral - are involved in public decisions on "key" policy issues, as well as the various local actors (including non-governmental ones) that might somehow be affected by the decisions to be taken.

In 2007, this model was integrated by the approval of the first Regional bill in Europe dealing with the topic of participation in public decision-making (Tuscany's Law No. 69). In particular, art. 20 of Law No. 69 added to art. 10 of Law No. 49/1999 the following paragraph: "*2 bis. Regional plans and programmes must specify the share of available resources dedicated to the organisation of participatory processes and to be determined on a sufficient basis to guarantee their effective fulfilment; participation in the regional plans and programmes is promoted exclusively by the Regional Government*". The next articles of Law No. 69 further specify the policy domains where the establishment of participatory processes has become mandatory. These include: Regional Law No. 1/2005 in the topic of urban planning; Regional Law No. 40/2005 regarding the universal health service; Regional Law No. 41/2005 on social citizenship rights; Regional Law No. 25/1998 regarding the management of waste disposal; Regional Law No. 1/2004 on the development of information society.

Under the provisions of the above set of Regional Laws, the outline of a typical, "standard" decision-making process could be depicted as per the following diagram.

The process stages highlighted in the "Involvement" boxes encompass the classical "four levels" of the (traditional and/or electronic) Governance model first introduced by [16, 17] - namely:

• *Information dissemination*, or the distribution of information that is complete, objective, reliable, relevant, easy to find and to understand;

• *Consultation*, or the involvement of citizens and stakeholders in a joint exercise that has clear goals and rules, defining both its limits and the government's obligation to account for the use of its results;

• *Concertation*, or a more advanced interaction than simply feedback provision as for the case of consultation; dealing with negotiation and mutual composition of confronted interests;

• *Active participation*, or the proper integration of citizens' will and "wisdom" into government's decision-making.

Curiously enough, while the diagram below can well be conceived of as a process, structured and detailed by a number of Regional laws and regulations, most activities in the process are still carried out "offline" (for instance, the management of meetings with local stakeholders), or at best through several independent Web 1.0 applications (e.g. Regional government's sectorial portals): in either case, no or little effort has been done so far towards a unitary view – supported by advanced ICT applications – of the integrated and interlaced nature of the various process stages.

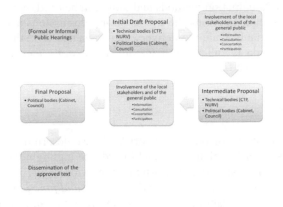

Fig. 3. AS-IS policy-making process in the Tuscany Region[7]

In short, what we are facing here is a kind of *mismatch between availability and usage* of process technology in public administration. This can become increasingly evident in the years to come, where the Region itself foresees the involvement of an increasing number of people into shared decision making on a growing variety of policy processes. The rationale for that is still related to the Regional Law No. 69 of 2007, which recognizes and guarantees to everyone (including foreigners) the right to participate in public sector's decision-making. Under the provisions of the Law, any citizen, association or institution located in Tuscany may request the activation of a participatory process on major investment projects, development programmes and initiatives, of regional and/or local relevance. There are three dates during a year, by which citizens can submit such a request: March and July 31st, and November 30th. The outcome of the public debate is not binding, but the process must be finalised in 6 months time only. If the majority of public opinion is against, those who brought the project in may waive it or support a different version, or insist on the original formulation providing appropriate reasons thereof. In any case, a more informed decision from the competent authority will be allowed and certainly, if the debate has been lively and participated, it would be hard for a public body not to take its results into account.

Thus, the Regional Law, which has become fully operational by early 2009, with the appointment of the Regional Authority on Participation and the start-up of the first participatory processes launched under its provisions, aspires to open up a "third way" between participatory and representative democracy, through a more intense involvement of citizens on a discussion and deliberation about the "big issues" of public interest, avoiding any waste of time in the process and possibly any protests after the political decisions are finally taken.

Currently, the Regional Government envisages to setup and experiment on a multi-channel decision-making support environment that could ultimately involve all key stakeholders and the entire Tuscan population (approx. 3,6 million people from 287 municipalities), in compliance with the provisions of Law No. 69/2007. In this

---

[7] Adapted from: Regional Cabinet decision No. 2 of 6th November 2006.

scenario, several eParticipation methods and tools can be used, where co-location and co-presence of participants during the consultations, discussions and deliberations are becoming less important, while the delivery and exchange of multimedia (text, audio and video) information is enhanced, thanks to the ubiquity and usability of devices and applications employed.

5   Discussion

What are the implications of our framework and case description for the definition and appraisal of sustainable eParticipation? In order to highlight them, we would like to borrow a definition of sustainability originally provided by [13], that is *"the ability of an ecosystem to maintain (its) ecological processes and functions, biodiversity, and productivity over time"*. Adapting it to our perspective, this becomes *the ability of a participatory decision-making process to maintain juridical compliance, legitimacy, social value, efficiency and productivity over time*.

Why is this definition different from the previously commented ones? First, it does not focus on eParticipation as such. We don't even speak of electronically supported interactions between citizens and governments; our attention particularly goes to the implications arising from the addition of (offline and/or online) participation to state-of-the-art legislative, regulatory or policy-making processes (workflows). In fact, as it emerges from the Tuscan experience, either a discontinuous change in the existing system of governance occurs, or even the best performing (e-)Participation trial or practice will remain 'experimental' or 'pilot' forever. On the other hand, what needs to be further explored is the set of conditions under which a migration from 'self-referential' to 'inclusive' (or 'participatory') decision-making may not endanger the stability of the underlying political and administrative environment. Thus, making institutional change an option that at least in principle, could be considered as viable and ultimately sustainable.

Secondly, while an element of 'continuity over time' is being kept in association with our new definition of sustainable participation, this avoids the partly tautological results surveyed in Section 2 and outlined in Table 1 above. Here, continuity refers to what has been called *Institutional Compliance*, namely, the possibility to "embed" the participatory methods and tools experimented into the legal, organisational, political and social infrastructures of a governance system. Being a multifaceted concept, that form of compliance can be split up into a variety of procedural attributes, namely five, which are introduced and described later in this Section.

What does this definition add up to the current evaluation research? First of all, we posit that relevant areas for sustainable institutional change in the public sector – whether eParticipation related or not - cover the key process dimensions of *juridical compliance, legitimacy, social value, efficiency* and *productivity over time*. Whatever P/P leaves these unchanged (if not improved), candidates itself to provide a positive contribution in that direction. In particular, we posit that sustainable participation will emerge whenever these five dimensions are not jeopardised, compromised, or are left unaltered, by the introduction of participatory elements into a given decision-making process regarding issues of public relevance. Empirical testing is recommended of these five aspects upon evaluation of every eParticipation project, as we expressly did for the sustainability assessment of our own Preparatory Action [9], when we tried to migrate away from a mere reporting of Project outcomes, and to acknowledge the long-term impact of the 'assets' generated on the overall governance system of each specific public sector authority involved.

In order to provide an operational description for each of the five dimensions of sustainability introduced, we propose to see them as attributes that clarify and specify the actual meaning of sustainability, much in the same way as in the literature on sustainable development the same term takes on different meanings according to the attributes adjoined to it[8]. Thus, in analogy to the notions of, say, juridical, ethical, or political sustainability of growth and development, we now introduce the following qualifying statements for the sustainability of eParticipation:

Juridical Compliance. A legislative or policy-making process is said to be juridically compliant whenever it can be fairly acknowledged by a neutral third party (in particular, at one extreme, by Administrative Justice) to lay beneath the scope and provisions of existing laws and regulations in the subject area addressed. A variant of the above statement – particularly apt to Common Law countries, such as the UK etc. – can make reference to a (weaker, yet more encompassing) compliance with the legal and/or statutory aims of a public sector organisation and/or with previous rulings of administrative Courts. From this set of references, a first attribute of sustainable participation can be derived: *It is said to be sustainable a participatory decision-making process that is able to maintain its previous degree of juridical compliance unaltered.*

Legitimacy. A legislative or policy-making process is said to be legitimate whenever it is approved by a majority of adult population (in particular, by a majority of the voters in general, either national or local, elections). To us, legitimacy has a different meaning with respect to juridical compliance. For instance, the opposing parties to a governing majority may find some or all of their decisions as lacking legitimacy, yet being able to demonstrate that they also break-up some existing norm (if not a Constitutional principle) is a totally different matter. Moreover, one of the key features of representative democracy is the political legitimisation of governments by means of periodic (free and transparent) elections. Nonetheless, more trust and better acceptance of ruling governments in the eyes of the citizens are often associated with the creation of more and better spaces for involvement in decision-making. From this definition, a second attribute of sustainable participation can be derived: *It is said to be sustainable a participatory decision-making process that is able to increase the level of its political legitimacy over time.*

Social Value. The concept of social value is broader than the one of social capital, as it also includes subjective aspects of citizens' well-being, such as their ability to participate in making decisions that affect themselves. Changes in social value may occur over time, because of e.g. changes in the dominant moral vision, the evolution of religious beliefs, changes in the economy, technological innovation, demographic

---

[8] See [13] and also http://www.ec.gc.ca/soer-ree/English/SOER/ 1996 report/Doc/1-5-2- 6-1.cfm

shifts, scientific findings, etc. On the other hand, it is a known fact that communities able to engage their fellow citizens in activities of social relevance are also the most successful in reaching sustainable development targets[9]. In short, a legislative or policy-making process actually creates social value if it enhances collaboration and civic engagement of citizens and stakeholders. From this definition, a third attribute of sustainable participation can be derived: *It is said to be sustainable a participatory decision-making process that is able to create more, or at least no less, social value than its previous (non participatory) instances.*

Efficiency. It may sound odd that the notion of efficiency - already defined as the ratio between outputs (or results) of a P/P and the inputs (or resources) that were necessary to support its activities[10] – is now moved from the implementation to the evaluation stage. In fact, one of the known difficulties related to such concept is that neither the outputs, nor the inputs, of a given P/P are all measurable quantitatively and/or by one common measurement unit. This is why we adopt here a stricter notion of efficiency, which is nonetheless particularly useful in highlighting the importance of achieving financial savings, or at least keeping costs invariant, by the integration of participation in the existing institutional framework[11]. Following this concept, a fourth attribute of sustainable participation can be derived: *It is said to be sustainable a participatory decision-making process that is able to reduce operational costs or at least keep them invariant with respect to its previous (non participatory) instances.*

Productivity. Formally speaking, productivity might appear the reverse of efficiency, i.e. the ratio between outputs and inputs of a P/P. Even in this case, we adopt a stricter notion that focuses on a specific aspect of public administration: the productivity rate of employees and managers[12]. Following this concept, a fifth attribute of sustainable participation can be derived: *It is said to be sustainable a participatory decision-making process that is able to increase public officials' productivity over time.*

Taken together, the two latter propositions underlie the fact that – without a clear advantage in terms of cost savings or productivity gains for the organisation involved – the success of eParticipation will continue to be mostly dependent on the sporadic prevalence of passionate idealists and/or ICT enthusiasts within existing communities of civil servants and elected officials.

---

[9] For example, the UK based project PatientOpinion (http://www.patientopinion.org.uk) invites patients to comment, review and rate the services they have received at healthcare facilities and allow them comparing the reviews of other patients (like in several hotel booking portals).

[10] In short, working with greater efficiency means doing more with the same, or the same with less.

[11] This can be done in many different ways: one good example is given by the US project entitled Peer-to-Patent (http://www.peertopatent.org), which has opened up to the general public's participation the patent examination process, thus reducing the delays in examining some applications.

[12] Again, there are many possible ways to increase this: today, the so-called Web 2.0 applications are growingly used in the public sector, not only for "crowdsourcing" new ideas and contributions from the Internet population, but also as to support the capacity of civil servants to handle, assess, give response to citizens inquiries.

6 Conclusions

The big challenge of future research and practice on eParticipation, is to assess the conditions under which civic engagement and citizens empowerment can become "embedded" components of new and more advanced (digital) governance systems.

In this paper, we have introduced a new and possibly more advanced definition of sustainable eParticipation, based on five fundamental dimensions, which can be used to assess the level of potential integration of a participatory practice or trial within the legal, political, social and organisational contexts of the public sector institutions involved. Empirical investigation is recommended to assess the potential of our model by testing the five propositions delineated above.

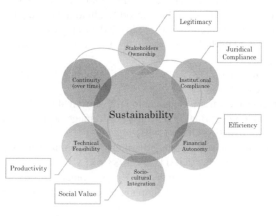

Fig. 4. New/Old Concept Mapping

Compared with Figure 1, reflecting the state of the art of theoretical reflections on sustainability, our new concept can be graphically represented as above.

Like the diagram shows, our definition takes on "continuity over time" as a central trait of sustainability, though with a different and less tautological meaning as it was explained in Section 5. Furthermore, it overlaps to the "institutional compliance" concept, leaving the remaining dimensions (also differently named) in a subordinate or explanatory position. We expect that the proposed taxonomy should be beneficial to future experiments (and evaluation thereof), being able to define and encompass all the different aspects of more direct relevance and impact for eParticipation designers and policy makers alike.

Acknowledgments. This research was made possible in part by a co-funding of the European Commission to the IDEAL-EU project, a Preparatory Action in the area of eParticipation. However, the opinions expressed in this paper are solely of the author and do not involve any of the EU institutions.

References

1. Aichholzer, G., Westholm, H.: Evaluating eParticipation Projects: Practical Examples and Outline of an Evaluation Framework. European Journal of ePractice 7 (March 2009) ISSN: 1988-625X

2. Aichholzer, G., Allhutter, D., Freschi, A.C., Lippa, B., Macintosh, A., Moss, G., Westholm, H.: eParticipation Evaluation and Impact. DEMO-Net Project Deliverable No. 13.3 (2008)
3. Bicking, M., Wimmer, M.: eParticipation Projects Evaluation Methodology. MOMENTUM Deliverable No. 2.5 (2008), http://www.ep-momentum.eu (accessed)
4. Coleman, S., Macintosh, A., Schneeberger, A.: eParticipation Research Direction based on Barriers, Challenges and Needs. DEMO-Net Project Deliverable No. 12.3 (2007)
5. Development Researchers' Network: Monitoring and Evaluation for NGOs Projects. A Manual for FORUM SOLINT, Forum Valutazione No. 14, pp. 105–173 (2002)
6. European Commission: Evaluation in the European Commission: A Guide to the Evaluation Procedures and Structures currently operational in the Commission's External Cooperation Programmes. Brussels, EuropeAid Evaluation Office (2001)
7. Ferro, E., Molinari, F.: Making Sense of Gov 2.0 Strategies: No Citizens, No Party. In: Proceedings of the eDEM09 Conference on Electronic Democracy, Vienna, Austria, September 7-8 (2009)
8. Henderson, M., Henderson, P.: Associates: E-democracy Evaluation Framework (2005) (unpublished manuscript)
9. IDEAL-EU Project Consortium: Deliverable D7.1 Sustainability Report (2009)
10. Interamerican Development Bank: Evaluation: A Management Tool for Improving Project Performance. IBD Evaluation Office (1997)
11. Islam, M.S.: Towards a sustainable e-Participation Implementation Model. European Journal of ePractice 5 (October 2008) ISSN: 1988-625X
12. Kalampokis, E., Tambouris, E., Tarabanis, K.: A Domain Model for eParticipation. In: Proceedings of the 3rd International Conference on Internet and Web Applications and Services (2008)
13. Kaufmann, M.R., Graham, R.T., Boyce Jr., D.A., Moir, W.H., Perry, L., Reynolds, R.T., Bassett, R.L., Mehlhop, P., Edminster, C.B., Block, W.M., Corn, P.S.: An ecological basis for ecosystem management. Fort Collins, Colorado: U.S. Department of Agriculture Forest Service, Rocky Mountain Forest and Range Experiment Station and Southwestern Region. USDA Forest Service General Technical Report RM-246 (1994)
14. Macintosh, A.: Characterizing e-Participation in Policy-Making. In: Proceedings of the 37th Hawaii International Conference on System Sciences (2004), http://csdl2.computer.org/comp/proceedings/hicss/2004/2056/05/205650117a.pdf
15. MOMENTUM White Paper: Report on the Objectives, Structure and Status of eParticipation Initiative Projects in the European Union eParticipation Workprogramme (June 2009), http://www.ep-momentum.eu (accessed)
16. OECD: Citizens as Partners: Information, Consultation and Public Participation in Policy-making. OECD Publishing, Paris (2001a)
17. OECD: Engaging Citizens in Policy-making: Information, Consultation and Public Participation. OECD Public Management Policy Brief No. 10. (2001b), http://www.oecd.org/dataoecd/24/34/2384040.pdf (accessed)
18. Osimo, D.: Web 2.0 in Government: Why and How? JRC/IPTS Scientific and Technical Reports (2008) ISSN 1018-5593
19. Panopoulou, E., Tambouris, E., Tarabanis, K.: Framework for eParticipation Good Practice. European eParticipation Study Deliverable D4.1b, 2nd version (November 2008)

20. Sommerlad, E., et al.: A guide to local evaluation. London, Tavistock Institute of Human Relations, Evaluation Development and Review Unit (1992)
21. Tambouris, E., Liotas, N., Tarabanis, K.: A Framework for Assessing eParticipation Projects and Tools. In: Proceedings of the 40th Hawaii International Conference on System Sciences (2007a)
22. Tambouris, E., Liotas, N., Kaliviotis, D., Tarabanis, K.: A Framework for Scoping eParticipation. In: Proceedings of the 8th Annual International Digital Government Research Conference (2007b)
23. Wimmer, M.A.: Ontology for an e-Participation Virtual Resource Centre. In: Proceedings of the ICEGOV2007, Macao, China, December 10-13 (2007)

Widening the Disciplinary Scope of eParticipation. Reflections after a Research on Tourism and Cultural Heritage

Francesca Ricciardi[1] and Patrizia Lombardi[2]

[1] Università Cattolica di Milano, Italy
[2] Politecnico di Torino, Italy
Francesca.ricciardi@unicatt.it, patrizia.lombardi@polito.it

Abstract. Cultural Heritage and Tourism Development may be strong driving factors for local policies and may have great importance in strategic decision making at territorial level; then, they may be important subjects for eParticipation studies. But this paper demonstrates, through a literature review, that today's disciplinary shape of eParticipation as a research field is not suitable to effectively investigate participatory processes related to Tourism and Cultural Heritage. Then, by presenting a field research, which took place in the Italian city of Genoa, and by confronting its outcomes with some most widespread disciplinary eParticipation underpinnings, the paper seeks to identify some areas where a widened disciplinary scope is particularly needed. Finally, we propose a new disciplinary framework, suitable to address also Cultural Heritage and Tourism Development eParticipation processes.

Keywords: eParticipation, participatory planning, tourism, cultural heritage, ICT.

1 Introduction

"eParticipation involves the extension and transformation of participation in societal democratic and consultative processes mediated by information and communication technologies (ICT), primarily the Internet. (…) It aims to support active citizenship with the latest technology developments, increasing access to and availability of participation in order to promote fair and efficient society and government". [1] Theoretical discussions involving participation span a large range of disciplines (for example, participatory management, or participatory design); but eParticipation normally focuses on participatory processes connected with political or public interest decision-making, and is consequently strictly connected to sister disciplines such as eGovernment [2] and eDemocracy [3] [4].

On the other side, eParticipation is a young disciplinary field, whose boundaries are still under discussion and whose theoretical underpinnings are still under elaboration [1]. Many issues related to public interest and political and administrative decision-making are still scarcely investigated in eParticipation studies.

E. Tambouris, A. Macintosh, and O. Glassey (Eds.): ePart 2010, LNCS 6229, pp. 140–150, 2010.
© IFIP International Federation for Information Processing 2010

For example, cultural heritage and tourism development may be unique driving factors for local policies and may have great importance in strategic decision making at territorial level [5]; then, they may be important subjects for eParticipation studies. This paper demonstrates, through a literature review, that in today's disciplinary scenario eParticipation researches involving tourism and cultural heritage management processes are very few, and scarcely supported by methodological and theoretical frameworks. The method and the outcomes of this literature review are presented in Paragraph 2.

Paragraph 3 will present a three-years field research (in which one of the authors of this paper was involved) focused on developing an e-participatory / e-governance model for cultural tourism development of the city of Genoa, Italy.

Then, paragraph 4 will seek to use the experience and the outcomes of Genoa field research, along with the outcomes of literature search, to identify some areas of widening and improvement of the eParticipation disciplinary framework.

Finally, Paragraph 5 will propose a new disciplinary framework, in which the areas of needed widening and improvement identified are addressed. In particular, this study will suggest a description of possible eParticipation (i) *Actors*, (ii) *Activities*, and (iii) *Effects*, aimed at classifying, through Concept Matrixes suitable also for evaluation purposes, eParticipation studies and experiences, included those which are related to Cultural Heritage and Tourism management.

In the Conclusions, the outcomes of our theory-building effort will be synthesized, and some areas of improvement and further research will be identified.

2   Tourism and Cultural Heritage Management Issues within E-Participation Literature

Tourism and Cultural Heritage management almost always involves planning activity at city, regional and/or national level; it often implies Public Authorities (P.A.) decision-making, government processes and political commitment [6].

This makes Tourism and Cultural Heritage (CH) management a potentially fertile field for e-participation.

For example, Go, Lee and Russo [7] remark the possible positive impact of ICTs when both citizens and (cultural) tourists actively participate in policy and decision making processes. Innes and Bohr [8] highlight the importance of involving local communities in cultural tourism decision making, to take into account the complexity of concrete local culture and local problems, and to keep development processes well balanced.

Sigala and Leslie [9] note that transforming a site into a tourism destination may have negative socio-cultural consequences, and identify e-participation as a possible tool to face the problem.

Nevertheless, e-participation is very rarely applied in tourism and cultural heritage *actual* management and decision-making processes [10]; moreover, the presence of e-participation in tourism/CH literature is poor and often limited to generic complaints, ideas and suggestions, as we will seek to demonstrate below.

To examine the role of Cultural Heritage and Tourism Development issues in today's eParticipation journal publications, a literature search was conducted in February 2010.

The following on-line Databases were selected as particularly important for e-participation issues: Econlit, E-Journals, Business Source Premier.

Four searches were conducted in this Databases, through the EBSCO search engine.

The first query asked to search writings including the words "e-participation" (or "eParticipation") and "tourism" in the Abstract. The result was 0: no writing included those two terms in the Abstract.

A second query asked to find writings including "participation" (without "e-") and "tourism" in the Abstract. 134 writings were found, many of which were not relevant in that the term "participation" was not related to the concepts of "discussion" and "decision making" (e.g. "participation in revenues"). 17 writings included just generic complaints (e.g. "local community participation to planning and decision making should be enhanced"). Four writings were actually focused on participatory and collaborative planning in Tourism /Cultural Heritage management processes. Among these four writings, two included somehow generalizable hypotheses about success factors in participatory processes: Bahaire and Elliott-White [11] interestingly highlight the conflicts and contradictions, in tourism planning and development, between public-private sector partnerships (based on elite groups and entrepreneurial city management) and public participation. Yuksel [12] notes, after a statistical analysis, that along with other structural and cultural factors, residents' perceptions of the intensity of clientelist relations between the local authority and other stakeholders may significantly decrease active participation of citizens in developmental issues, and in tourism planning particularly.

In no writing, among the 134 provided by the search system, ICTs were identified as a driver or a significant factor for enhancing participation in tourism /CH management and planning.

A third search was launched, asking the system to find writings including "e-government" and "tourism" in the Abstract. The system found 7 writings, but none of them focused on the issue of using ICTs to promote public participation in discussion and decision-making on tourism development and CH management. The 7 writings focused on top-down classical management issues (and on tourism promotion above all) without investigating if, and under what conditions, ICT tools could be also used for bottom-up participation.

A fourth search was launched, using "e-governance" and "tourism" as keywords. Only one writing was found [13]. In this paper, the authors present an e-governance model developed for cultural tourism in the Italian city of Genoa. The purpose is to involve the stakeholders (citizens and tourists included) in discussions and decisions about on-line promotion and communication of the city's cultural heritage and tourism attractions. In this project, thus, people are involved in a precise, limited decision-making process, which does not imply more complex processes of city planning or participatory design: the aim is to provide, with the aid of participants, more effective e-services for tourists.

This field research will be one main basis of our theoretical proposal, and will be more thoroughly described in the following paragraphs.

To complete this survey on the role of CH / tourism related issues in e-participation studies, we have taken into consideration the systematic literature review conducted in 2008 by Sæbø,, Rose and Skiftenes Flak [1], aimed at characterizing e-participation as a research field.

The authors, after analyzing 131 writings deemed highly relevant, among the 651 yielded by the keyword search, describe the disciplinary boundaries and key concepts of eParticipation, which can be drawn from literature. Firstly, the authors identify what are, according to literature, eParticipation *Actors*, dividing them into 4 groups: citizens, politicians, government institutions, voluntary organizations. Secondly, the authors list eParticipation *Activities* described in literature: eVoting, online political discourse, online decision making, eActivism, eConsultation, eCampaigning, ePetitoning. The authors explicitly say that in their model "pure information exchange activities lie outside the scope of eParticipation because there is no participative element" (p. 410).

Then, the authors describe the *contextual factors* influencing eParticipation identified in literature, namely: information availability, net infrastructures, underlying technologies (i.e. HW/SW), accessibility, policy and legal issues, governmental organization. In Sæbø,, Rose and Skiftenes Flak's work, more general factors influencing participation, such as trust in government or conflicting interests, are not mentioned, letting it be understood that the analyzed 131 writings had not investigated such issues.

Finally, the authors describe what are, according to the literature they analyzed, eParticipation *effects*, and possible eParticipation *evaluation metrics*. The authors complain that the analyzed literature is quite poor as for these issues, and in fact both the list of eParticipation effects (civic engagement; deliberative and democratic effects) and of eParticipation evaluation metrics (quantity of participation; demographic of participants; tone and style in online activities) appear, even at a first glance, generic and unsatisfactory.

3   The Genoa Field Research

The City of Genoa is an internationally renowned centre of culture and heritage. Its reputation grew in 2004 when it was nominated 'The European Capital of Culture'. Amongst its many cultural sites and attractions, of most interest to the visitors are the Unesco word heritage site Palazzi dei Rolli, the City Museum, Strada Nuova, Palazzo Rosso, Ducale Palace, Luzzati Museum, Spinola Palace, Sea Museum (Galata), Genoa Aquarium, Luzzati Museum, Spinola Palace, and the National Gallery. The city has recently embraced a strategic policy to transform the port, culture, and tourism as main vehicles of economic revival based on social inclusion, urban integration, and sustainable development, with ICT playing a major role. A recent study conducted by a number of researchers of the ISAAC project [14] found that the city's main web portal is a true gateway to information on tourism attractions, local museums, historic buildings, urban squares, and cultural events. Yet, the content is developed and presented by the city tourism authorities only and there is no communication with the users as regards its type, quality, user preferences, and so forth. At the same time, local heritage providers use only limited digital media in the promotion of their attractions. To improve electronic services and widen access and participation in cultural heritage development, the city of Genoa has chosen to participate in the EU FP6 Project ISAAC "Integrated e-Services for Advanced Access to Heritage in Cultural Tourist Destinations" and to develop the e-governance system in close collaboration with 'Fondazione Eni Enrico Mattei' [15].

From April to October 2007, four focus groups involving tourist, residents, local service providers and external service providers separately, were administered with thirty-seven participants aiming at (i) exploring their local heritage perceptions, (ii) selecting the most relevant heritage sites for Genoa, and (iii) identifying the most appropriate e-services for each of the selected sites. An on-line debate continued among the participants remotely in the following three weeks. The second phase consisted of an on-site focus group session held in February 2008, involving fifteen tourists, residents and service providers together that aimed to identify the priority of e-services defined in the first phase.

The e-governance website (www.isaac-genovaculture.eu) was structured in three main sections, each with a different function: information, communication and participation. The information section aimed at providing information and sensitize people about local cultural heritage resources. Here users are passive learners about local heritage and the available opportunities. The communication section aimed at creating a virtual public space for exchanging general opinions and ideas about cultural heritage among the citizens. Here, the users become authors of the web content. Finally, the participation section aimed at creating a more advanced level of interaction between decision makers and users with the latter getting involved in the decision-making process.

The first round of the face-to-face focus groups provided important insights about how users perceive and value local heritage in Genoa and their differences. Local and external services providers, for example, identified some 36 and 30 cultural heritage sites respectively, out of the 58 sites chosen by all participants. This shows that service providers are much more aware of local cultural heritage offers than residents and tourists, suggesting insufficient 'access' to cultural heritage supply by residents and tourists in the local tourism promotional activities.

Furthermore, when each user group was asked to associate added value to the territory – historical, cultural, tourist, social, environmental and emotional – by the selected cultural sites, service providers seemed more prone to capture cultural and historical values while tourists and residents placed more attention on social, environmental and emotional values. Furthermore, tourists in general emphasized more environmental values as compared to the residents, which shows that the latter associate sites with experiences, hence territorial identity and value of place have a stronger relevance to the visitors than to local residents. So the issue of access to heritage for the local residents comes out again strong. Interestingly enough, some of the participants attributed rather unexpected and 'unusual' values to sites, like the 'Ancient Port', 'Aquarium' and the 'Lanterna', which reinforces the notion that cultural heritage users have subjective and changeable perceptions of it, therefore, its ongoing monitoring becomes essential to ensure sustainable management of the sector. For further details, see [13] and [15].

4   Challenges to the Disciplinary Boundaries

The Genoa field research, when compared with the disciplinary shape of eParticipation as described by [1], reveals several aspects where a widening of disciplinary scope and frameworks is needed.

In fact, Sæbø, Rose and Skiftenes Flak's list of eParticipation *actors* (Citizens, Politicians, Government Institutions, and Voluntary Organizations) does not include several actors that were actually crucial in Genoa research, i.e. Tourists (who may not be Citizens of the country/region/city where decision making takes place), Researchers, Businesses and Business Groups. Moreover, other potentially important actors of e-participation could be: Lobbies/Groups of Interest, Professionals involved in planning / design activities, Press and Journalists (many e-consultation activities, for example, are organized by the newspapers' web sites today). Important contradictions and conflicts may raise between these diverse Actors, and these contradictions and conflicts should be considered an important subject of studies in research focused on participatory activities, be they supported by new technologies or not.

Moreover, another important outcome of the Genoa experience is that eParticipation activities demonstrated themselves as not "spontaneous": even for the "mere" content management processes, they require efforts, which are often overlooked or underestimated. Thus, eParticipation needs the motivated commitment of at least one Actor; when the Actor who took the initiative loses its interest in the eParticipation acivity (in the Genoa case, when ISAAC group ended its research) the activity is likely to be abandoned by all the other Actors.

On the other side, Sæbø,, Rose and Skiftenes Flak's list of eParticipation *activites*, though rich and articulated, does not include discussion and knowledge sharing [1]. Sæbø,, Rose and Skiftenes Flak, in fact, think that information availability is part of the context, i.e. a *prerequisite* of eParticipation, just like net infrastructures or software applications. But the field experience of Genoa, and in particular the potentialities of ISAAC platform, showed that it is often impossible, in practice, to separate the moment of making information available from the moment of participation: information is often created *during* discussion, and then information sharing has revealed, during Genoa field research, as a possible eParticipation activity in itself.

The Genoa experience allowed also a rethinking of what could or should be the eParticipation *effects*, with particular regard to increased awareness of actors, increased territorial value, enhanced civil rights, improved territorial services. The enlarged lists of eParticipation Actors and eParticipation Activities that we propose will be more thoroughly presented in the next paragraph, along with a description of the main eParticipation effects we identified.

5   A Renewed Disciplinary Framework

On the basis of the field research experience, of our literature analysis and of our experience as researchers and as practitioners, we propose a new draft of disciplinary framework, with a widened scope, including 3 categories of entities: eParticipation Actors, eParticipation Activities, eParticipation Effects.

Whilst for the first two categories our list stems from [1], just with several added Actors and Activities that Sæbø, Rose and Skiftenes Flak did not mention, for the third category we propose a list organized in a completely different way.

eParticipation possible Actors:
1. Citizens
2. Politicians
3. Governmental Institutions
4. Voluntary Organizations
5. Users and Customers of the Territorial System (e.g. Tourists)
6. Businesses and Business Groups
7. Lobbies and Groups of Interests
8. Professionals involved in Territorial Planning activities
9. Researchers and scholars
10. Press and Journalists.

eParticipation possible Activities:
a) Discussion and knowledge sharing (aimed at or related to civil participation in public-interest decision making)
b) eVoting
c) online political discourse
d) online decision making
e) eActivism
f) eConsultation
g) eCampaigning
h) ePetitoning

eParticipation expected Effects:
I   Improved Civic Awareness
II   Improved Civic Engagement
III   Enhanced Civil Rights
IV   Increased Territorial Value
V   Improved Territorial Services

The category *eParticipation (expected) Effects* deserves some more thorough comments. We propose to include *Civic Awareness* in this category because participatory activity, independently from actual decision-making, implies discussion, knowledge sharing and consequently a growth in awareness on the part of (ideally) all the Actors. For example, public officers may become more aware of concrete implications of adopted policies; citizens may want to monitor the outcomes of decision-making processes they (or their representatives) were involved in. It is important to note that the mere existence and use of e-participation tools does not imply, in itself, improved civic awareness: for example, [16] asserts that simplistic and distorted political information easily spreads throughout the web; and this phenomenon, far from enhancing civic awareness, tends to undermine it.

Engagement, on the other side, was included in Sæbø, Rose and Skiftenes Flak's framework. Improved civic engagement on the part of Actors may be one possible effect of eParticipation. But also this concept is problematic, because whilst many authors optimistically think that new technology cam be powerful triggers to enhance civic engagement (e.g. [17] [18]), many other authors highlight that there is little correlation between the increasing facilitations provided by e-tools and actual enhancing in civic engagement [19] [20] [21].

Civil Rights, which may or should be enhanced by successful eParticipation activities, could be (but are not limited to): protection from discriminations; equal access to care, education and culture; inclusion and participation in civil society and politics; freedom of expression and communication.

Whilst eParticipation Effects I, II and III mainly involve eParticipation Actors, by identifying eParticipation Effects IV and V we have concentrated on what could or should be the expected outcomes of eParticipation from a general point of view. Successful eParticipation activities, in fact, being aimed at improving decision-making processes, should result in concrete improvements in the real world, on a territorial basis. Improvements due to good decision-making at political and administrative level may be very numerous and different in nature; here, we have concentrated on two aspects, which of course are not exhaustive, but are representative of the issues raised by the Genoa field research.

eParticipation effect IV refers to the fact that good decision-making should result in measurable improvement of territorial assets. Such improvement could be effectively described and measured using the concept of Territorial Value. Literature on environmental economics has highlighted the ability of CH to produce "intrinsic" and "extrinsic" values. The concept of "territorial value" is one of the most important in this field [26]. It refers to the tangible and intangible linkages and relationships between Cultural Heritage and the (urban) context. This value is very important for tourism sector as it refers to public consciousness and perception of values: that's why we propose to include it in the Framework.

Also eParticipation Effect V refers to an effect of participatory activity that may involve the whole socio-territorial context, and not only eParticipation Actors. The expression *Improved Territorial Services* spans a very large range of possible good (e)Participation effects. For example, the Genoa field research was aimed at designing an on-line portal included several e-services for tourists. Moreover, the participatory activity provided information on how many real-world services, such as bus lines, could be re-organized to better meet the Actors' needs.

This framework allows to describe each specific eParticipation initiative with specific concept matrixes. For example, the Genoa project could be synthetically represented as follows:

For each activated crossing between eParticipation *Actors* and eParticipation *Activities*, expected eParticipation *Effects* can be identified: for example, the participation into the activity of eConsultation, on the part of Tourists (as Users/Customers of the territorial system) was expected to result in *improved web-based services* for Genoa tourism promotion.

Table 1. The classification of Genoa field research into the eParticipation Framework

Activities → Actors ↓	Discussion	eVoting	Online Pol. Discourse	Decision Making	eActivism	EConsultat.	ECampaign.	ePetitioning
Citizens	x			x		x		
Politicians								
Governmental Institutions	x			x		x		
Voluntary Oganizations								
Users and Customers of the Territorial System	x			x		x		
Businesses and Business Groups	x			x		x		
Lobbies and Groups of Interests								
Professionals involved in territorial Planning activities								
RESEARCHERS AND SCHOLARS (Triggering Actor)	x			x				
Press and Journalists.								

Improved e-services (Tourism Portal)

This Concept Matrix, once filled in detail with all the expected Effects of eParticipation, could also be used as a basis for eParticipation evaluation: comparing the a-priori matrix, filled with a description of *expected* Effects, with an a-posteriori matrix, filled with a description of *actual* Effects, could be a very interesting goal for eParticipation research, and could trigger an interesting debate on qualitative and quantitative metrics, and on the study of cause-effect relationships within (e)Participation processes.

6 Conclusions

This paper has presented a theory building research, which is qualitative in nature. In such a research approach [22] [23], field research was not meant to theory testing (which is normally quantitative in nature), but to point out theoretical / disciplinary lacks, to propose new frameworks (which will need testing in following phases) and to explore possible methodological innovations.

A single case study, such as the Genoa case, would not be epistemologically sufficient in a quantitative, theory-testing research; but in the context of theory building research, even a single, meaningful case study can provide several hints for theoretic proposals [24].

The Genoa case, in particular, being developed in form of Action Research [25], yielded several, practice-founded challenges to existing disciplinary frameworks, and was therefore deemed a good starting point to trigger a theoretical reflection.

With respect to the recognized framework of eParticipation discipline, for which we have referred to Sæbø,, Rose and Skiftenes Flak's seminal work [1], we have proposed a threefold framework, based on widened definitions of the categories of eParticipation Actors and eParticipation Activites, and on a re-organized definition of the category of eParticipation Effects. We seeked to define eParticipation (expected) Effects in a form which may be suitable also for providing a basis for eParticipation evaluation metrics.

We do not expect the proposed Framework to be considered exhaustive. The lists of eParticipation Actors, Activities and Effects will be certainly improved if compared and contrasted with many other case studies, in the context of eParticipation research community. When the theory building efforts yield a more experienced framework, it should undergo several theory-testing research processes. Then, and only then, could the eParticipation Framework be presented as sound.

It is the hope of present study's authors that this work will elicit further discussion and research within the eParticipation research community. In particular, for limited length of the paper, the key research streams focusing on eParticipation enabling (contextual) factors and on eParticipation evaluation metrics have been only mentioned here. However, it is recognized that these issues are fundamental in establishing the disciplinary field, and, therefore, should be included in the framework. This task will be the subject of a future research.

References

1. Sæbø, Ø., Rose, J., Skiftenes Flak, L.: The shape of eParticipation: Characterizing an emerging research area. Government Information Quarterly 25(3), 400–428 (2008)
2. Grönlund, Ä., Horan, T.: Introducing e-GOV: History, definitions and issues. Communications of the AIS 15, 713–729 (2005)
3. Macintosh, A.: Characterizing e-participation in policy-making. In: Proceedings of the 37th Annual Hawaii International Conference on System Sciences. Computer Society Press (2004)
4. Coleman, S.: Personal communication, Demo-net Web-site (2007), http://www.demo-net.org
5. Svensson, B., Vensson, B., Flagestad, A.: A governance perspective on destination development – Exploring partnerships, clusters and innovations systems. Tourism Review 60(2), 32–37 (2005)
6. Go, F., Govers, R.: Integrated quality management for tourist destinations: A European perspective on achieving competitiveness. Tourism Management 21(1), 79–88 (2000)
7. Go, F.M., Lee, R.M., Russo, A.P.: E-heritage in the globalizing society: enabling crosscultural engagement through ICT. Information Technology and Tourism 6(1), 55–68 (2003)
8. Innes, J.E., Booher, D.E.: Consensus building and complex adaptive systems. A framework for evaluating collaborative planning. American Planning Association Journal 65(4), 412–423 (1999)
9. Sigala, M., Leslie, D.: International Cultural Tourism: Management Implications and Cases. Elsevier Butterworth-Heinemann, Oxford (2005)

10. Ciborra, C., Lanzara, G.F.: The transaction costs analysis of the customer-supplier relationships in product development. In: Baskin, A.B., Kovacs, G., Jacucci, G.K. (eds.) Cooperative Knowledge Processing for Engineering Design. Kluwer, Norwell (1999)
11. Bahaire, T., Elliott-White, M.: Community Participation in Tourism Planning and Development in the Historic City of York, England. Current Issues in Tourism 2(2-3), 243–276 (1999)
12. Yuksel, F.: Perceived Clientelism: Effects On Residents' Evaluation of Municipal Services and Their Intentions for Participation in Tourism Development Projects. Journal of Hospitality and Tourism Research 32(2), 187–208 (2008)
13. Paskaleva-Shapira, K., Azorin, J.A., Chiabai, A.: Enhancing digital access to local heritage by e-governance: innovations in theory and practice from Genoa, Italy. Innovation: The European Journal of Social Science Research, 1469-8412 21(4), 389–405 (2008)
14. Mitsche, N., Bauernfeind, U., Lombardi, P., Ciaffi, D., Guida, A., Paskaleva-Shapira, K., Besson, E.: ISAAC-Deliverable 1.1 Report on current digitisation and cultural interpretation in the cities of Amsterdam, Leipzig and Genoa, 28/02/07 (2007)
15. Chiabai, A., Lombardi, P., Chiarullo, L., Rocca, L., Paskaleva-Shapira, K., Brancia, A.: An e-Governance System for Managing Cultural Heritage in Urban Tourist Destinations: The Case of Genoa. In: Cunningham, P., Cunningham, M. (eds.) Collaboration and the Knowledge Economy: Issues, Applications, Case Studies. IOS Press, Amsterdam (2008)
16. Koch, A.: Cyber citizen or cyborg citizen: Baudrillard, political agency, and the commons in virtual politics. Journal of Mass Media Ethics 20(2/3), 159–175 (2005)
17. Jensen, J.L.: Virtual democratic dialogue? Bringing together citizens and politicians. The International Journal of Government and Democracy in the Information Age 8(1/2), 29–47 (2003)
18. Chang, W.Y.: Online civic participation, and political empowerment: Online media and public opinion formation in Korea. Media, Culture and Society 27(6), 925–935 (2005)
19. Albrecht, S.: Whose voice is heard in online deliberation? A study of participation and representation in political debates on the Internet. Information, Communication and Society 9(1), 62–82 (2006)
20. Dahlberg, L.: The Internet and democratic discourse: Exploring the prospects of online deliberative forums extending the public sphere. Information, Communication and Society 4(4), 615–633 (2001)
21. Schneider, S.M.: Creating a democratic public sphere through political discussion. A case study of abortion conversation on the Internet. Social Science Computer Review 14(4), 373–393 (1996)
22. Järvinen, P.: On Research Methods. Opinpaya Oy, Tampere (1999)
23. Eisenhardt, K.M.: Building Theories from Case Study Research. Academy of Management Review 14(4), 532–550 (1989)
24. Yin, R.K.: Case Study research: Design and Methods. Sage Publ., Beverly Hills (1989)
25. Hult, M., Lennung, S.Å.: Towards a definition of Action research: a note and bibliography. Journal of management Syudies 17, 241–250 (1980)
26. Dematteis, G., Governa, F.: Territorialità, sviluppo locale, sostenibilità: il modello Slot, Franco Angeli, Milano (2005)

A Survey on Participation at Geneva's Constituent Assembly

Olivier Glassey

Swiss Public Administration Network (SPAN) and Swiss Graduate School of Public
Administration (IDHEAP), Route de la Maladière 21, CH-1022 Lausanne
Olivier.Glassey@idheap.unil.ch

Abstract. In February 2008 the people of Geneva voted in favor of a new
Constitution to replace the current one, written in 1847 and considered by many
to be out of line with today's society. The main objective of this research was to
analyze participation during the process of writing a new Constitution. In the
first part of this paper we set the context of our study and in the second we
describe our research methodology and analysis framework. In the last section
we describe our findings regarding actors and processes of participation and
eParticipation, as well as underlying communication and coordination channels.

Keywords: participation, constitution, eDemocracy, framework, case study.

1 Introduction

Between November 2008 and February 2010 we surveyed the communication and
coordination mechanisms of selected stakeholders in order to analyze participation
and eParticipation at the Constituent Assembly in the Canton of Geneva in
Switzerland. In previous work [1] we described our analysis framework and presented
preliminary results of this ongoing research project. This current paper contains the
complete results of our research.

This first section describes the context in which this study takes place, i.e. the work
of a Constituent Assembly to write a new Constitution for the Canton of Geneva. The
second section explains our research methodology and analysis framework; in the last
part of this paper we discuss our results.

1.1 Geneva's Constitution

Geneva is a republic since 1535 when the city became the capital of the Protestant
Reformation. The first Constitution adopted in 1543 was largely based on the "Edits
Civils" written by John Calvin. Although Geneva was a French department between
1798 (when it was invaded by Napoleon's army) and 1813, it was mostly independent
until joining the Swiss Confederation in 1815.

In 1846 James Fazy led a revolution that overthrew the conservative government
and subsequently wrote the 1847's Constitution that is still ruling the Canton,
although it has been modified many times over that period. This text is now the oldest

E. Tambouris, A. Macintosh, and O. Glassey (Eds.): ePart 2010, LNCS 6229, pp. 151–161, 2010.
© IFIP International Federation for Information Processing 2010

of the 26 Cantonal Constitutions in Switzerland and many believed that its language, structure and content are not adequate anymore [2].

In 1999 the parliamentary group of the "Parti Radical" proposed a bill in order to completely revise Geneva's Constitution, but without success. In 2005 an association called "Une nouvelle Constitution pour Genève" (a New Constitution for Geneva) was set up. Its front man was a famous law professor, Andreas Auer, and its members came from all political parties and from the civil society. They were ready to launch a popular initiative requiring a new Constitution as the government was reluctant to do so, but after long negotiations a vote was organized. In February 2008 the people of Geneva accepted a constitutional law allowing for a new Constitution in the Canton.

1.2 Election of the Constituent Assembly

In October 2008 the people of Geneva elected 80 members of the new Constituent Assembly. This was no easy task for citizens as there were 530 candidates and 18 lists to choose from. Half of these lists were presented by traditional political parties and the other nine lists represented heterogeneous interest groups (business associations, home-owners, women, retired people, and so on). Funding for the campaign was also very heterogeneous: from 5'000 Swiss Francs (about 3'500 Euros) for the women's list to 200'000 (140'000 Euros) for the business associations' list.

The quorum for a list to be elected was initially 7%, but the Parliament lowered it to 3% in order to have a wider participation. However one cannot say that the initial members of this Assembly were really representative of Geneva's people: only 14 women were elected (although two elected men resigned in order to leave their position to women from the same left-wing party) and the average age of members was 56. Furthermore only three lists outside traditional parties made the quorum:

- The lobby of pensioned people (Avivo) got 9 seats; it must be said that Christian Grobet, the leader of this list, was a member of various legislative and executive authorities in Geneva from 1967 until 2005, thus this list is not completely "outside" political parties.
- The g[e]'avance list represented business and employers' lobbies and it was attributed 6 seats.
- The FAGE (Federation of Geneva's Associations) is the umbrella organization of 480 associations of all types (parents, culture, human rights, ecology, Attac, pacifism, consumers, social integration, gays, development, etc.); the associations' list obtained almost 4% of the votes (with a quorum at 3%) and thus obtained 3 seats.

The participation rate being of 33 % (about 10% less than the average participation), one can conclude that giving Geneva a new Constitution was not a popular issue and that only "traditional" or "politicized" voters accomplished their electoral duties. The political balance of the Constituent Assembly was also similar to the Parliament of Geneva: 43 seats for right wing parties and 37 for the left.

2 Research Methodology and Analysis Framework

This section describes the dimensions of participation, eParticipation, and eDemocracy that we build upon them in order to define our analysis framework.

2.1 Participation and eParticipation

According to [3] eParticipation is an emerging research area which lacks a clear literature base or research approach. In their review of the field, they identified and analyzed 99 articles that are considered to be highly relevant to eParticipation. [3] write in their introduction that governments seek to encourage participation in order to improve the efficiency, acceptance, and legitimacy of political processes. They identify the main stakeholders of participation as citizens, non-governmental organizations, lobbyists and pressure groups, who want to influence the political system, as well as the opinion forming processes. Various information and communication technologies (ICTs) are available for eParticipation: discussion forums, electronic voting systems, group decision support systems, and web logging (blogs). However traditional methods for citizen participation (charettes, citizens' juries or panels, focus groups, consensus conferences, public hearings, deliberative polls, etc.) are still very widely used and must be taken into account when studying eParticipation.

[4] defines eDemocracy as the use of information and communication technologies to engage citizens, to support the democratic decision-making processes and to strengthen representative democracy. She furthermore writes that the democratic decision-making processes can be divided into two main categories: one addressing the electoral process, including e-voting, and the other addressing citizen e-participation in democratic decision-making. [5] give a working definition of eParticipation as the use of ICTs to support information provision and "top-down" engagement, i.e. government-led initiatives, or "ground-up" efforts to empower citizens, civil society organizations and other democratically constituted groups to gain the support of their elected representatives.

There are many examples of surveys on eDemocracy, such as [6] who take the case of Switzerland where citizens are often called to the polls either to vote for parties and candidates or, even more often, to decide on direct-democratic votes at the three different political levels. In their paper on "smart-voting" they analyze what they call voting assistance applications, i.e. tools where citizens can compare their positions on various political issues to those of parties or candidates. They mention the Dutch "Stemwijzer" system, first introduced in 1998 and they provide in-depth information on the Swiss smartvote website.

Even if eParticipation is a relatively new research field, projects and tools are increasing thanks to governmental support [7]. Furthermore a number of research projects such as Demo-Net.org have been funded worldwide to pave the way.

2.2 Analysis Framework

Our main objective is to survey communication and coordination mechanisms for participation and eParticipation, thus we defined an analysis framework integrating two central **variables**:

- Communication and coordination **channels**.
- **Levels** of participation.

To investigate traditional and electronic communication **channels** we adapted the approach used by [8] for its case study on participation and eParticipation in Germany, where he used the three arenas of political communications defined by [9]. Table 1 shows these three communications modes and the systems or actors involved in political communication, as well as the vectors used to carry this communication. We made a distinction between **traditional participation** vectors and ICT-enabled channels (**eParticipation**).

Table 1. Communication/Coordination Modes and Channels for Participation

Communication / Coordination mode	System / Actors	Traditional Participation	eParticipation
Institutional		Elections	eVoting
	Representative Democracy	Consultation: citizen forums, public hearings or any formal consultation procedure	eVoting
	Direct Democracy	Voting, referendums, initiatives	eConsultation
Mediated	Mass Media	Articles, opinions, interviews, editorials, readers letters, polls, phone calls, etc.	
	Parties Interest groups Trade unions	Parliamentary groups Lobbies Strikes Meetings, campaigns, street or door-to-door communication, tracts, mailings, negotiation	Websites, forums, wikis, emails, chats, ePolls, webcasts, social networks, mobile communications, Web 2.0, etc.
Informal	Citizens Associations Networks	Street or door-to-door communication, tracts, free radios, local TVs, cafés, clubs, etc.	

As for our second variable, we relied on the five **levels** used by [7] in their framework to assess eParticipation:

- (e-)Informing
- (e-)Consulting
- (e-)Involving
- (e-)Collaborating
- (e-)Empowerment

We do realize the limitations of such an approach, and we agree with [10] who states that eParticipation analysis models are typically ladder type and share two assumptions: progress is equaled with more sophisticated use of technology, and direct democracy is seen as the most advanced democracy model. However we think it is useful to characterize the results of our survey.

In addition to these two main dimensions, we added the distinction proposed in the previous section by [5]: **top-down** initiated participation vs. **bottom-up** participation.

Finally we used two additional concepts in order to describe and characterize the context of participation and eParticipation:

- **Process:** we rely on the deliberation lifecycle defined by [11] in their comprehensive framework to analyze deliberative decision making: issue emergence, issue structuring, issue analysis, deliberation, decision, monitoring and evaluation.
- **Stakeholders:** we describe them according to the generic stakeholders of eParticipation workflows defined by [12]: owners, decision-makers, practitioners, moderators and participants.

2.3 Selection of Stakeholders and Methodology

In order to apply our analysis framework, we selected a sample of **stakeholders** involved in institutional, mediated and informal communication:

- The "Parti Radical Genevois" (PRG) is a progressive right-wing party that has a long history in Geneva; it was born in 1841-42 during the first revolutionary movements in the Canton and it was led by James Fazy, the author of the 1847's Constitution that is still in effect today. We selected it because PRD is rather representative of traditional parties and political structures.
- "Les Verts" are Geneva's green party. It was founded in 1983 by various members of environmental and anti-nuclear associations. The Green party is now a well-established party with, amongst others, two elected members of the executive government in Geneva (which comprises seven ministers). We decided to survey them because they are a newer party, created by members of the civil society and based on a more associative operational mode.
- We already introduced the Federation of Geneva's Associations (FAGE) in section 1: it is the umbrella organization of 480 associations. We integrated them in our study because they are very typical of networked communication and participation.
- The "Tribune de Genève" (TDG): we chose it because it is Geneva's main printed newspaper and it furthermore provides a blog platform to its readers; most blogs related to the Constituent Assembly are hosted at the TDG.
- The Communication Bureau of the Constituent Assembly: this is the official communication channel of the Assembly.
- The Plenary Assembly, where deliberation and decision-making takes place.

This survey is **qualitative** and based on two investigation methods:

- Periodical review of **secondary sources**: all identified websites, blogs, forums, wikis, and publicly available working documents related to the Constituent Assembly.
- **Semi-structured interviews** with representatives of the stakeholders listed above.

We used a standardized **interview guide** (with adaptations when necessary, e.g. when interviewing elected members or "outsiders"). It was based on the following questions:

- How do you prepare plenary sessions of the Constituent Assembly?
- How do you make decisions (e.g. regarding voting at plenary sessions)?
- How are you organized regarding participation / consultation of your members? Of citizens?
- How do you manage documents and information produced by the Constituent Assembly?
- How do you communicate around your work?
- Do you use information and communication technology for your work (mail, wiki, office suites, document servers, blogs, etc.)?
- Do you see any opportunities for eParticipation at the Constituent Assembly?

3   Results

In this section the results of our survey are presented according to the dimensions we defined in our analysis framework. We will not go into the details of our analysis and we will try to highlight only the key findings.

3.1   Communication and Coordination Channels in Participation

We will use the dimensions defined in Table 1 to describe our findings in terms of communication and coordination channels.

On **institutional** participation: the Constitutional Assembly's first task was to define its own operational rules, as the constitutional law did not contain any information on execution. These rules defined several innovative possibilities (in comparison to standard parliamentary policies in Switzerland). They allowed several interesting participatory tools:

- **Petitions:** any person or group can submit a proposal to the Constituent Assembly under the form of a petition; petitions are transferred to the relevant thematic commission that then decides whether they want to take it into account.
- **Collective proposals:** a proposal signed by at least 500 citizens has to be handled by the relevant thematic commission and should be answered in a chapter of the commission's report; at the time of writing, around 20 collective proposals were submitted.
- **Public hearings:** the Assembly can hear any representative of the civil society or of interest groups, as well as members of the public sector from Geneva, and from other Cantons or countries; this concept of public hearing

did not previously exist in Switzerland, where hearings are privately held in commissions.

- **Plenary Assembly:** all members, commissions, groups or circles can make proposals and submit amendments. Minutes of the plenary sessions are published
- **Thematic commissions:** 5 thematic commissions (fundamental rights, political rights, institutions, territory, roles of the State and finance) as well as a coordination commission were set up. They work on thematic content and can organize hearings (private or public) and they already provided preliminary reports.
- **Groups:** all members elected on a list belong to a common group; each group received funding for a parliamentary assistant; an elected member that would quit his group could not take part in thematic commissions anymore; groups can be heard at the plenary assembly upon request.
- **Circles:** elected members that have common interests can form a circle; circles must be formed of at least three members; members can be part of several groups; circles can be heard at the plenary assembly upon request; for the time being there are circles dedicated to sustainable development, youth, SMEs, and culture.

Although several innovative participation channels were defined there is no eParticipation at the institutional level. However bottom-up participation is supported, mainly with collective proposals and petitions. Institutional communication is quite traditional, although press releases, minutes and thematic reports are published online.

On **mediated** participation:

- **Parties:** The "Parti Radical Genevois" has only one participation channel, the *Caucus*, where elected members and the party's leaders define their positions. "Les Verts" also have a *Caucus* operating in a similar way, and they additionally work with so-called *"resources groups"* where members of the party debate and make recommendations on given issues. The "FAGE" has set up several participation channels: *colloquiums* or meetings where any member of the 480 federated organizations can attend and make their opinion known; *competence poles* that are organized similarly to resources groups mentioned above; *common objectives*, where a minimal and common set of requirements for all 480 associations is defined.
- **Media:** The local press, radio and TV provide minimal coverage of the Constituent Assembly, and it does not seem to raise much interest. However the blog platform of the "Tribune de Genève" is very active, with around 20 elected members and one group having their own blog. Furthermore two or three elected members comment the plenary sessions on Twitter; one of them even launched a contest to propose an introduction to the new Constitution. Last, the main source of information and place of exchange on the Constituent Assembly is a blog called "La Gazette de la Constituante" maintained by a journalist of the "Tribune de Genève".
- **Interest groups, associations:** Most of the collective proposals mentioned above were initiated and supported by these groups.

Here again several interesting participation channels were developed, but eParticipation is still rather limited: one blog platform and a few "tweets". In parties we found mainly top-down supported participation, with the exception of the FAGE where bottom-up participation is made possible through the possibility of colloquium's attendance for any member of any represented association.

On **informal** participation: few citizens comment on the blogs and follow the "tweets" mentioned above. Participation channels remain very traditional with the possibility of submitting a petition or of signing a collective proposal.

3.2 Levels of Participation

In Fig. 1 we positioned our various stakeholders regarding their participation level and their participation approach. This graph is given as an indication only, as it was not created on the basis of quantitative indicators, but rather on the author's perceptions, e.g. the mass media is typically a top-down informing process, elected members that have a blog or use Twitter are informing on a more bottom-up basis, the FAGE supports involvement through colloquiums, and so on.

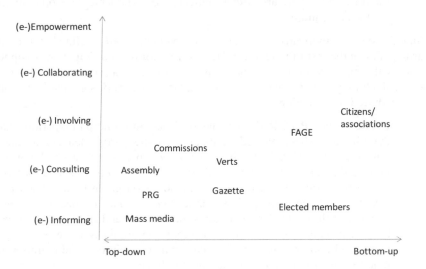

Fig. 1. Stakeholders positioning regarding **participation levels** and **participation approaches**

With a quick look at this figure one can conclude that the main supported participation processes are informing and consulting, and barely involving. We are thus quite far from our "ideal" participation where all stakeholders could be empowered.

3.3 Stakeholders and Processes in Participation

Table 2 is an effort to characterize stakeholders in terms of the typology defined by [12]. We have already defined what commissions, groups and circles were in §3.1 and others such as media and citizens are quite self-explanatory. Let us briefly explain some additional stakeholders listed in the table:

- The **Presidency** is made of four members elected by the Constituent Assembly and it is mainly in charge of applying rules and monitoring the operations of the Assembly (and of signing acts).
- The **Bureau** is formed of one delegate per group of the Constituent Assembly and is mainly responsible for planning, organizing, budgeting external relations.
- The **General Secretary** supports the work of the Constituent Assembly; it comprises legal and administrative workers that are hired by the Assembly.

Table 2. Participation at Geneva's Constituent Assembly in terms of Actors and Tasks

Stakeholders	Description	Tasks
Owners	Citizens	Vote and elections
Decisions-makers	Elected members	Debate and vote in plenary sessions
Practitioners	Bureau, General Secretary, Presidency, Commissions, Groups, Circles	Organize tasks of Constituent Assembly and prepare proposals
Moderators	Media, experts	Comment on Assembly's work and provide input (e.g. in public hearings)
Participants	Citizens, associations, interest groups	Prepare petitions or collective proposals

Table 3 characterizes the participation channels described in §3.1 regarding the deliberation life-cycle defined by [11].

Table 3. Participation and Deliberative Processes at Geneva's Constituent Assembly

Process	Instruments	Description
Issue emergence	Petitions, collective proposals	Any person or group can submit ideas
Issue structuring Issue analysis	Commissions, Circles, Groups, Public hearings	Commissions prepare proposals under the forms of articles or general principles; groups and circles can be heard by the Bureau upon request; the Assembly can hear any representative of the civil society, interest groups or public authorities.
Deliberation	Plenary sessions	The Assembly deliberates on proposals and amendments.
Decision	Plenary sessions	Decision are made by majority rule
Monitoring and Evaluation	N/A	

4 Conclusion and Future Work

This survey was conducted in an exploratory mode, as the Constituent Assembly was just elected when we began and nothing was in place. Indeed during the first months elected members did not even have an email address and there was no secretary or any support staff. As sessions went along, the Assembly defined its own policies and operational rules. Before we started our survey we had the analysis framework defined in Table 1, and when new requirements appeared we added variables such as levels and approaches of participation, processes and stakeholders.

We believe this context of a Constituent Assembly to be very interesting to investigate participation, as it is rather different from many projects where citizens participate on generic societal issues or very specific topics such as local territorial planning. Indeed, the redaction of a new Constitution really resides at the heart of democratic processes. Our key findings were not so much of a surprise: participation was made mainly through institutional channels with a top-down approach (such as public hearings and thematic consultations); although some interesting bottom-up and mediated channels were set up, most notably the collective proposal. Moreover, eParticipation was rather limited, with a number of elected members using a blog or Twitter to communicate.

As our analysis framework was build in an exploratory manner and suited for a specific context, it needs to be refined and validated in order to be more generic. Along with partners from Switzerland and Germany we are currently preparing a research proposal on participation at the local level and this will be a perfect test-bed to do so.

References

1. Glassey, O.: Writing a New Constitution for Geneva: An Analysis of Participation Mechanisms. In: Tambouris, E., Macintosh, A. (eds.) Electronic Participation, Proceedings of Ongoing Research, ePart 2009, 1st International Conference, Linz, Austria (2009)
2. Schmitt, N.: Quelques réflexions comparatives à propos de l'élection d'une assemblée constituante à Genève (2008),
   http://www.federalism.ch/files/Newsletter/742_19/constituant e-geneve.pdf
3. Sanford, C.S., Rose, J.: Characterizing eParticipation. International Journal of Information Management 27, 406–421 (2007)
4. Macintosh, A.: Characterizing e-Participation in Policy-Making. In: Proceedings of the 37th Annual Hawaii International Conference on System Sciences, HICSS-37 (2004)
5. Macintosh, A., Whyte, A.: Evaluating how eParticipation changes local democracy. In: Irani, Z., Ghoneim, A. (eds.) Proceedings of the eGovernment Workshop. Brunel University, London (2006)
6. Ladner, A., Felder, G., Schädel, L.: From e-voting to smart-voting – e-Tools in and for elections and direct democracy in Switzerland. IDHEAP Working Paper 4/2008 (2008)
7. Tambouris, E., Liotas, N., Tarabanis, K.: A Framework for Assessing eParticipation Projects and Tools. In: Proceedings of the 40th Annual Hawaii International Conference on System Sciences, HICSS-40 (2007)

8. Mambrey, P.: From Participation to e-Participation: The German Case. In: Janowski, T., Pardo, T. (eds.) Proceedings of the 2nd International Conference on Theory and Practice of Electronic Governance (ICEGov), Cairo, Egypt (2008)
9. Habermas, J.: The Theory of Communicative Action. Beacon Press, London (1981)
10. Grönlund, A.: ICT Is Not Participation Is Not Democracy – eParticipation Development Models Revisited. In: Macintosh, A., Tambouris, E. (eds.) ePart 2009. LNCS, vol. 5694, pp. 175–185. Springer, Heidelberg (2009)
11. Passas, A.A., Tsekos, T.N.: A Procedural Model for Public Deliberation. In: Tambouris, E., Macintosh, A. (eds.) Electronic Participation. LNCS, vol. 5694, Springer, Heidelberg (2009)
12. Colombo, C., Kujnstelj, M., Molinari, F., Todorovski, L.: Workflow Modeling for Participatory Policy Design: Lessons form Three European Regions. In: Macintosh, A., Tambouris, E. (eds.) Electronic Participation. LNCS, vol. 5694. Springer, Heidelberg (2009)

A Regional Model for E-Participation in the EU: Evaluation and Lessons Learned from VoicE

Sabrina Scherer and Maria A. Wimmer

University of Koblenz-Landau, Institute for IS Research,
Research Group e-Government,
Universitätsstraße 1, 56070 Koblenz, Germany
{scherer,wimmer}@uni-koblenz.de

Abstract. Attracting and motivating citizens to participate actively in online discussions of European policies turns out not to be easy. In the VoicE project, a regional e-participation model has been developed to deal with this challenge. The results and lessons learned from the project VoicE are of particular importance for the follow-up project VoiceS. This way, VoicE and VoiceS incorporate ongoing evaluation through an iterative design cycle. In this paper, we present the scientific evaluation method and results whether the regional e-participation model of VoicE is an appropriate means to attract citizens for European policies and to motivate citizens to participate in discussions. The methodology is based on a layered model of e-participation evaluation. Subsequently, this paper examines to what degree the approach chosen in the project delivers suitable insights for establishing successful e-participation platforms on a European level and what lessons can be learned.

Keywords: E-Participation, Evaluation, E-Consultation.

1 Introduction

The VoicE[1] project is designed as a trial project, implementing a regional model of e-participation in the European Union (EU), which places a high emphasis on platform marketing, editorial preparation and integration into the surrounding political institutions [1]. In this regard, VoicE provides two regional platforms[2] serving as interfaces between decision-makers in the EU and citizens in the regional contexts. In terms of contents, the project focuses on the policy field of consumer protection. On both platforms, general information on the topics, a news section, polling functionality ("Question of the Month") and a discussion forum ("civil forum") are included. For the distribution of content also RSS feeds, Twitter messages, social bookmarking and newsletters are used. Texts are available in German on the Baden-Württemberg and in Spanish and Valencian on the Valencia instance. Fig. 1 shows a screenshot of the German platform. The feasibility of such an approach is of

---

[1] VoicE- Giving European people a voice in EU legislation, www.give-your-voice.eu
[2] Baden Württemberg, Germany (http://www.bw-voice.eu) and Valencia, Spain
(http://www.voice.gva.es). Platform functionalities are described e.g. in [7].

E. Tambouris, A. Macintosh, and O. Glassey (Eds.): ePart 2010, LNCS 6229, pp. 162–173, 2010.

particular importance, as the follow-up project VoiceS[3] continues the aims of the VoicE project (which was finished in December, 2009) and complements the platform by adding a series of new features such as a serious game and semantics [2]. This way, VoicE and VoiceS incorporate ongoing evaluation (as recommended by [3]) in an iterative design cycle [4].

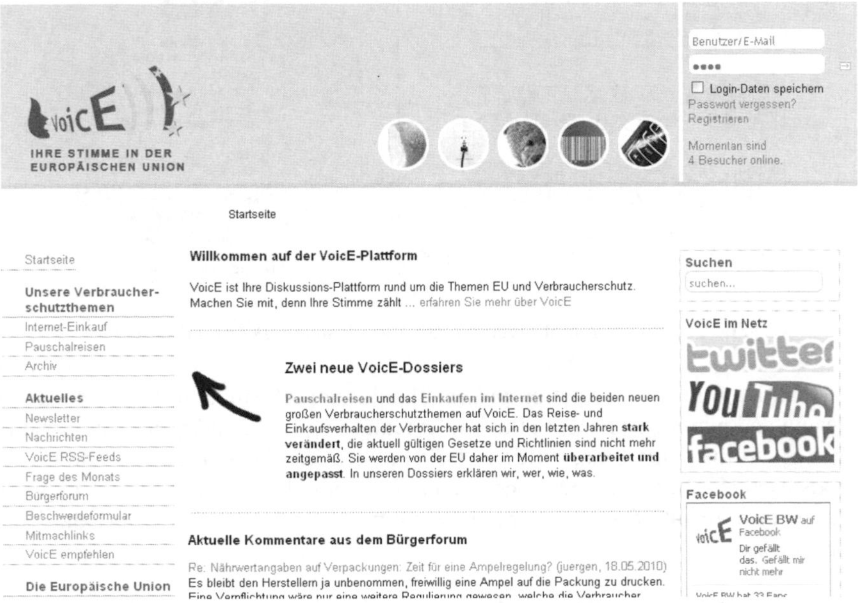

Fig. 1. Screenshot of www.bw-voice.eu (accessed in May, 2010)

This paper examines to what degree the approach chosen in VoicE delivers suitable tools for establishing successful e-participation platforms on a European level and what lessons can be learned for VoiceS. Section 2 introduces the evaluation methodology applied. Section 3 presents the evaluation results. Section 4 summarises lessons learned from the VoicE project. Section 5 gives a conclusion and an outlook on resulting activities for VoiceS to take lessons learned into consideration.

2   Evaluation Methodology

Evaluation of the VoicE project aims to assess if the regional e-participation model of VoicE is an appropriate means to attract citizens for European policies and to motivate them to participate in discussions. Fig. 2 further details this research question into three ones. The methodology applied to answer these questions is based on the layered model of e-participation evaluation of Macintosh and Whyte [5]. It integrates the project, socio-technical and democratic perspective on an

---

[3] VoiceS – Integrating Semantics, Social Software and Serious Games into eParticipation, www.eu-voices.eu

e-participation exercise. Fig. 2 shows how the evaluation perspectives of [5] feed into the individual research questions formulated to evaluate VoicE.

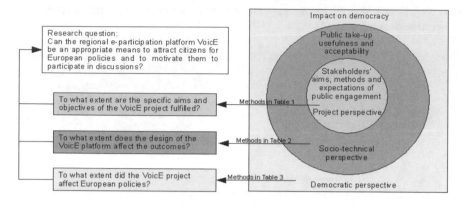

Fig. 2. Application of layered evaluation framework (based on [5])

Evaluation of an e-participation project should be performed at different stages: in the design and planning phase, in the implementation phase, and focusing on the final results [6]. At the same time, different stakeholders should be involved and different methods used [5]. In this respect, the evaluation methodology applied in VoicE bases on a number of results from applying different methods during the VoicE and VoiceS project life cycles:

I.   **Planning and implementation phase of VoicE:**
1.   Requirements for the VoicE system were based on surveys with citizens and politicians.[4]
2.   Field observations were collected with different platform versions [7].
3.   Website statistics were tracked since the launch of the pilots.[5]
II.   **Requirements analysis in VoiceS:**
4.   Requirements were formulated for VoiceS[6].
5.   Analysis of legislative procedures in the EU[6] was performed.
III.   **Evaluation phase of VoicE:**
6.   An online end user evaluation questionnaire was distributed among citizens to gather information about their perception of the VoicE platform (January - November 2009 and filled out by 21 users). It was also envisaged to ask MEPs for their perception, but only one MEP participated in the survey.[5]
7.   A survey undertaken in July/August 2009 among visitors of the German VoicE platform investigated, how web 2.0 contents and features are accepted in general

---

[4] VoicE Deliverable D2.1. End-users' requirements report. Internal (5, 2008).
[5] VoicE Deliverable D6.6 Evaluation report, including lessons learned. Internal (1, 2010).
[6] VoiceS Deliverable D2.1 Requirements analysis report: Specification of (user) requirements for the VoiceS platform with focus on process models and user roles. Internal (5, 2009).

by the users and if the use of such features has an added value to the project. The online questionnaire was filled out by 164 respondents[7].

8. Surveys with experts on e-participation were conducted in the frame of the MOMENTUM[8] project with the aim to evaluate VoicE [8]: Answers from three experts were provided anonymously to the VoicE team.[5]

9. Analysis of the quantity and quality of users' contributions were based on the approach of Märker [9].[5]

10. Polls on bw-voice.eu and voice.gva.es were asking users in December 2009 for their perception regarding their link to European politics. 18 answers were recorded on bw-voice.eu and 61 on voice.gva.es.[5]

The DEMO-net evaluation framework proposes a number of criteria for evaluating the perspectives. It provides indicators and measures as well as methods to get the data [6].

Table 1, Table 2 and Table 3 list the evaluation criteria and respective methods applied in the VoicE evaluation as described before (numbers for the methods indicate the methods referred to in the list above).

Table 1. Evaluation criteria and methods for project perspective

Criteria	Applied methods
Engaging with a wider audience	3, 10, Media review, evaluator assessment
Obtaining better-informed opinions	6, 8, 9, evaluator assessment
Scope of deliberation	9
Effectiveness	Estimation of time spend
Feedback	6, 9, 10
Process quality	6,8, desk research
Sustainability	6, 7, 8

Table 2. Evaluation criteria and methods for socio-technical perspective

Criteria	Applied methods
Social acceptability	1, 6, 7, 8, evaluator assessment, analysis of system concept
Usefulness	1, 2, 4, 6, 7, 8, evaluator assessment, website analysis
Usability	2, 5, 6, website analysis, evaluator assessment

Evaluation results derived are presented in the subsequent section. Quantitative and qualitative results are not presented in detail for lack of space. Instead, we refer to the papers and deliverables mentioned above for more details.

---

[7] VoicE report: Bedeutung und Gegenstand von Web 2.0 Technologien im Rahmen von bestehenden E-Partizipations-Projekten der Europäischen Kommission und besondere Analyse dieser Technologien im Bezug auf das Projekt VoicE/VoiceS (8, 2009).

[8] MOMENTUM – Monitoring, Coordinating and Promoting the European Union eParticipation Projects and Initiatives, www.ep-momentum.eu

Table 3. Evaluation criteria and methods for democratic perspective

Criteria	Applied methods
Representation	4, 5, 8, evaluator assessment, desk research
Engagement	6, 7, 8, 3, 9, 10, website analysis
Transparency	6, 7, 8, 9
Conflict and consensus	9, interview with moderators, website analysis
Political equality	8, 3
Community control	5, 6, 7, 8

3 Evaluation Results

In section 3.1 general results and outcomes are introduced. The evaluation results, which are focusing on project, socio-technical and democratic perspectives, are presented in sections 3.2, 3.3 and 3.4.

3.1 General Results and Outcomes

The evaluation of numbers of visits and unique visitors show that - as a result of extensive dissemination activities - the VoicE platform was widely recognised. Yet, the website statistics also show that the majority of users only visit the platforms short-time. To get a basic idea of how VoicE services are accepted, the functionality and frequency of use is briefly described subsequently. The participants from the survey in method 7 were asked, which feature of the Internet platform they used or intended to use. Table 4 shows the corresponding figures.

Table 4. VoicE platform functions and their (considered) usage (N=164)

Service	Yes.	No.	I am not sure.	I do not know.
Question of the month	**51.8%**	23.8%	12.8%	11.6%
Forum	27.4%	**34.1%**	28.7%	9.8%
Read news	**73.8%**	12.8%	7.9%	5.5%
Subscribe newsletter	22.6%	**53.0%**	17.7%	6.7%
RSS-Service	7.9%	36.6%	16.5%	**39.0%**
Search	**51.8%**	21.3%	15.9%	11.0%
Twitter	7.9%	**49.4%**	20.7%	22.0%
Social bookmarking	11.0%	**51.2%**	22.0%	15.9%
Information provision	**50.6%**	21.3%	19.5%	8.5%

The "Questions of the Month" are succinct polls that change on the platform in a monthly frequency to collect citizens' opinions on specific questions. Often, these are used to put forward a question in the name of a politician. Such questions are mainly of type yes/no answers. In some cases, a third possibility in the form of "I do not know" or "I did not think about it" is inserted. The trend of users' participation is increasing in both regions. On average, about 90 users answer the questions per month.

The citizens' forum is a discussion area where users can write their opinions and comments and exchange their views. It is divided into the various discussion topics (toy safety, food, energy, market watch, and telecommunication), and "general topics". Participation in the forum is possible for unregistered users since summer 2009. The majority of threads is viewed between 1,000 and several thousand times. Based on the frequency of views, an importance for the Internet platform and attention of the user can be attested. However, the active participation is too low in comparison to page visits. VoicE therefore needs to intensify its work to find proper participation possibilities, which are noticed by both, citizens and politicians. With the "Letter to Brussels" initiatives, MEPs should be directly informed about the opinions of their voters from the regions. It was planned that MEPs formulate a reply and send this to the VoicE team (for publication on the website) or discuss in the forum. One problem is that few reactions of the politicians discourage citizens to invest their time in further discussions. Vice versa, input of only few citizens discourage politicians to invest their time in reactions. Despite rather low participation of citizens and political stakeholders, the "Letter to Brussels" initiative gives an idea and impression for further activities. It should also be noticed that such an initiative needs to be established to increase the number of participants (on both sides – citizens and politicians).

3.2 Project Perspective

The analysis is focussing on the specific aims and objectives of the project.

Engaging with a wider audience: VoicE contributes in two ways to engage people: informing about participation possibilities and motivating people to participate first time. The majority of platform visitors is from Baden-Württemberg and Valencia respectively. This is due to the fact that most dissemination activities are performed in these regions. Strong efforts are made to promote the platforms using different online and offline channels. Online marketing (newsletters, emails etc.) turned out much more useful and effective than offline marketing. The target groups (citizens in both regions) are very diverse in age, social background, interests etc. However, the social profile of involved people could not be analysed because such data are not available[9]. In consequence, dissemination material produced and activities performed as well as the look-and-feel of the platform were not customised for a specific age or social group. It seems that this decision negatively influenced the attractiveness of VoicE. In general, individual participation and networking on both platforms was rather low. Concentration and focus on a smaller target group might be considered in the future.

Obtaining better informed decisions: Studies show that the majority of European citizens has little knowledge about the EU, its institutions and its functions. They also underline that a number of citizens do not have an idea of the EU's influence on national legislation [10, 11]. The VoicE platform aims to inform users about such issues. An evaluator assessed the website contents as texts being comprehensive and in general easily understandable, but too long. The last issue rather deters users from reading. In contrast, news on the website are rather short and up-to-date, sometimes

---

[9] Registration is not necessary to actively participate in the VoiceE platform.

linked with the forum and provide important background information about the topics. In general, a high information factor of the platform was underlined by 20 of 21 respondents of the end user evaluation questionnaire. They agreed that the platform provides proper tools to sufficiently inform them about the topics under discussion. Hence it can be stated that VoicE enhances the scope of expertise of informing citizens.

Scope of deliberation: The interactivity among the participants of the citizens' forum is rather little and most comments are rather short, consisting of 3 or 4 sentences. Almost all start entries originate from moderators. One positive aspect is that in the majority of cases, the work of the moderators focused on explanations with regards to content, summarisations, or posting motivating questions.

Most comments keep the issue of discussion and reasonably deal with it. Only in few cases, postings were obviously malevolent or nonsense. The overall majority of comments refers to individual experience and what might be called common sense. These comments are not built upon inter-subjectively available data and stringent argumentative figures. Thus, the discussion consists more or less of individual positions put opposite each other or underline a position (as already explained in other evaluations, see [12]). Nevertheless, it was manageable to summarise the discussions and derive a common final statement. The platform does not provide an argumentation visualisation of options and no technical support to summarise comments.

Effectiveness: Efforts spent in VoicE cannot be evaluated against offline processes because there was no comparable initiative. It is not possible to compare saved costs and time. The only figures, which can be evaluated, are average hours spent per week for moderation of discussions, updating information, posting news, and general efforts to keep the platform alive. The figures are similar on both platforms, whereas the effort for moderation is a little higher on one platform caused in the fact that more discussions took place there. Most effort is spent to search and post news to keep the platforms up-to-date. When comparing traditional with electronic participation opportunities, lack of knowledge of people in such services needs to be noted. Addressing the effectiveness from a user perspective, the project could not achieve the objective that users' voice was really heard (see next point). Time spent by users seem to be rather low, as website statistics show.

Feedback: Feedback of politicians was rather low and unsatisfying for the users. Only one MEP answered two times in the bw-voice.eu forum. No other reactions were recognised on the different letters, which the organisers from Valencia and BW sent to MEPs. The politician who answered the evaluation questionnaire stressed the lack of time as reason for not participating in the discussions. In this regard, the offered participation processes are not sufficiently transparent. It does not become clear to the user, which information or decisions of the ongoing process are available and where impact or at least influence can be achieved. This is caused in the fact that consulted MEPs do not provide a feedback. Indeed, the VoicE platform visualises the EU decision making process, even though it might be helpful to provide a simpler version of the process focussing on the explanations how the contributions feed into the process. Explicit information on expectable feedback should be provided to participants on their inputs. This could not be provided in VoicE because it was not clear what MEPs do and how they react on the citizens' opinions forwarded by the project. Here a stronger adaption on political processes is necessary.

Process quality: The design process of the VoicE portal was an iterative and well-defined process. It was influenced by the heuristic analysis performed by project partners and the empirical testing with pilot users. It turned out useful to improve the system [7]. This usability engineering process has been approved by the results of the evaluation regarding usefulness and usability of the system (see section 3.3).

The quality of the participation processes was evaluated by analysing its appropriateness, appeal and economics. The objectives of the participation processes should be better communicated to target groups. It should also be pointed out what happens with the discussions and how users can participate in the legislative process. The participation processes need to be analysed for their appropriateness to the topic.

Sustainability: In this regard, the respondents of the end user evaluation questionnaire (see method 6) were asked if they would continue using the VoicE platform. The question if the topics discussed attract them to return to the platform was positively answered by all 21 respondents. The question of the "visit frequency and continuity" was also part of the questionnaire for the analysis of web 2.0 tools (see method 7) for e-participation. A "return" to VoicE (N=164) is intended by 75.4% of the one time visitors, 95.2% of the two times visitors, 90% of three or four time visitors and 100% of 5 times or more visitors. In summary, the data show a positive signal for the sustainability of VoicE regarding VoiceS if weak points are eliminated. In particular the consumer protection topics discussed would attract users to return to the platform.

3.3 Socio-Technical Perspective

This evaluation perspective investigates the usefulness, usage and acceptability of the platform regarding users and processes.

Social acceptability: It can be stated that information presented is accurate, complete and reliable. Privacy of information is performed by the controlled access to information. The user's password is used for the authentication mechanisms. To participate in the forum and in online, the user does not need to register, but needs to provide email and user name. The email is not visible to other users. The data necessary for registration in the platform are minimal (user name, e-mail, password).

Usefulness: Commonly used platform functions include reading news and information provision offerings. Polls are the only form of active participation, which is frequently used by the participants. Social bookmarks and Twitter are rather unused. Participation in the citizens' forum is a core component of the possibility of active participation in VoicE but rather not used in this form.

The user surveys (see methods 6 and 7) show that users do not miss any specific functionalities and services, which they may know from other participation experiences. But experts recommend the usage of further communication and community building functionalities. It was e.g. proposed by one expert to consider a kind of petitioning tool instead of or in addition to aggregating discussion results by a moderator. It can be concluded that tools provided are useful and appropriate for this kind of participation. Experts recommended making the tools more interactive. Resulting from the low number of active participants in the platform and expert statements the participation processes should be reconsidered. In this context, the participation tools should be adapted.

Usability: A good usability was stated by survey respondents and experts even if there are some minor usability flaws, which should be eliminated. The technologies and tools deployed are perceived rather accessible for all (because "essential parts of the content are available in audio format") even if not according to WCAG standards. In general, the usability of the VoicE platform resulted from a comprehensive usability engineering process.

3.4 Democratic Perspective

This perspective aims to understand to what extent the VoicE affects the democratic goals.

Representation: Provided information is correct, comprehensive and easily understandable (cf. section 3.2) and therefore enhances the understanding in this form of representative democracy. This is of significant importance as the general knowledge in the EU is rather low (see e.g. [10, 11]). VoicE aimed to enhance especially the role of MEPs by making it more visible and by offering citizens the chance to give their opinions on recent activities in the EU. The low support from the side of European politicians hindered this.

Engagement: The objectives of the project address the level of engagement in informing and consultation. While the first was fully reached, the second was only partly reached. Information on (electronic) participation possibilities is rather rare. One example is the petitioning procedure, which is explained on the Valencia platform but not yet on the German one. The same is the case with knowledge about existing initiatives e.g. running consultations of the EC, which is rather sparse on both platforms. General willingness of users to actively participate in political topics is rather low, even if they are interested in the topic. For those persons who are willing to actively participate, VoicE contributed partly to this decision. But the attractiveness and participation possibilities should be improved to engage more visitors. In conclusion to this, VoicE is rather used as information than as participation offering.

Transparency: The VoicE pilot has increased transparency of EU politics partly by providing simple explanations of the EU legislative procedures, the institutions and consumer protection issues as well as by publishing the latest news on these issues. A strength of VoicE in this regard is the dynamic tool showing progress of legislation process. This should be even more brought to the fore and used to explain the legislative process in general in an interactive way. The possibilities for influencing the decision-making process were not yet made sufficiently transparent.

Conflict and consensus: The VoicE platform supports the divergence of opinions and the deliberation about a topic in the forum. In general, the level of agreement in the discussions is rather high. But there are also deliberations about pros and cons of issues among the participants. The moderators need to manage the diversity when summarising the discussions e.g. for a "Letter to Brussels". In this context, it should be considered, as recommended by the experts, to use a kind of petition tool and provide the opportunity for the users to summarise their opinions themselves.

Political equality: The project shows strong potential for greater inclusiveness. There were signs that participants were mostly not previously "engaged" in political decision making. But there are no numbers available about the political, ethical, cultural, social etc. variety of users.

Community control: Most users are rather unsatisfied with the influence they reached in the legislative process. They do not think that - or are not sure if - their contributions will be further considered. The majority of these respondents did not expect higher achievements and they see the citizens' forum, polls and letter to Brussels to be of low to medium importance for the politicians. More efforts need to be made to improve participation rates by e.g. facilitating electronic debates, fostering participation on the same topics offline, making the final impact clear. Citizen engagement also needs to be linked appropriately to decision making processes.

4 Lessons Learned

The lessons learned are provided along six topics:

Regional approach: The question if regional e-participation is an appropriate means to interest citizens for European policies and motivate them to participate was analysed. Analysis evidences that the regional approach attracts citizens to visit the website and in some cases also to participate. A number of platform visitors from the regions confirm that they have now a better or slightly better link to European politics. The regional focus helps citizens to recognise the direct effects of European politics on their own life. Therefore the EU comes closer to the citizens. However, as the provision of participation opportunities on EU level is rather low (and often has no real impact on the decision-making process), it is a hard task to reach an impact with citizens' participation. Hence, a regional e-participation model towards the EU is supportive to attract citizens' interest. Yet to have a voice in Brussels, citizen participation must be linked directly with decision-making at Parliament level.

Heterogeneous target groups: As VoicE's target group is quite diverse and because a one-approach-for-all strategy was decided, it was difficult to reach many people of different age groups and with different (political) interests with no particular address. A rather serious look-and-feel does not attract users who are familiar with web 2.0 websites as e.g. younger citizens. On the other side, another look could deter older citizens from visiting the platform. The same can be assessed for the topics discussed. The biggest flaws in unmotivated participation in political decision making resulted from the low impact of participation and the low participation of politicians on the platform.

Involvement of politicians could not be successfully implemented in VoicE. It was only possible to involve politicians superficially and only if no further work was requested from them (e.g. with the question of the month). Only one MEP felt up to react on user comments and a letter to Brussels with some posts in the forum. Politicians are overcharged with their usual work and a huge amount of participation possibilities that ask them to contribute.

Relevance of the topic: The topic of discussion is crucial for an e-participation initiative. In VoicE the users were to a lesser extent interested in European politics than in consumer protection topics. It is important that participants are directly concerned by the topic selected.

Use of technologies: The use of each technology needs to be seen in the overall participation context. Tools used need not only to be adapted to the user requirements but also to the participation processes. The use of web 2.0 technologies does not ensure high user participation regardless how nice and easy to use they are.

Participation processes: It is key for a successful e-participation initiative that there are well-defined participative processes and that outcomes have an impact. In VoicE, this could not be achieved because politicians did not include users' contributions in their decision making processes. Other participation opportunities should be envisaged.

5 Conclusion and Outlook

In this contribution we investigated whether the VoicE model of regional e-participation is suitable to attract users for European politics. The analysis evidenced that regionalised information and up-to-date news provide a proper means to inform and attract citizens. Most platform visitors appreciated the information offerings. Even though the wider target group is rather not interested in active participation, some visitors discussed EU legislation and the impact on the VoicE platform. Some challenges of wider citizen participation lay in the need for targeted tools for older vs. younger citizens. Likewise, interests in political topics vary among different ages. A future version of the VoicE platform should become more interactive. If participation of citizens in EU politics shall be successful, e-participation initiatives need to achieve an impact. This means that participation processes need to be aligned to show how citizens' contributions will be further considered in the decision making processes. Likewise, politicians and citizens need to get into direct dialogue, i.e. also politicians need to be ready to interact with the citizenship. E-participation initiatives such as the VoicE project need therefore to be linked up with the processes provided by the European Union (e.g. running consultations or petitions from the European Parliament).

The VoicE consortium can address these points in VoiceS. Resulting from the evaluation, a number of activities are envisaged in the VoiceS project:

1. Promotion activities and the look-and-feel of the website should be focused to specific conditions of the diverse target groups. In VoiceS, it is envisaged to concentrate activities to the specific target group of younger citizens.
2. Involvement of MEPs and other politicians should be triggered with a well-defined participation process going along with media coverage.
3. Information texts should be shortened and elaborated for the targeted group.
4. The participation processes should be made more transparent.
5. The platform should get more interactive. The discussion forum should be replaced by a comment functionality.

Acknowledgment. VoicE and VoiceS are co-funded by the European Commission under the eParticipation Preparatory Action. This publication reflects the views only of the authors, and the Commission cannot be held responsible for any use which may be made of the information contained therein.

References

[1] Holzner, M., Schneider, C.: Consumer Protection, European Decision-Making and the Regions - the eParticipation Project VoicE. In: Cunningham, P., Cunningham, M. (eds.) Collaboration and the Knowledge Economy: Issues, Applications, Case Studies Part 1, pp. 351–356. IOS Press, Amsterdam (2008) ISBN 978158603924-0

[2] Scherer, S., Holzner, M., Karamagioli, E., Lorenz, M., Schepers, J., Wimmer, M.A.: Integrating Semantics, Social Software and Serious Games into eParticipation: The VoiceS Project. In: Tambouris, E., Macintosh, A. (eds.) Electronic Participation: Proceedings of Ongoing Research, General Development Issues and Projects of ePart 2009, pp. 151–158. Trauner Verlag, Linz (2009)

[3] Millard, J.: eParticipation recommendations - focusing on the European level. Deliverable 5.1, Study and supply services on the development of eParticipation in the EU (July 2009)

[4] Scherer, S., Wimmer, M.A., Ventzke, S.: Hands-on guideline for e-participation initiatives. In: Proceedings of the E-Government and E-Services (EGES) conference 2010. IFIP AICT. Springer, Heidelberg (2010) (to appear in September 2010)

[5] Macintosh, A., Whyte, A.: Towards an evaluation framework for eParticipation. Transforming Government: People, Process and Policy 2(1), 16–30 (2008)

[6] Lippa, B., Aichholzer, G., Allhutter, D., Freschi, A.C., Macintosh, A., Westholm, H.: D 13.3: eParticipation Evaluation and Impact. DEMO-net (2008) (Deliverable)

[7] Scherer, S., Karamagioli, E., Titorencu, M., Schepers, J., Wimmer, M.A., Koulolias, V.: Usability Engineering in eParticipation. European Journal of ePractice (7) (2009)

[8] Bicking, M., Wimmer, M.A.: Evaluation framework to assess eParticipation projects in Europe. In: Tambouris, E., Macintosh, A. (eds.) Electronic Participation: Proceedings of Ongoing Research, General Development Issues and Projects of ePart 2009, Schriftenreihe Informatik, vol. 31, pp. 73–82. Trauner Verlag, Linz (2009)

[9] Märker, O.: Evaluation von E-Partizipation. In: E-Partizipation: Beteiligungsprojekte im Internet. Beiträge zur Demokratieentwicklung, vol. 21, pp. 252–281. Stiftung Mitarbeit, Bonn (2007)

[10] EUROBAROMETER: Public Opinion in the European Union. National Report, Executive Summary: Germany 70, Eurobarometer (2008)

[11] EUROBAROMETER: Public Opinion in the European Union. First Results 70, Eurobarometer (December 2008); Fieldwork (October–November 2008); Publication (December 2008)

[12] Scherer, S., Neuroth, C., Schefbeck, G., Wimmer, M.A.: Enabling eParticipation of the Youth in the Public Debate on Legislation in Austria: A Critical Reflection. In: Macintosh, A., Tambouris, E. (eds.) ePart 2009. LNCS, vol. 5694, pp. 151–162. Springer, Heidelberg (2009)

Service Guidelines of Public Meeting's Webcasts: An Experience

Mario A. Bochicchio and Antonella Longo

Università del Salento – Dipartimento di Ingegneria dell'Innovazione
Lecce, Italy
{mario.bochicchio,antonella.longo}@unisalento.it

Abstract. In Italy, public meeting webcasts are frequently adopted by local public administrations to support the "information provision" process. This is supposed to increase the citizens' awareness and participation to public life. In the paper, the experience gathered from the design of both the architecture of a webcasting system and the "webcast's production and distribution process" is presented. The system implementation is discussed referring to a large Italian Public Agency.

Keywords: Webcasting, information provision, broadcasting of public meeting.

1 Introduction and Background

In a transparent and accountable Public Administration critical decisions are often deliberated during public meetings. These meetings are based on strict rules and their detailed agendas must be published prior to the meeting date, together with related documentation, to allow all interested citizens and administrators actively participating.

Actually the advent of eParticipation has changed the meaning of Government transparency. Historically, the definition sounded like "show us what you have done"; however, this leaves citizens and the media with the less than ideal option of complaining to or complimenting the government after the fact. According to the main goals of the EU policy defined in the eGovernment Action Plan 2006, an alternative and more appropriate definition was created: "let me participate in what you're doing as you're doing it". This new definition leads to two main approaches [14]: the first type simply provides a central source for information about the government and its activities. An example for this kind of initiative is government websites. The second type, based on Web2.0 technology, make massive text-based, audio, and visual records of government activity (meetings of Community groups, Parliamentary debates, or Council Committees) available to citizens' computer screens (i.e. Webcasting). Webcasts can be viewed in real-time (live Webcasts) or they can be archived to let people watch them at a later time (on-demand Webcast).

Alas, this "movie-like" approach is not practical if videos are longer than 10-15 minutes. Net-citizens, in fact, are accustomed to Web browsers and search engines for surfing and retrieving "fine grained" multimedia contents (like in YouTube), in contrast with the "coarse grained" scenario of many Council meetings and

E. Tambouris, A. Macintosh, and O. Glassey (Eds.): ePart 2010, LNCS 6229, pp. 174–183, 2010.
© IFIP International Federation for Information Processing 2010

Parliamentary debates, whose videos can last even several hours. Obviously, large video sequences can be cut and annotated with titles and short description or even minutes and translations, to better support the "Web approach" based on search, click and surf operations. Actually the topic of video annotation is not new in the research literature, where a huge number of tools have been developed and described [1-9] to make them searchable also on the Web. These tools have evolved from simple text annotators to semantic tagging systems for online communities to produce rich, structured metadata and annotations based on standard mark-up languages [4, 6].

The application of these tools and techniques to improve the transparency is very promising but, in general, it is not sufficient to transform the movie-oriented digital meetings into media-rich applications valuable to Net citizens and e-participation [10]. Indeed the quality of the annotations depends on many factors, like the granularity (the average length of the atomic videoclips) and the definition of a suitable standard for metadata: this topic is a hot issue in eParticipation research, due to the unsustainable variety of non-standardized and proprietary formats used by each public agency for publishing its own information [12].

The overall quality also depend on the "production process", and in particular on the definition of a "validation and publishing procedure" based on a pre-agreed thesaurus of terms and phrases used from the indexers. A further requirement is about accessibility, in order to support the eParticipation of citizens with disabilities.

Various research and industrial tools have been analyzed which annotate video fragments, deliver webcast (both live and on-demand) video/audio contents, arrange contents or add accessibility features to existing multimedia content [16], but to our knowledge there is no integrated platform supporting all the previous features in the transparency perspective and which also provides the following:

- support an approved thesaurus and an agreed set of rules for annotating the video/audio recordings or adding appropriate metadata to digital documents or public meetings minutes
- workflow for content validation before its online publication
- searchability of public meeting webcasts by Web search engines
- ability to produce statistics (indicators) about the politicians participation to the public meetings, the time spent for each topic, etc.

In addition to these functional objectives, other important requirements include ease of use, simplicity, minimal learning curve, low cost of implementation and maintenance, the adoption of standard formats and protocols for digital encoding, storage and transmission. The aim of the VIEW system here described is to satisfy all these requirements, and to describe its implementation in a large Italian Municipality.

The structure of the paper is the following: the usage scenario is presented in section 2. The system architecture and main technical aspects are presented in section 3. A description of the user interface is given in section 4. Section 5 is about the evaluation of VIEW in a real case and Section 6 is for conclusions and future works.

2 The Usage Scenario

Italy is a large, southern European country with a strong, growing economy and a high level of internet usage, especially amongst the younger generation. It is also a country with a heavily bureaucratized, multi-tiered, semi-federal government.

The population density ranges from extremely low in the countryside to extremely high in the urban areas. Thus, local eParticipation initiatives in Italy have many demographic backgrounds against which to be set.

The Italian government is divided into 4 levels: a Central Government, twenty Regional Governments, 110 Provinces and about 800 Municipalities.

This level of government enjoys a fair amount of autonomy in decision-making as well as significant financial support from higher levels of government.

In this scenario the issue of providing local authorities with transparency Web tools is a big challenge. Even if Web technologies provide means so that the government's critical decisions must be deliberated on and made during public meetings (e.g. Municipal Councils) or hearings and these public meetings must be accessible to anyone and everywhere, live and on-demand, Government agencies have always seen making public records accessible as an extra step or job, to be done off-line after the Council. This is the main reason why a system enabling annotating video/audio records during the public meeting process, is considered critical for improving servant efficiency and effectiveness. The scenario envisioned is that of a system able both to live broadcast public Municipal Council meetings and to provide remotely located administrative jurists (indexers) with a client for real-time annotating the broadcasted video.

Indexers' tasks are to create the meeting agenda, to link it with the corresponding video fragment and to attach related documents (minutes, annexes, reports, etc). During the live event, the indexer can add the speaker's name, the topic, start and stop time, his/her political party, his/her role in the meeting (Major, Meeting chairman, external guest). The system must contextually support indexers, for example, by automatically completing the speaker's name, the topic or political party thanks to a preloaded vocabulary preventively agreed with the meeting chairman. Once the meeting is over and the integrated public record is saved, the meeting chairman is notified by email. He accesses the pre-staging area, validates annotations, hyperlinks and attached documents and publishes the item. Once the new content is online, citizens can browse public meeting using the navigation tree displaying the agenda and the speakers for each topic or using a general purpose search engine to look up speaker, topic or any other specific annotation inserted by the indexer. The search engine retrieves the web page with the whole annotated video, then the user can refine the search filtering by dates, time intervals, speakers and subjects, in order to retrieve the specific video fragments.

3 VIEW: System Architecture

VIEW is an information system allowing:

- the live and on-demand webcast of multimedia content
- the real time annotation of videos and the addition of files,

- the definition of a standard vocabulary, validated by the Council Chair and used by the servants during the real time video annotation
- the validation of the multimedia objects before their online publication
- the retrieval of these multimedia objects by Web searches (i.e. Google, Yahoo, etc.) and a detailed search, based on SQL queries, once the user on the Municipal portal

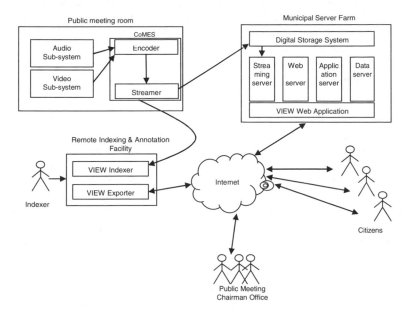

Fig. 1. VIEW architecture

The synchronization system is based on timestamps added on the continuous media, which tag the video and allow the linkage among the video, the annotation and the other documents. The whole system has been implemented with Microsoft technologies (VB.NET and ASPX.NET, using the .NET 2.0 Framework) and is made up of three main modules. The "public meetings room", in the upper left corner of Figure 1, provides the continuous media source (audio and video streaming) from the meeting room. The CoMES (Continuous Media Encoding and Streaming) component encodes audio and video streaming and synchronizes the local clock with those at the Remote Indexing and Annotation Facility to guarantee a unique temporal reference. The outcome streaming is sent both to the digital storage facility, via a dedicated line on the Municipal Network, for the live broadcast (via a streaming server) and to the remote indexer, via a dedicated domestic ADSL line, for annotations. The server farm, in the upper right corner of Figure 1, provides:

- the storage space for 5 years of digital meetings (4 TB on line plus a tape unit for automatic backup;
- the media server (a local MS Media Server on Win 2003 Server, connected to a 6 Mb/s Internet connection, plus a remote backup server, in hosting).

- the Web server   and the application server (MS IIS with .NET 2.0 framework);
- the data server (a MS SQL Server 2005 with full text extensions);
- the VIEW Web platform, which includes the following features:

1. the Citizen Front End, serving the live meeting interface, the on-demand interface (archived public meetings) and the internal search engine, to look up specific topics, meetings, speakers or associate documents;
2. the Exporter Front End, i.e. the interface used by Indexers to prepare new indexed and annotated video according to the style guide and the publishing workflow ;
3. the Meeting Chair Front End, used to modify, approve and publish each meeting.

The Remote Indexing & Annotation Facility, in the lower left part of Figure 1, is based on two main applications, the VIEW Indexer and the VIEW Exporter (both developed in VB.NET). The Indexer and the Exporter are used to annotate the continuous media coming from the public meeting with the metadata agreed with the Meeting Chair (i.e. the speakers' name, its role in the meeting, the name of its political party, the exact start/stop time and the subject of the speech), using the vocabulary previously defined, and to link it with the relevant documents (minutes, agenda, annexes etc.). The Exporter is in charge to pack each new group of metadata, to send it to the server farm and to install each part (html pages, temporal indexes, annotations, attached documents, minutes, …) in the corresponding farm component.

The video player embedded in the Web interface is the Microsoft Media Player and the synchronization between the tree elements (topic/subtopic/speakers) and the audio/video fragments is based on a purposely-developed multibrowser javascript library and on the adoption of the .asx metafiles (Microsoft advanced stream redirector and markup language) suitable to extract and browse "on the fly" specific video fragments from continuous-media streams, just relying on temporal coordinates (like start-time, stop-time, length etc.).

The same features are also developed with:

1. the Smil markup language together with the Quicktime-Server/Quicktime media-player (from Apple) or the Real-Server/RealPlayer (from Real Media);
2. the Flash runtime plugin and the ActionScript programming language together with the Flash Media Server (from Adobe).

Even if VIEW fully supports both technologies, the diffusion of the Microsoft Media Player and the low cost of the Microsoft Media Server are very attractive for many public agencies. Other similar or newer solutions based on the ogg vorbis or on the MPEG-4 video formats and on various markup techniques like CMML, MPEG-7, RDF etc. are under analysis and evaluation.

In order to implement the searchability of annotated video meetings, VIEW generates contents that can be retrieved both by Web search engines (like Google or Yahoo) and by an internal specialized search engine. The double support is achieved thanks to the introduction of a little redundancy: static .html pages including all metadata, temporal markers and text annotations are created for all archived meeting. These pages are crawled and indexed by all the Web search engine, but the granularity of the retrieval is the whole public meeting. Then, the internal VIEW search engine can be invoked, to refine the answer. The internal search engine is based on a purposely-designed relational data model including speakers, their politic parties, their role in the meetings, the date and hour of each meeting and speech and its topic; the database is able to track all the changing aspects (party, role, name, sex, ..) of each speaker, and to periodically extract statistics about the time spoken by each party, the respect of the time limits, the most discussed topics (in terms of time spent and number of speeches) etc. The adoption of free runtime distribution of the MS SQL Server 2005 with the full-text extensions enables most of the advanced linguistic features (extended query language, stemming algorithms, stop-word elimination, domain-specific dictionaries, double-word and multi-word identification, …) typical of all modern search engines.

4   User Interface

As shown in Figure 2 and Figure 3, the main application layout for citizen's interface is based on three panels. They are framed by a rectangular area on the top (for the main navigation and the search engine) and a lateral grey part, which are due to the Institution communication style guidelines. The left panel contains the meeting agenda represented as a tree of topics, nested subtopics and speakers' names. Each speaker (i.e. each leaf of the tree) is linked to the corresponding speech (audio/video fragment), displayed in the upper part of central panel, while in the bottom part, minutes and short descriptions are visualized, if available. The related documentation (like the planned agenda, the .pdf documents) is visualized at the bottom of the right panel. The upper central bar is for breadcrumb trails, status information and archive searching. Figure 3 shows the result of a "simple research". The left hand panel has been substituted by a speeches' list coming from the search engine while the upper part of the right panel contains a set of fields for search refinement.

Fig. 2. The layout of the main page of VIEW

Fig. 3. The result of a "simple search" action

The creation and modification of a digital public meeting is possible through the main interface of the Indexer, displayed in Figure 4. The indexing/annotation session starts together with the meeting's live broadcast. From that moment on, it is possible to create the detailed agenda (as a table of contents) adding and linking the annotations (topics/subtopics, speakers' name, start/stop time, attached documents, …) to the video clip in real-time. At the end of the meeting annotations, links, temporal markers and attached documents are used to create both:

-   the static web pages constituting the archive (Figure 2);
-   the relational data structures stored in the database which will enable the advanced search options (right panel, Figure 3) .

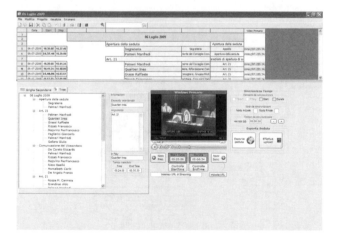

Fig. 4. VIEW Indexer - main interface

Accessibility for disabled peoples is taken into account through high-contrast and character-magnified interfaces (upper right icons in Figure 2 and Figure 3).

5 Evaluation

The motivation of VIEW can be summarized in the following points:

1. to minimize the cost, the effort and the time required to transform a public meeting in online eParticipation event;
2. to maximize the searchability of the multimedia contents produced and the easiness of use;

VIEW is not a general purpose authoring environment to create hypervideos, but it is a specific, optimized platform for the large community of government agencies interested in fostering efficient transparency in eParticipation.

We chose two specific case studies to evaluate the system. We identified these case studies on the basis of existing established collaborations with two public Institutions, a big Municipality in the Lombardia Region and a local agency of Apuglia Region.

This first case study involved a 12 months collaboration with the chairman's office of the City Council, in charge of documenting and publishing activities concerning the Council public meetings. The collaboration aimed at tuning the public meeting annotation and publishing process up and to analyze the gap with another publishing system used by the office in the previous five years.

The second case study concerned an eParticipation initiative of Apulia Region, involving specific communities (some thousands of citizens) to discuss and reformulate three important regional laws about sport, health and urban organization.

Both the case studies are based on the use of VIEW, which was used by public servants for acquiring, annotating and publishing the meetings. In both the cases the test was preceded by a training session (8 hours in a 5 people class) during which after a session of presentation of the platform, servant were invited to try the platform. The trainers included a jurist, explaining the legislative and administrative foundations of the platform, a functional analyst, who described the use of the system and a usability expert, in order to qualitatively observe how the class should have interacted with the platform and discover usability and interaction bugs. The general feedback was positive both on the layout and navigation design and on functional aspects.

In the case of the City Council, since each officer used a personal annotation style, variable in time, inconsistent with the other officers and prone to discussions with the Council Chairman, they agreed to model the annotation procedure and to agree about detailed annotation guidelines, which have been included in the Indexer software component, as thesaurus and online suggestions to support the indexing and annotation task. This produced dramatic improvements in the time to publish each meeting, in the quality of the detailed agenda and, most of all, as a side effect, it reduced the overall time spent by the office to search information. The same relevant improvement can be achieved in each public meeting with a well defined structure, like the City Council.

Moreover the comparative analysis with the previously used system also revealed that the major advantages perceived by the users were the ability to:

1. publish each indexed and annotated meeting within few hours from the end of the event, rather than in a week or more;
2. easily associate relevant documents (agenda, minutes, annexes, reports etc.) to the published meeting;
3. perform both simple and advanced search in published meetings;
4. reduce the publishing costs from 4000 €/meeting to 1000 €/meeting;
5. increase the overall number of published meetings, and the accountability and the transparency level perceived by citizens.

The main issues they highlighted during the test and evaluation sessions are:

1. The current multibrowser support, based on Javascript, HTML and CSS, is heavy to maintain while new browsers and new browser-versions come out. A completely new, Flash-based user interface is under evaluation to overcome the problem, together with a more general, non proprietary (in the sense of multi-vendor) and stable solution
2. The officers in charge of indexing and annotating the meetings ask more and more to be enabled to use the platform via wi-fi and mobile. Anyway, frequent line interruptions and low bandwidth of mobile or domestic lines hinder this feature;
3. While is frequent the request from citizens to add social tagging tools, Municipalities are unable to undertake the burden derived by supervise public comments in the official council meeting pages.

6   Conclusions and Future Works

VIEW is an example of tool to easily and effectively transform movie-oriented public meeting recordings into Web oriented, interactive applications for eParticipation. After 12 months of experimental usage, VIEW is a mature and stable tool, ready to be industrialized and deployed on large scale but, as for similar initiatives, we argue that the organizational structure of local administration and government agencies is not ready to accept it, while preferring home made, less-than-optimal solutions.

Our case studies revealed a range of potentials and issues that deserve further investigation. In particular, we are planning to investigate the following improvements and extensions:

1. the web user interface should become more portable and compatible with the existing and future web browsers;
2. the remote indexing & annotation facility should become nomadic or mobile;
3. the system should be extended with social tagging features, providing the officers with tools able to efficiently manage a huge amount of comments ;
4. a standardized vocabulary and formats are necessary for cross-agency search, in order to compare the behavior of different public administrations (e.g. different municipalities) on a given topic (e.g. how to organize the urban garbage collection).

References

1. Hurst, W., Stiegler, P.: User interfaces for browsing and navigation of continuous multimedia data. In: Proceedings of NordiCHI, Arhus, Denmark, pp. 267–270 (2002)
2. Davis, J., Huttenlocher, D.: The CoNote System for Shared Annotations (1995), http://www.cs.cornell.edu/home/dph/annotation/annotations.html
3. Money, A.G., Agius, H.: Video summarisation: A conceptual framework and survey of the state of the art. Journal of Visual Communication and Image Representation 19(2), 121–143 (2008)
4. Pfeiffer, S., Parker, C., Schremmer, C.: Annodex: a simple architecture to enable hyperlinking, search & retrieval of time–continuous data on the Web. In: Proceedings of the 5th ACM SIGMM international workshop on Multimedia information retrieval
5. Jansen, J., Bulterman, D.C.: SMIL State: an architecture and implementation for adaptive time-based web applications. Multimedia Tools and Applications 43(3) (July 2009)
6. Schroeter, R., Hunter, J., Newman, A.: Annotating Relationships Between Multiple Mixed-Media Digital Objects by Extending Annotea. In: Franconi, E., Kifer, M., May, W. (eds.) ESWC 2007. LNCS, vol. 4519, pp. 533–548. Springer, Heidelberg (2007)
7. Metavid, http://metavid.org/wiki/MetaVidWiki_Software
8. Aubert, O., Prié, Y.: Advene: an open-source framework for integrating and visualising audiovisual metadata. In: Proc. of ACM Multimedia Conference on Open Source Competition: Technical presentation and overview paper, Augsburg (September 2007)
9. INFORMEDIA Project at CMU, http://www.informedia.cs.cmu.edu/pubs/byyear.asp
10. Granicus, http://www.granicus.com/Streaming-Media-Government.aspx
11. Christel, A.G., Yan, M.G., Hauptmann, R.: Video Retrieval based on Semantic Concepts. Proceedings of the IEEE 96(4), 602–622 (2008), doi:10.1109/JPROC.2008.916355
12. Peristeras, V., Mentzas, G., Tarabanis, K.A., Abecker, A.: Transforming E-government and E-participation through IT. IEEE Intelligent Systems, 14–19 (September/October 2009)
13. Saebo, O., Rose, J., Skiftenes Flak, L.: The shape of eParticipation: Characterizing an emerging research area. Government Information Quarterly 25(3), 400–428 (2008) ISSN 0740-624X, doi: 10.1016/j.giq.2007.04.007
14. Peart, M., Diaz, J.R.: Taking stock: local e-democracy in Europe and the USA. International Journal of Electronic Governance 1(4), 400-433(34) (2008)
15. DEMO-net: the eParticipation Network of Excellence, http://www.demo-net.org/
16. Zhang, C., Rui, Y., Crawford, J., Heacm, L.: An Automated End-to-End Lecture Capture and Broadcasting System. Transactions on Multimedia Computing, Communications and Applications 4(1) (January 2008)
17. http://212.239.56.103/newconsiglio/archivio/archivio.aspx

Semantic Web Standards and Ontologies for Legislative Drafting Support

Tommaso Agnoloni and Daniela Tiscornia

ITTIG-CNR, Via de' Barucci 20, Florence, Italy
{agnoloni,tiscornia}@ittig.cnr.it

Abstract. Machine readable open public data and the issue of multilingual web are open challenges promising to transform the relationship between citizens and European institutions. In this context the DA-LOS[1] project aims at ensuring coherence and alignment in the legislative language, providing law-makers with knowledge management tools to improve the control over the multilingual complexity of European legislation and over the linguistic and conceptual issues involved in its transposition into national laws. This paper describes the design and implementation activities performed on the basis of a set of parallel texts in different languages on a specific legal topic. Natural language processing techniques have been applied to automatically build lexicons for each language. Lexical and conceptual multilingual alignment has been accomplished exploiting terms position in parallel documents. An ontology describing entities involved in the chosen domain has been developed in order to provide a semantic description of terms in lexicons. A modular integration of such resources, represented in RDF/OWL standard format, allowed their effective and flexible access from a legislative drafting application prototype, able to enrich legal documents with terms mark-up and semantic annotations.

Keywords: Machine-Readable Open Data, Multilingual Legal Ontologies, Natural Language Processing, XML Authoring.

1 Introduction

A process of standardization of document formats, their unique identification and their annotation in machine readable format is being carried on in recent years under the impulse of web technologies. The envisaged goal is to make electronic documents interoperable among different systems, meaningfully interlinked in a web of documents and at the end more effectively accessible by human and artificial agents. Legal documents (norms, procedures, court decisions) due to their particular relevance in an effective and transparent democracy and their pervasiveness in all the fields of citizens' activities are natural candidate to be affected by such innovations. Moreover they are the outcomes of a complex, distributed and expensive bureaucratic machine whose reengineering in the light of

---

[1] DrAfting Legislation with Ontology-based Support.

E. Tambouris, A. Macintosh, and O. Glassey (Eds.): ePart 2010, LNCS 6229, pp. 184–196, 2010.

the availability of information technologies would produce huge potential benefits. Quality in European and national legislation is actually one of the main purposes of the current initiatives of the European Commission. In the Mandelkern report on better regulation [1] the need for a coordinated action by Member States was solicited to simplify the EU regulatory environment, to enhance the quality of EU legislation as well as to rationalise the transposition of European directives into national law. Coherence, interoperability and harmonization in the legislative knowledge of, and control over, the legal lexicon is therefore considered as a precondition for improving the quality of legislative language and for facilitating access to legislation by legal experts and citizens. In a multilingual environment and, in particular, in EU regulations, only the awareness of the subtleties of legal lexicon in the different languages can enable drafters to maintain coherence among different linguistic versions of the same text, as well as over their transposition in national laws. The DALOS project launched within the "eParticipation" framework of the EU Commission, tackled these problems from different point of views. Providing a legislative drafting environment able to produce legislative documents in a standard compliant interoperable XML format from the very beginning of their proposal. Integrating domain knowledge, conceptual and lexical resources in the editing tool in order to help and constrain the legislator to the use of shared and understandable (clear and effective) legal concepts within the legislation. Tackling the multilingual issue of European law providing cross-language and cross-culture shared and aligned legal concepts in order to favour uniform adoption and implementations of European regulations and directives in member states. Providing an initial nucleus of *Linked Data* on a specific domain capable of automatically contextualize, explain and rephrase relevant concepts through the semantic connection with relevant related resources on the web. The DALOS outcome have been essentially twofold: propose an authoring tool enabling the production of documents in standard reusable format annotated with respect to tags stored in an knowledge resource accessible from a user friendly environment. Propose and implement a methodology to encode, by extraction from a corpus of documents, the domain knowledge on a specific subject as the outcome of previous legislation and decisions on the subject to be reused in new document production and put in comparison with different linguistic versions for legal translation assistance and standardized for use in annotation of documents.

2   Semantic Web Technologies and Legal Information

The web as it has developed in the last decades is basically a web of interlinked documents. It is based over a few basic technologies URI, HTTP, HTML *i.e.* a standard for resources identification, a transfer protocol, a markup language enabling the display of documents in web browsers with typographical informations and hyperlinking to other documents. The huge potential of such innovation is evident in its everyday use. In recent years however the web is evolving from a global information space of interlinked documents to a web of data, i.e. a global distributed, flexible and queryable database. The linked data initiative [2] in fact aims at providing on the Web machine-readable data, complementing the human-readable documents that constitute the major part of the current Web. The goal is to allow computer-based agents to be much more efficient in assisting users and performing automated tasks on their behalf, thus realising the vision of the Semantic Web. In order to accomplish that an additional set of specification on the top of existing ones have been proposed and standardized by the W3C consortium in order to achieve standardized machine readable document formats (XML), a flexible relational model of data (RDF) and an ontology specification language (OWL) enabling the definition of concepts and conceptual relations and the computation of conceptual inferences. XML (eXtensible Markup Language) provide the technology to ensure interoperability at the syntactic level, i.e. provides the mean to make documents readable and interchangeable among different systems using standardized and open document format for which numerous tools and applications have been developed and are widely available. Moreover any specific portion of documents or additional data on documents (metadata) can be structured in meaningful elements that can be read and interpreted by software applications. Syntactic interoperability is then ensured by the definition of common data structures, e.g. XML Schema to which a class of documents must comply (document validation). This already opens a scenario where a shift from documents to specific piece of information and from natural language to processable data takes place. Moreover technological barriers once format standards have been established and adopted on a large scale would be removed enabling a high potential of information exchange and reuse among different heterogeneous systems. RDF (Resource Descriprtion Framework) is the data model enabling the definition of typed links among data from different sources on the web just like in the current Hypertext web, hyperlinks establish (untyped) links among HTML documents. The RDF model encodes data in the form of *subject, predicate, object* triples. The subject and object of a triple are both URIs that each identify a resource, or a URI and a string respectively. The predicate specifies how the subject and the object are related. Thus RDF triples can be thought as link among items in different data sets analogous to hypertext links connecting one HTML document to another. RDF enables us to include in the documents machine understandable statements on relevant objects and their properties. An RDF triple can state for example that two resources, a person A and a document B, both identified by a URI are related by the fact that A is the author of B. Such resources can be stored in different data sets exposed on the web thus creating a web of data. Semantic interoperability on the other hand aims at ensuring that the exchanged information is interpeted by communicating parties (human or artificial agents) with a shared meaning. This can be accomplished by the definition of semantic resources e.g. shared terminology, thesauri or ontologies ensuring that data elements are interpreted in the same way by explicitly tagging their content with reference to an encoded shared conceptualization. Semantic interoperability assets, e.g. taxonomies or code lists, are moreover particularly relevant in the multilingual and multicultural context of the European Union where data exchange faces the obstacles of linguistic and jurisdictional barriers [2]. Actually semantic web technologies are also the key to tackle the challenge of a multilingual web by enabling the connection of language independent conceptualizations with lexical databases and semantic networks enabling language dependent access to resources. The RDF data model can in fact be used to publish data in a language-independent fashion and connect them with language dependent resources in order to enable users to access data in their own language. In the Legal Information field many initiatives have been promoted to implement semantic technologies in document production, storage and presentation. A standardization process in document formats both for the annotation of their textual content (specific normative text elements like *heading, section, article, paragraph, reference* or formatted text like *tables, lists*) and additional metadata (like *subject classification, publication date, enacting authority, relatioship among acts*) is being carried at National and European level. See [3] for an overview. At the European level the CEN/Metalex[3] initiative aims at becoming the standard interchange format for legal documents by implementing a metalevel of mapping among national document formats. The implementation of Semantic Web technologies in the Legislative field, focusing on the addition of computer processable information to legal documents, according to shared standards, facilitates for example the integration between:

- the production of documents and the management of their workflow
- the use of a shared consistent terminology among different implementation of the same legal concept in different legislative interventions on a topic or in different national implementations of a legislative provision.
- the distribution, access and reuse of the resulting documents and information for citizens (enhanced with such interlinked meta-information)

During the drafting phase for example machine processable data can be added to the various versions of a document in order to facilitate the subsequent retrieval of a specific version of a document and to keep track of its workflow. These same data (for instance the specification of the structure of a document, its authors, its life-cycle, etc.) can enrich the document when they are published, and can be used to provide information concerning the procedure through which the document has been produced. The approach of the Semantic Web facilitates on the one hand (from the "back office" side) legal drafting, the maintenance of legal sources for example enabling "point-in-time" access to in-force legislation or the implementation of normative references for easy navigation among cited documents, and the management of legislative workflows and procedures. On the other hand (on the "front office" side), the publicity and transparency of procedures and information, the dialogue between sub-national, national, and international institutions, and community stakeholders at every stage of the Legislation formation and debate. Machine readable data in fact, enabling the separation between content and presentation allow for straightforward implementation of

---

[2] www.semic.eu
[3] www.metalex.eu

e-consultation applications during the whole legislative process. See also [4] for an overview of information technology impact on e-participation. According to the described scenario the DALOS project contribution have been essentially to:

1. Encode by extraction from a corpus of documents the domain knowledge on a specific subject as the outcome of previous legislation and decisions on the subject to be reused in new document editing and standardized for use in semantic annotation of content.
2. Tackle the multilinguality issue by providing a formal structure integrating language independent conceptualization encoded in a domain ontology connected with WordNet-like structured lexical resources providing language dependent lexicalizations.
3. Link multilingual lexicalizations of relevant concepts on a domain with their original context of use or definition in source document-fragments.
4. Integrate in a standard compliant XML authoring tool for legislative documents the access to external knowledge, lexical and documental multilingual resources for drafting support and document annotation from a non-technical user friendly environment.

In particular DALOS aims on one hand at ensuring that legal drafters and decision-makers have control over the legal language at national and European level, by providing law-makers with linguistic and knowledge management tools to be accessed in the legislative processes. On the other hand at guaranteeing open access to resulting data by implementing open document standards for favouring their subsequent reuse. The methodological approach proposed in DALOS for the design of the domain knowledge resource consists of three main activities:

1. semi-automatic term extraction from a set of selected documents by using NLP (Natural Language Processing) tools;
2. construction of a domain ontology;
3. integration of ontologies, lexical resources and documents.

The next three sections will focus on these points. Finally the integration of access instruments to the semantic resources from a Legislative XML drafting environment is described in Sect. 6

3   Building Aligned Lexicons

The starting point for the construction of the lexicons is a selected corpus of documents on the domain of "protection of consumers" economic and legal interests, including Directives, Regulation and Case Law on the subject. From a methodological point of view, of great importance is the fact that the source documents for the construction of the resource are made available in parallel translations in the EU languages because of the obligation for European Institutions to publish directives in the national languages of the member states, making possible a subsequent automatic terms and concepts alignment. Domain lexicons in the four European languages (Italian, English, Spanish, Dutch) supported in DALOS have been constructed in a semiautomatic way applying Natural Language Processing techniques to the set of selected documents. For the extraction of Italian terms we used T2K (Text–to–Knowledge), a hybrid ontology learning system combining linguistic technologies and statistical techniques [5]. For the other languages two term extraction applications have been used. TermExtractor [6] offers a comprehensive package of algorithms for the selection of relevant terms from any text corpus. GATE [7], developed by the University of Sheffield, is a framework for Language Engineering (LE) applications which supports efficient and robust text processing. A key requisite for both the automatic tools was the possibility to keep track of the links to document fragments in the domain corpora from which each relevant term has been extracted. To this end a preliminary fragmentation of each document in its formal partitions (paragraphs of normative documents *e.g. Part, Article* etc.) have been performed. More important, this made possible the exploitation of the peculiarity of the domain corpus to be parallel. Interlingual alignment could in fact be automatically established exploiting the origin of extracted terms in different languages from parallel contexts. A particular treatment is reserved to terms identified by automatic tools to be definitions, *i.e.* terms preceding a definition in the directives. For this terms a translation in the different languages keeping the original meaning is guaranteed. Defined terms are highlighted in the lexicons and corresponding definitions are entirely reported in the knowledge base as special contexts. After a manual clean-up phase due to the noise introduced by automatic tools, the average size of the four lexicons is about 1500 terms. The automatic construction of lexicons should be seen as a starting point for the setup of a dynamically growing resource. A manual update of the lexicons will be possible and should be done at a second stage directly by the users through terms insertion, deletion and inter-linguistic alignments editing.

4   Building Domain Ontology

The DALOS domain ontology is the result of an intellectual activity aimed at describing the domain of the consumer protection, chosen for the pilot case. It has been implemented as an extension of the Core Legal Ontology (CLO)[4] [8] developed on top of DOLCE foundational ontology [9] and on the "Descriptions and Situations" (DnS) ontology [10] within the DOLCE+ library[5]. Such an extension is addressed to cope with the entities of the chosen domain and their legal specificities. In this knowledge architecture the role of a core legal ontology is to provide well established entities/concepts which belong to the general theory of law, bridging the gap between domain-specific concepts and the abstract categories of formal upper level or foundational ontologies such as,

---

[4] http://www.loa-cnr.it/ontologies/CLO/CoreLegal.owl
[5] DOLCE+ library, http://dolce.semanticweb.org

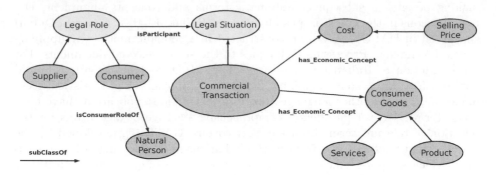

Fig. 1. Extract of the DALOS domain ontology

in our case, DOLCE. The domain ontology is therefore populated by the conceptual entities which characterize the consumer protection domain. The chosen approach in the ontology design has been to encode knowledge grounded on source text in order to avoid any forced concept harmonization. The first assumption is that all concepts that appear as definitions in the Dalos corpus are representative of the domain and, as a consequence, that several concepts *used* in the definitional contexts pertain to the ontology as well, representing the basic properties or, in other words, the 'intensional meaning' of the relevant concepts. Furthermore the domain Ontology contains generic situations having a legal relevance in the chosen domain. Such domain-specific concepts are classified according to more general notions, imported from CLO, as `Legal_role` and `Legal_situation`. An example of some concepts obtained by the definitions of the consumer law (as `Commercial_ transaction`, `Consumer`, `Supplier`, etc.) playing specific roles ([10]) is given in Fig. 1. The first version of the Ontological layer contains 118 named classes.

5   Integrating Resources

One of the aim of the DALOS project was the construction of a knowledge base including ontologies and lexicons in different languages to be accessed in a flexible way in order to accomplish different tasks like drafting, consultation, document retrieving, assisted translation. In order to allow the integration of all the available resources in a single knowledge base, they have been chosen to be represented in the RDF/OWL language.

5.1   Lexicons

For lexicon structure formalization, a meta-level ontology describing the WordNet semantic has been used. This is based on three classes: *Synset*, *WordSense* and *Word*. A WordNet synset is a set of one or more uninflected word forms (lemmas) with a synonymous meaning: for example *trial, proceedings, law suit*

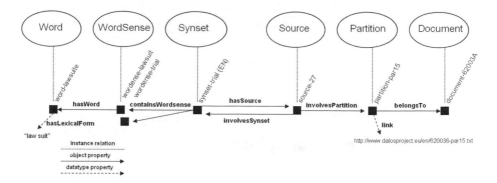

Fig. 2. Low level description of the English lexical resource "synset-trial" and one of its references to a EU directive

form a noun synset because they can be used to refer to the same concept. In this meta-level ontology the classes Synset, WordSense and Word and the properties relating instances of such classes are defined. Each Synset object is a set of WordSense objects since polysemous terms are distinct in wordsenses. In practice, each entry of a DALOS lexicon is represented as a synset object, *i.e.* a set of word objects in a particular meaning and one or more lexical forms associated (variants). This conversion from a WordNet like data structure in RDF is described at the W3C site [6].

5.2 Dalos Corpus

Another meta-level ontology has been used to represent links, namely *sources*, between terms and document fragments in the DALOS corpus. Here the main classes are *Document, Partition* and *Source* whose instances are directly linked with instances of Synset. The Partition and Document classes represent the DALOS corpus fragments and documents and both have a datatype property specifying the location where the text can be accessed on-line. These two meta-level ontologies give a low level description of lexical resources and document fragments (Fig. 2).

5.3 Concept Layer

In order to integrate multilingual lexicons and references to documents with the domain ontology on Consumer Protection, a middle layer containing objects of type *Concept* has been implemented. These objects represent language independent concepts, *i.e.* objects representing a unique particular meaning that can be differently expressed in different languages. In a multilingual environment they can be seen as pivot entities that link the corresponding synsets through the *hasLexicalization* property. For this reason Concept objects identifiers (URI)

---

[6] RDF/OWL Representation of WordNet, http://www.w3.org/TR/wordnet-rdf/

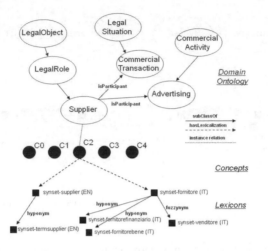

Fig. 3. Extract of the DALOS KB. The "C2" concept is classified in the ontology as a "Supplier" and has two lexicalizations for two different languages.

are language independent as shown in Fig. 3. The integration of lexicons with the domain ontology is then obtained through a classification of the concepts in the ontological classes. Moreover, on the *Concept* class, properties of partial matching like *narrowMatch* and *broaderMatch* are defined in order to implement relations of non perfect equivalence.

5.4   Domain Ontology

The Concept objects act as a sort of middle layer that mediates between linguistic aspects of terms and semantic/conceptual ones. It is then clear how synset resources in this knowledge base show both low level features deriving from their belonging to a lexicon in a specific language and invariant with respect to the domain, and high level feature deriving from their association to a concept object. In fact, when applying the domain ontology, concepts assume new roles and particular properties that are valid only in the Consumer Protection semantic sphere. Thus, for each synset it is possible to list both its linguistic relations, typically WordNet relations, and its semantic relations with other synsets in the same or in a different lexicon. Fig. 3 depicts most of the DALOS knowledge system, from ontology classes to lexical synsets. In this section it has been described how the DALOS knowledge base, a resource including ontologies, multilingual lexicons and documental corpus, has been designed and integrated. See also [11] for a theoretical foundation of heterogeneous knowledge resources integration. Particular attention has been paid to modularity, limiting as much as possible the coupling between lexicons and ontologies through the introduction of *Concept* objects middle layer in order to favour:

– a modular use of the single knowledge components;
– maintenance and evolution;
– knowledge reuse and sharing;
– processability of the ontology by applications;
– collaborative ontology development;
– distributed reuse on the web.

In this view it is then possible for an application or an agent to exploit only the lexicons without applying the ontology and using only lexical properties and interlingual alignments. Otherwise it could be possible to select a single lexicon in order to work in a mono-lingual environment with or without sources. Many kind of applications can benefit of the availability of the described resources, for example an information retrieval system or a legal drafting application. This second case is described in the following section as an implemented prototype of use.

6   The Application Prototype

An application prototype has been developed within the project in order to show how the DALOS resource can be accessed and exploited to provide multilingual lexical and semantic support in legislative documents drafting concerning the "consumer protection" domain.

xmLegesEditor[7] is an open source legislative drafting environment developed at ITTIG-CNR [12] for supporting the adoption of legal national standards (XML and URN NIR[8] standards). Briefly, xmLegesEditor is a visual XML editor able to support legislative drafters in the production of standard compliant normative documents, providing advanced features for structural and semantic markup. The DALOS extension of xmLegesEditor provides integrated access from the drafting environment to the knowledge resource produced in DALOS. Conforming to the modular structure of the knowledge model described in previous section, the application modules for accessing the resources have been designed to be able to selectively exploit the single components of the knowledge base in a dynamic and transparent way. The chosen language in the application for example, determines the lexicon to be loaded. Moreover, dealing with a large (and presumably increasing) amount of data, arises a number of interesting efficiency problems especially in a User Interactive application like an editing environment where response time has a crucial importance.

These have been faced by setting up solutions using:

– precalculation of needed inferences in order to limit to the least necessary runtime reasoning;
– an independent segmentation system for selective loading of data;
– a caching system for dynamically loading and disposing data.

This gave significant result in the application prototype integration in terms of time response and resources use.

---

[7] http://www.xmleges.org
[8] NormeInRete, http://www.normeinrete.it

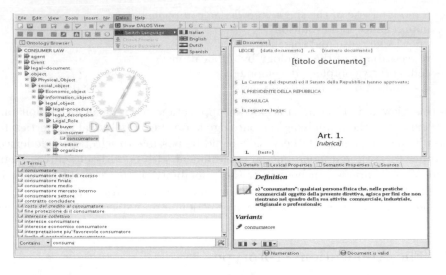

Fig. 4. A screenshot of xmLegesEditor DALOS prototype

6.1   Accessing DALOS Resources within the Application Prototype

Following its multiple components architecture a set of views on the Knowledge Base have been been implemented in the editing environment to provide access to the different resources (Fig. 4). Once the KB in a specific language is loaded in the application, users can access the controlled vocabulary from different perspectives exploiting

- terms classification accessed from a browsable hierarchical view of the ontology;
- direct search of terms in the lexicon from a plain list view from which the user can perform textual queries over the lexical forms of the extracted synsets
- access to detailed information over a synset as well as to hyperlinked external document fragments in the domain corpus where each term, as well as its variants, have been defined or used;
- view and browsing on sets of terms clustered according to their lexical relations (*i.e.* "hyponymy" , "fuzzynymy") or semantic relations *i.e.* relations inherited from the relations between the ontological classes under which each synset is classified (see sect. 5)
- interlingual relations provided by terms alignment for "horizontal" browsing in the multilingual resource

Starting form an initial core of loaded objects, additional information are dynamically loaded as needed following user interaction.

7   Conclusions

The main purpose of the DALOS project is to provide law-makers with linguistic and knowledge management tools to be used in the legislative processes, in particular within the phase of legislative drafting. The aim is to keep control over the legal language, especially in a multilingual environment, as the EU legislation one, enhancing the quality of the legislative production, as well as the accessibility and alignment of legislation at European level through explicit tagging of metainformation expressed in standard machine readable format.

In this paper the DALOS knowledge base design and implementation is presented, including NLP techniques used to create lexicons and their integration with a domain ontology. Finally the use of the DALOS resource in xmLegesEditor legislative drafting environment has been shown, along with facilities aiming at enhancing the quality of legislative texts.

The availability of a document archive marked up with a vocabulary of normalized terms derived by the DALOS resource can also be useful in documents indexing to provide enhanced retrieval services. Moreover, as terms in XML texts will be linked to the ontology, it will be possible to provide more advanced query features exploiting semantics for extracting norms or document fragments using more complex retrieval inferences.

The application prototype (the integrated environment composed by the drafting tool and the knowledge resource) has been tested and evaluated within the project by legislative offices of the Italian Parliament and CNIPA (Italian Minister of Reforms and Innovations in Public Administration / National Center for Information Technology in Public Administration) and by other public administration users in the Netherlands and Spain.

References

1. Mandelkern group on better regulation. final report, Tech. rep., European Commission (November 13, 2001)
2. Bizer, C., Heath, T., Berners-Lee, T.: Linked Data: The story so far. International Journal on Semantic Web & Information Systems 5(3), 1–22 (2009)
3. Biasiotti, M., Francesconi, E., Palmirani, M., Sartor, G., Vitali, F.: Legal informatics and management of legislative documents. Tech. Rep. Working Paper No 2, Global Center for ICT in Parliament (2008)
4. Peristeras, V., Mentzas, G., Tarabanis, K.A., Abecker, A.: Transforming E-government and E-participation through IT 24(5), 14–19 (2009)
5. Dell'Orletta, F., Lenci, A., Marchi, S., Montemagni, S., Pirrelli, V.: Text-2-knowledge: una piattaforma linguistico-computazionale per l'estrazione di conoscenza da testi. In: Proceedings of the SLI-2006 Conference, Vercelli, pp. 20–28 (2006)
6. Sclano, F., Velardi, P.: Termextractor: a web application to learn the shared terminology of emergent web communities. In: Proceedings of the 3rd International Conference on Interoperability for Enterprise Software and Applications, I-ESA 2007 (2007)
7. Cunningham, H., Maynard, D., Bontcheva, K., Tablan, V.: Gate: A framework and graphical development environment for robust nlp tools and applications. In: Proceedings of the 40th Anniversary Meeting of the Association for Computational Linguistics, ACL'02 (2002)

8. Gangemi, A., Sagri, M., Tiscornia, D.: A constructive framework for legal ontologies. In: Benjamins, R., Casanovas, P., Gangemi, A., Selic, B. (eds.) Law and the Semantic Web. Springer, Heidelberg (2005)
9. Gangemi, A., Guarino, N., Masolo, C., Oltramari, A., Schneider, L.: Sweetening ontologies with dolce. In: Gómez-Pérez, A., Benjamins, V.R. (eds.) EKAW 2002. LNCS (LNAI), vol. 2473, p. 166. Springer, Heidelberg (2002)
10. Masolo, C., Vieu, L., Bottazzi, E., Catenacci, C., Ferrario, R., Gangemi, A., Guarino, N.: Social roles and their descriptions. In: Welty, C. (ed.) Proceedings of the Ninth International Conference on the Principles of Knowledge Representation and Reasoning, Whistler (2004)
11. Picca, D., Gliozzo, A., Gangemi, A.: LMM: an OWL-DL metamodel to represent heterogeneous lexical knowledge. In: Proceedings of LREC, Marrakech, Morocco, May 28-30 (2008)
12. Agnoloni, T., Francesconi, E., Spinosa, P.: xmLegesEditor: an opensource visual XML editor for supporting legal national standards. In: Proceedings of the V Legislative XML Workshop, pp. 239–251. European Press Academic Publishing (2007)

Using Gis Tools to Support E_Participation – A Systematic Evaluation

Euripidis Loukis[1], Alexander Xenakis[2], Rob Peters[3], and Yannis Charalabidis[1]

[1] University of the Aegean, Gorgyras Str., Karlovassi 83200, Greece
{eloukis,yannisx}@ aegean.gr
[2] Panteion University, Syggrou Avenue 136, Athens 17672, Greece
a.xenakis@panteion.gr
[3] Zenc BV, Alexanderstraat 18, Den Haag 2514 JM, Netherlands
rob.peters@zenc.nl

Abstract. In this paper a systematic evaluation is presented of an e-participation platform based on GIS tools. The evaluation methodology is founded on the Technology Acceptance Model (TAM), which has been elaborated and adapted to this particular type of IS, taking into account the particular objectives and capabilities of this platform. Our main evaluation dimensions were usage, ease of use, functional usefulness, political usefulness and importance of discussion topic; each of them has been analyzed into a number of sub-dimensions. Using this methodology five pilot applications of this platform in 'real-life' situations and problems have been evaluated with both quantitative and qualitative techniques. Finally it has been concluded that the use of GIS tools can provide significant value in the area of e–participation, which however depends on a number of context factors, such as citizens' computer literacy and familiarization, trust to the political system, interest of the sponsoring public authorities, appropriate promotion, importance of the topic under discussion and quantity and quality of reference information appended on the digital maps by public authorities.

Keywords: geographical information systems (GIS), e-participation, evaluation, technology acceptance model (TAM).

1 Introduction

A relatively new concept in the area of e-participation is the use of digital maps and geographic information systems (GIS) for supporting and enhancing on-line deliberations, by offering to the participants the capability to upload and access geographically referenced multimedia content concerning various aspects of the topics under discussion, especially with regard to spatial planning, environmental and energy issues [1] – [2]. Though there has been some previous literature concerning the use of GIS in the area of e-participation, which is briefly reviewed later in section 2, there is a lack of systematic evaluations of such efforts, based on sound theoretical

E. Tambouris, A. Macintosh, and O. Glassey (Eds.): ePart 2010, LNCS 6229, pp. 197–210, 2010.

foundations, which would provide more complete and reliable conclusions about the potential of GIS in e-participation and the context factors affecting it.

This paper contributes to filling this research gap by presenting a systematic evaluation of an e-participation platform based on GIS tools, which has been developed as part of the FEED project (www.feed-project.eu) co-financed by the European Commission under its e-Participation Initiative. This project aimed at improving the quality of implementation of European legal acts concerning energy and environment by enabling enhanced maps/GIS-based interaction between regional/local government and citizens. For achieving these objectives an advanced e-participation platform was developed, which allows citizens and government organizations to share quickly and easily multimedia content they have generated themselves (e.g. a picture or video produced even through a simple mobile phone, which shows a problem or documents an opinion/position concerning in a particular geographical location or area) through a map interface [1] – [2]. Every user of this platform (citizen or public organization) can upload multimedia documents on the topic under discussion and associate it with a particular geographical location or area, and also search (using the digital map or/and the semantic annotation of all documents) for relevant content provided by other citizens or public administrations. Beyond this powerful interaction mechanism, the platform offers additional interaction capabilities through forum and petition functionalities. These capabilities were expected to result in a significant improvement of the quantity and quality of interaction among citizens, and also with public administrations, concerning the formulation of public policies and decisions.

In the following sections we present the evaluation of five 'real-life' pilot applications of this platform in five quite different national contexts (Greece, Czech Republic, Slovakia, UK and Netherlands) as part of the FEED project. In section 2 we provide a brief review of previous literature on the use of GIS for supporting public participation, while in section 3 we describe the evaluation methodology. Section 4 presents the main results from the evaluation of each pilot application, while in section 5 results are discussed and final conclusions are drawn.

2 Background

In the pertinent literature it has been recognized that GIS have a great potential in the area of e-participation for supporting resolution of conflict among stakeholders concerning various public policies, and assisting in reaching decisions that are acceptable to the majority of them, through consensus-building approaches based on awareness of the spatial dimensions and implications of problems (e.g. [3]). GIS can present maps with different layers and also perform various spatial analyses based on them. However, it has been argued that GIS technology itself is highly complex, so it can be effectively used mainly by specialists. In [4] it is argued that an integration of maps and multi-criteria decision making tools through data visualization can improve the understanding of decision situations, and lead to better outcomes of the decision making process; the authors propose to achieve such integration through an interactive and dynamic visualization of criteria and decision spaces. Nonetheless, it is noted that we need to approach GIS as a socially constructed technology, including not just hardware and software but also practice, laws, organizational arrangements, and knowledge which are necessary for its use [5].

Public Participatory Geographical Information Systems (PP GIS) is a research area that focuses on the exploitation of GIS by the general public supporting their participation in government decision-making processes. Its main objective is to expand the use of GIS to the general public and non-governmental organizations that are not usually represented in traditional top-down GIS projects [6], [7]. In recent years, applications supporting Public Participatory GIS increasingly use the Internet as a platform for communication and dissemination of information [8]. These applications range from Internet-based spatial multimedia systems to conventional field-based participatory development methods with a modest GIS component. However, there is a lack of systematic evaluations of such Public Participatory GIS, based on sound theoretical foundations. The abovementioned FEED platform is an example of such a Public Participatory GIS, and in the following sections we are describing the systematic evaluation of it, contributing to filling this research gap.

3 Evaluation Methodology

For evaluating the five pilot applications of this advanced e-participation platform a methodology was formulated based on the Technology Acceptance Model (TAM), which provides a mature and well established framework for evaluating IS [9] – [13]. Therefore our main evaluation dimensions were usage, ease of use and usefulness. Each of them was further elaborated and adapted to the objectives, capabilities and specificities of this platform. In particular:

I) The usage of the platform was evaluated by assessing the extent of using it for getting information on the topic under discussion and for contributing postings about it in the forum.

II) The ease of use was evaluated by assessing how easy it was for the users to use the platform in general and also its the main capabilities: to search for and find information using the map, to access the postings of the other users or add a new posting.

III) The usefulness dimension, taking into account that a user of such a platform has both functional objectives (e.g. read information and postings on the topic under discussion, and enter his/her own contributions) and political objectives (influence decisions and public policies on the topic under discussion), was divided into sub-dimensions: the 'functional usefulness' and the 'political usefulness'. The former was evaluated by assessing to what extend the users find that the map interface and the information uploaded on it enabled them to get better informed on the topic under discussion and to contribute more informed postings in the forum discussion, and also to what extend the forum postings of others increased their knowledge on the discussion topic. The latter was evaluated by assessing what level of e-participation the users believe that was achieved (using the classification proposed by OECD [14] – [15]): one-dimensional information provision from government to citizens, consultation with citizens (aiming at simply collecting their opinions), engagement (meant as consultation affecting government decisions) and citizens' empowering), and whether they believe that the visions and ideas they entered in the forum will be further considered by the government, and also their general satisfaction. Furthermore, taking into account that the value for the citizens of the e-consultations conducted through the platform depends also on the importance of the discussion topics, we used it as an additional evaluation sub-dimension. It was evaluated by assessing how important the users find the topics of the electronic discussions, and also to what extent they attract the users to use the platform again in the future.

Each of the above evaluation dimensions was assessed using both quantitative and qualitative techniques. The quantitative evaluation involved the distribution of questionnaires to the users of the platform in the each of the five different pilots deployed. The questionnaire included an initial section with questions concerning respondent's demographic data (concerning age, sex and education), followed by four sections corresponding to the above evaluation dimensions (usage, ease of use, functional and political usefulness and discussion topics). We received an average of 40 filled questionnaires per pilot, with exception of the Dutch pilot, for which a different evaluation approach was adopted, as explained below.

Additionally the responsible partner for each pilot organized a qualitative in-depth discussion in a small focus group of 4-5 persons (participants in the e-consultation and employees of the corresponding sponsoring public organization). The objective of these discussions was to understand in more depth than through the questionnaire what these persons see as main strengths weaknesses of the platform with respect to ease of use and usefulness. The main topics of these in-depth discussions were:

- Ease of use (what is the general impression of these persons concerning the ease-of-use of the platform, what functionalities they found easy-to-use, and what functionalities they found difficult-to-use, etc.).
- Functional usefulness (how useful they find the platform for getting information about the topic under discussion, for discussing about with other people and government, for learning new things from them, or other benefits it offers).
- Political usefulness (what the level of influence they believe can be achieved on government decisions about the topic under discussion).
- Importance of the topic under discussion

The structure of the evaluation methodology is summarised below in Table 1.

Table 1. Structure of the evaluation methodology

	Demo-graphics	Usage	Ease of Use	Functional Usefulness	Political Usefulness	Topics Importance
Quantitative	+	+	+	+	+	+
Qualitative			+	+	+	+

Especially for the Dutch pilot application, which, as described in more detailed in 4.5 was the most sophisticated one and concerned some complex, critical and highly controversial decisions about the future of the Amsterdam region (associated with the development or not of new infrastructure and houses in a formerly 'green' area in Jmeer/Markermeer), a different and more detailed evaluation approach was adopted. In particular, all the capabilities of the platform (including both functionality and data) were presented in detail to 21 representatives of the main conflicting stakeholders (e.g. chambers of commerce, national government, regional government, building companies, non-government organizations, local community activist organisations), both the ones in favour and the ones against these new developments, who were then asked to evaluate through a questionnaire several usefulness and effectiveness related aspects of the platform. For this particular pilot we performed a more detailed analysis of the usefulness and effectiveness evaluation dimensions into several sub-dimensions, which reflect the particular characteristics of this situation and objectives of this pilot. These 'high-level' representatives of stakeholders had a very limited experience of using the platform themselves, so it was meaningless to ask them to evaluate its ease-of-use; at the same time the discussion topic was definitely of high importance, so there was no reason for asking these persons to evaluate its importance. For these reasons we decided to focus the evaluation of this pilot on a wide range of usefulness/effectiveness-related aspects of the platform.

In particular, these stakeholders were asked after the detailed presentation of the platform to assess initially through a questionnaire, and then in an in-depth qualitative discussion, to what extent it can assist them in the following basic aspects:

- keep track of the complex discussions taking place on these critical issues/questions,
- inform their constituency (i.e. the citizens they represent),
- understand relevant legislation and legal constraints,
- have more transparency in decision making,
- express and support the arguments of the stakeholder groups they represent,
- influence decision making,
- achieve consensus among conflicting groups and reduce the risk of ending up in a legal court,
- and finally have a better spatial planning process.

4 Evaluation Results

This section outlines the main results of platform evaluation in five pilot applications of it in 'real-life' situations and problems in five quite different national contexts (Greece, Czech Republic, Slovakia, UK and Netherlands), which were conducted as part of the FEED project.

4.1 The Greek Pilot Application

The Greek pilot application took place in the Municipality of Ano Liossia, which is a suburb in the north-western part of Athens, with a population of 26,500. The area has grown rapidly over the last 20 years. Its main problem is that it hosts the largest rubbish dump of Greece, which is currently serving about 4.5 million citizens of the greater Athens area, and is considered a severe danger for the environment and the public health. A considerable proportion of its citizens have low income, education and computer literacy.

The pilot included a public deliberation process supported by the platform about three important topics for Ano Liossia: a)The City Development Plan, which constitutes the main proposal of the local Municipality for the development of the area in the next five years; among others, it refers to urban planning, use of renewable energy sources and environmental protection. b)The Municipal City Park, which is being planned and discussed for almost a decade, however without any specific action taken up yet; it is a highly debated issue, as far as its place, size and specifications are concerned, having raised a number of disputes between citizens, local administration and central government. c)The future of this rubbish dump: for many years the local Municipalities along with the citizens demand the closure of it, and the construction of many smaller ones in several locations the greater Athens area, but no final decision has been made.

This pilot attracted mainly a young and educated part of this community, who used extensively the platform both for searching for and getting information and for posting opinions. However, the low computer literacy and educational level of this area and the fact that such a platform was a big innovation for this place were the main obstacles to the use of the platform by wider stakeholder groups. From an ease of use viewpoint, most of the respondents found the platform in general 'moderately easy' (52%) (and only 22% 'very easy', while another 22% found it 'not that easy'); with respect to its particular capabilities most (74%) found the forum 'very easy', while for the maps modules things are less clear: 50% found it 'moderately easy' and another 50% 'very easy'. Concerning the functional usefulness, most of the respondents find that the maps modules helped them 'to a considerable extent' to get informed on the topics under discussion (48%), to make better and more informed contributions to the forum discussion (59%) and to learn new things on the topics under discussion from the postings of the others (55%). As to the political usefulness, the majority believe that the outcome of this e-discussion will be higher than just getting informed: 34% believe that a 'consultation' level (provision of citizens' opinions to the local Municipality), and another 33% an 'engagement' level (serious impact on municipality decisions) has been achieved, however only 15% believe that the particular visions and ideas they expressed in the forum discussion will be further considered. Finally the quantitative analysis provides evidence that most respondents found the discussion topics very important (67%), and would be interested to return to use the platform in the future (96%). In total, the respondents are satisfied with this e-participation pilot (56% are 'satisfied' and 22% 'very satisfied').

The main conclusions of the qualitative discussion were that the system provided a good support to users through the provision of geographically and well organized content concerning important local Municipality decisions. However, it was mentioned that this pilot e-consultation based on such an advanced platform attracted mainly highly educated young citizens of this area, and to a much lower extent citizens of older ages and lower education and computer literacy, who are high important stakeholder groups, so their voice should be 'heard' by the local authorities. It was added that although there were efforts to promote the use of the platform, the main stakeholder groups were reluctant to adopt it, being quite sceptical towards the adoption of a new means of consultation: many did not believe that changing the means of debating the issue would lead to higher citizen empowerment and political influence. From the politicians' side it was noted that they did not believe in the platform very much as a decision making tool, but rather as a tool to understand voters' intentions towards the issues under discussion, especially before election time.

Therefore we can identify a number of context factors which had a negative impact on this pilot: low computer literacy and familiarization, and also low trust to the local political system and low interest of the sponsoring local public authorities (Municipality of Ano Liossia).

4.2 The Czech Pilot Application

The Czech pilot application took place in the city of Brno and the towns of Kunstat and Letovice, and included electronic public deliberations on planned waste management infrastructures in this area. Because this topic was of interest mainly for people with high awareness on cnvironmental issues, but of low interest for the 'general public' of this area (especially in a time of severe economic crisis), initially there were only few registrations; so it was necessary to organize many promotional campaigns, including e-mails to the registered users of a famous local environmental portal, which turned out to be successful. Finally this pilot attracted a satisfactory number young citizens, but of various educational levels, who used the platform extensively for searching for and getting information, and less for posting opinions. Concerning the ease of use, most of the respondents find 'very easy' both the platform in general (68%), and its main modules, the forum (66%) and the maps modules (61%). With respect to the functional usefulness, most of the respondents find that the maps modules helped them 'to a large extent' (34%) to get informed on the topics under discussion, to make better and more informed contributions to the forum discussion (37%) and to learn new things from the postings of others (46%), while another 27%, 24% and 22% respectively assess the assistance provided as 'considerable'. Also, as to political usefulness the majority believe that the outcome of this e-discussion will be higher than just getting better informed: 32% believe that a 'consultation' level is achieved (provision of citizens opinions to the local Municipalities), while 36% expect an 'engagement' level (serious impact on Municipalities decisions), though only 37% believe that the particular visions and ideas they expressed in the forum discussion will be further considered. Most of the respondents (however belonging to citizens registered in environmental portals, having thus high awareness in environmental issues) find the discussion topics 'very important' (67%). In total, there is a high satisfaction of citizen participants by the experience of using the platform (47% are 'satisfied' and another 17% 'highly satisfied'), and most of them (71%) would come back to use it in the future.

In the qualitative in-depth discussion that took place after the end of this pilot some interesting remarks were made concerning strengths and weaknesses of the platform. In particular, with respect to the ease of use of the platform the following strengths were identified:

- theme selection supported by GIS functionality is quite useful; also, it is possible to use GIS functionality, such as zoom, selection of area, etc., and this can be potentially improved by adding more GIS functionalities, such as overlapping, distances, etc.,
- content is available at the right place, it is at our disposal in a 'natural' way on the map, so it is not necessary to look for the content on various places,
- if offers the advantage of content classification, which makes the resulting conclusions from the it more clear and comprehensive,

- advanced capabilities for setting access rights and moderation; also, it is possible to protect the portal against direct attack and spam attack,

Also, at the same time the following weaknesses were mentioned:

-    localization problems: every application, which is localized from another initial language, tends to bring some features not common in the new language; also, some language relations are not reflected naturally,

- the need for users registration: this is a problem, since in the Czech Republic it is very often not to trust the official authorities.

With respect to the usefulness the following strengths were identified:

-   capability to share ideas among various levels of users, so it is possible that expert users can exchange opinions and ideas with non-specialist,

- capability to clearly see the geographical reference of topics and their context; the geographical connection of many important topics is not evident, but using digital maps this can be easily achieved,

- creation and sharing of content according to web 2.0 principles. Only the web 2.0 principles (numerous users create one extensive content) are capable of content creation in the desired quantity,

- the whole deliberation process on a particular public policy or decision is well documented and stored on digital media with all necessary information (documents provided by government organizations and citizens, and for each of them time, source, author, etc.); this makes it easy to create a well documented summary for decisions support (especially the help of content classification).

Also, at the same time the following weaknesses were mentioned:

- low quantity and quality of 'initial' reference content provided by government organizations can result in low interest and limited participation of citizens, since the success of this platform critically dependent on the content appended on the maps; only if the maps are interesting, and the documents appended on them are complete and updated, the portal can become interesting to the citizens,

- starting the discussion can be difficult, since it requires having at least a 'critical mass' of participants and uploaded content (such a platform is characterized by strong ''network effects': more participants and uploaded content make it more attractive for additional citizens to participate and upload more content); for this reason many promotional campaigns were required in order to have a sufficient number of participants.

- also the complexity of the topics discussed can restricted the interest and participation of the public; the experts, on the other hand, usually have other actual channels of expression of their opinions, so the interest usually does not come from this target group, at least in the desired quantity.

By combining the findings of the quantitative and the qualitative analysis, we can identify a number of a number of context factors which had a negative impact on this pilot: the low level of computer usage skills in this area in most age groups with the exception of the youth (taking into account that historically there has been a lower level of computer usage skills in the Eastern European countries, this was an obstacle in attracting older age groups); the topic of the discussion, which was not of high interest to the general public (especially in a time of severe economic crisis); also, the fact that young citizens still do not feel politically empowered, as they declare that they do not know if the views they expressed in the forum discussions will be further considered. On the contrary the extensive promotional activities conducted by the organizers of this pilot, using appropriate channels (sending e-mails to the registered users of a famous local environmental portals), had a positive impact on this pilot.

4.3   The UK Pilot Application

The UK pilot application was implemented in the city of Blackburn and Darwen, which is located in the Northern Counties of England, covering an administrative area of 137Km² and having a population of 137,470 persons. It was part of a wider consultation effort launched by the Unitary Authority of Blackburn with Darwen in 2009 in order to help shaping the future of this area. The central theme of this consultation, called Vision 2030, is how residents see this area now as well how they see it developing in the future. Its main questions are: i) Do you hope the borough will be centre of educational excellence with a world renowned university?, ii) Do you want it to be a hub of cutting edge businesses?, iii) Would you like it be viewed as the garden of the North West with award winning green spaces?, iv) Should our musical talent or food become famous nationwide? So this pilot included electronic public deliberations between citizens of this area about its future, both in general and on particular geographically referenced ideas and plans.

It should be noted that in this pilot the participants' group was more balanced from the age and education level perspective: we did not have predominantly young citizens, as in the pilots described in 5.1 and 5.2, but significant participants' percentages from various age groups (e.g. 35% were between 31 and 40 years old, 29% between 41 and 50 years old and 13% between 51 and 60 years old), and also from various educational levels (e.g. 45% had a university degree, while 34% had high school education). This reflects the high penetration of computers and Internet in various age and education level groups in UK. Concerning the ease of use most of the respondents found the platform in general 'very easy' (57%), while with respect to its particular modules most found the maps modules 'moderately easy' (52%) and the forum very easy (49%). With respect to functional usefulness things are not so clear: the respondents believe that they have been benefited more from the postings of the other participants in the forum than from the map and the information appended on it. In particular, 50% of the respondents believe that the map and the information appended on it helped them to a 'considerable extent' (29%) or 'large extent' (21%) to get informed on the topic under discussion, while the remaining 50% can see only limited or no help at all. Similarly, 46% of the respondents believe that the map and the information appended on it helped them to a 'considerable extent' (28%) or to a 'large extent' (18%) to make better and more informed posting in the forum, while the remaining 54% can see only limited or no help at all. However, 60% believe that the postings of the other participants helped them to learn new things on the topic under discussion to a 'considerable extent' (60%) or to a 'large extent' (20%). The political usefulness was higher in comparison with the other pilots: it should be noted that 63% believe that their visions and ideas expressed in the forum will be further considered by the local government (and the remaining 37% respond that they 'do not know', while nobody responds negatively), reflecting a higher level of trust to the local political system. With respect to the discussion topics most find them 'rather important' (50%), which is understandable, since the future visions under discussion will not affect their everyday lives in the short term, though one third (23%) find them 'very important'. In general, the respondents feel high level of satisfaction with this e-participation pilot, most of them being 'satisfied' (72%) and the remaining 'highly satisfied' (28%).

In the qualitative evaluation of the UK pilot the main points raised were that the platform and most of its modules were easy to use, though there were a few weak points identified with regard to navigation (e.g. were missing features for returning to the platform's start page, or for navigating through the different modules). The use of the forum in particular was found exceptionally easy for participating in the discussions held. However, it was remarked that the material initially appended on the map by the local authority was limited, and probably because of this citizens did not upload much their own documents (e.g. pictures, texts, etc.) either, and preferred mainly to enter posting sin the forum. This is compliant with the abovementioned result of the quantitative evaluation that citizens have been benefited more from the postings of the others in the forum than from the map and the information appended on it.

Based on the findings of the above quantitative and qualitative analyses we can identify two context factors which had a positive impact on this pilot: the high penetration of computers and Internet in various age and education level groups in UK (and not only in the young and educated citizens) and the higher trust to the local political system. Also, we can identify one factor which had a negative impact on the pilot: the limited material initially appended on the map by the local authority, which probably resulted in a reduced interest of the participants to upload their own content on it, who finally preferred to use the 'standard' and quite familiar to them forum functionalities, rather than the more advanced and innovative digital maps functionalities.

4.4 The Cross-Border Pilot Application

Also, a cross-border pilot was organized in cooperation between the Ministries of Environment of Czech Republic and Slovakia, taking advantage of the extensive collaboration between them after the split of Czechoslovakia in 1993. Both Ministries of the Environment are intensively working on the implementation of Framework Directive EU 2008/98/EC on waste management in order to develop their national legislation on this critical issue. For these reasons it was decided the main topic of this cross-country deliberation to be about waste management; also, it was decided to focus on the waste prevention, which is a key factor in any waste management strategy. Waste prevention is closely associated with improving manufacturing methods and influencing consumers to demand greener products and less packaging. In particular, this pilot included electronic discussions among young students who participated in the ENERSOL Conference about energy and environment.

The participants of this pilot were mainly young (56% of them were 21 and 30 years old) and of high educational level (55% were university degree holders and 17% postgraduate degree holders). With respect to ease of use they find 'very easy' the platform in general (83%), and also its main modules, the map module (78%) and the forum (78%). As to the functional usefulness they believe that the map and the information appended on it helped them (50% 'to a large extent' and 39% 'to a considerable extent') to get better informed on the topic under discussion and to make better and more informed postings about it in the forum. Also, they perceive high levels of <u>political usefulness</u>: most of the respondents (72%) believe that an 'engagement' level of e-participation has been achieved (characterised by serious impact on decisions), while 61% of them believe that the particular visions and ideas they expressed in the forum discussion will be further considered. Also, most of them (83%) find the <u>discussion topics</u> 'very important'. There was a high level of satisfaction in general from the use of the platform (45% were 'satisfied' and 44% 'highly satisfied'). A common qualitative evaluation was conducted for this cross-border pilot and for the Czech pilot, as their user groups had several common citizens, so the remarks mentioned in 5.2 are valid for this pilot as well.

The conclusions drawn from the evaluation of these cross-border pilots were by far the most positive of all pilots. We can identify two main context factors which had a positive impact on this pilot: the high educational level and computer skills of the participants, and also their high interest in the discussion topics.

4.5   The Dutch Pilot Application

In the Dutch pilot the platform was used as an electronic support and facilitation in an already existing highly confrontational debate in Jmeer/Markermeer (located in the wider Amsterdam area) about the installation or not of 60.000 new houses, road-infrastructure, bridges and support structure in a "green" area. This is a really difficult decision that local authorities have to make: on one hand it is necessary to expand the city of Amsterdam, and this area is the best alternative for this; however, on the other hand in this area there is a unique sweet water lake with European importance, protected by European directives on water management and Natura 2000 regimes. This pilot allowed us to investigate some important aspects of platform's usefulness for supporting and facilitating negotiations and consensus building on complex, critical and highly controversial government decisions and policies. As mentioned in section 5 the evaluation of this pilot focused on the political usefulness dimension, and was based on the responses of 21 representatives of the main conflicting stakeholders (e.g. chambers of commerce, national government, regional government, building companies, non-government organizations, local community activist organisations) in a questionnaire distributed to them, after having attended a detailed presentation of the platform. From the analysis of these responses the following quite interesting conclusions were drawn of the support this platform can provide in the main tasks of the decision making process:

- 88% of the respondents believe that the platform makes it 'easier', and another 6% 'much easier', to keep track of relevant discussions; so 92% in total perceive that it can support stakeholders in keeping track of the lengthy, complex and multi-participant discussions on such spatial planning issues,

- 68% of the respondents find that the platform makes it 'easier', and another 13% 'much easier', to depict the complexity and interconnection of issues; so 81% in total perceive that it supports a better presentation, visualization and communication of the complex and highly interconnected issues and questions that spatial planning poses,

- 57% believe that the platform makes it 'easier' to inform constituents (and all affected citizens in general) on the various issues and questions,

- 67% believe that the platform 'makes clearer' the various legal constraints,

- 50% perceive that the platform improves 'to some extent', and 6% 'to a large extent', the transparency of the decision making processes; so 56% in total believe that such a system can have a positive impact on the transparency in this sensitive and multi-stakeholder area of spatial planning, which is critical democratic principle,

- and finally 62% believe that this platform can help them to represent and support better their interests.

In the qualitative discussion the above participants agreed that the presentation of legal constraints, development plans, and also stakeholders' proposals, ideas and visions of the various on digital maps can be very useful in such 'difficult' situations of complex, critical, multi-stakeholder and highly controversial decisions. Most participants maintained the position that decision making is however something much more complex than the information provision and communication enabled by this platform; so they did not think that the platform would solve the real decision dilemmas and conflict of interests. They did agree that more information provision, communication and transparency were relevant for a good result of the deliberation outcome.

5 Discussion and Conclusions

In the previous sections of this paper we have presented a systematic evaluation of an advanced e-participation platform based on digital maps and GIS tools, which was conducted through five pilot applications of it in five quite different national contexts (Greece, Czech Republic, Slovakia, UK and Netherlands) as part of the FEED project. The evaluation methodology was founded on the TAM, which was elaborated and adapted to the particular characteristics, capabilities and objectives of this platform; our main evaluation dimensions were usage, ease of use, functional usefulness, political usefulness and importance of discussion topic, which were assessed using both quantitative and qualitative techniques.

With respect to ease of use, the platform has been assessed in all pilots (with the only exception of the Dutch pilot, in which ease of use was not assessed, for the reasons explained in section 4) as very easy or moderately easy. This indicates that though GIS tools, as mentioned in section 2, initially were tools for specialists, if we design appropriately their functionality and user-interfaces they can be used by the general public as well (at least by citizens with sufficient general education and computer skills) as tools for a better e-participation, especially on geographically referenced issues. Also, the platform was found in all pilots to have high or considerable functional usefulness (again with the only exception of Dutch pilot, in which we focused on the political usefulness), as it enables the users to get better informed on the topic under discussion by accessing geographically organized information on digital maps, to upload on the map and in this way communicate effectively their own information, ideas and suggestions, and also to participate in electronic discussions. However, in three of the pilots (Greek, Czech and Cross-border) the political usefulness perceived by the users was lower, as most users do not think that the ideas and visions they expressed in the forum discussions will be further considered by the local authorities; this seems to reflect a low level of trust to the local political system, which can be an important obstacle to e-participation and all forms of public participation in general. However, in total citizen participants were satisfied by the experience of using the platform, and most of them would come back to use it in the future.

Finally, the most sophisticated Dutch pilot allowed us to investigate some important aspects of its political usefulness for supporting and facilitating negotiations and consensus building with respect to complex and highly controversial government decisions and policies. In particular, it was found that the platform enables a better presentation, visualization and communication of the complex and highly interconnected issues and questions that spatial planning poses, and assists stakeholders in keeping track of lengthy, complex and multi-participant discussions on spatial planning issues; at the same time it allows representatives of the various stakeholders to inform better their constituents and to represent and support better their interests. Also, such a platform makes more clear the various complex and very often overlapping legal constraints that exist in spatial planning, and contributes to higher transparency of the whole decision making processes.

In general, the use of digital maps and GIS tools seems to provide a well accepted and useful additional feature to the e-consultation process; the combination of digital maps/GIS with forum tools was proven to be both usable by the general public, requiring a reasonable and acceptable amount of effort, and also useful. The use of maps to pinpoint relevant data seems to be a well accepted practice by citizen users in order to broaden their understanding of complex local problems and spatial suggestions. Therefore we can definitely conclude that such an advanced platform can provide significant value in the area of e-participation, which however depends on some factors of the context in which it is used, such as computer literacy and familiarization, trust to the political system, interest of the sponsoring public authorities, importance of the topic under discussion and quality of reference information appended on the maps by public authorities.

References

1. Loukis, E., Peters, R., Charalabidis, Y., Passas, S., Tsitsanis, T.: Using e-Maps and Semantic Annotation for Improving Citizens' and Administrations' Interaction. In: Proceedings of the European and Mediterranean Conference on Information Systems 2009 (2009)
2. Loukis, E., Peters, R., Charalabidis, Y., Passas, S., Howe, C.: Enhancing Deliberation for the Formulation and Application of Public Policy on the Environment and Energy Using Federated Content, Ontologies and Maps. In: Proceedings of the First International Conference on e-Participation (2009)
3. Carver, S.: Participation and Geographical Information: a position paper. In: Proceedings of ESF-NSF Workshop on Access to Geographic Information and Participatory Approaches Using Geographic Information (2001)
4. Jankowski, P., Andrienko, N., Andrienko, G.L.: Map-Centered Exploratory Approach to Multiple Criteria Spatial Decision Making. International Journal of Geographical Information Science 15(2), 101–127 (2002)
5. Innes, J.E., Simpson, D.M.: Implementing GIS for Planning. Journal of the American Planning Association 59(2), 230–236 (2002)

6. Talen, E.: Bottom-Up GIS: A New Tool for Individual and Group Expression in Participatory Planning. Journal of the American Planning Association 66(3), 279–294 (2000)
7. Ghose, R., Elwood, S.: Public Participation GIS and Local Political Context: Propositions and Research Directions. URISA Journal Special Issue on Access and Participatory Issues 15(2), 17–24 (2003)
8. Kingston, R.: Web Based PP GIS in the United Kingdom. In: Craig, et al. (eds.) Community Participation and Geographic Information Systems, pp. 101–112. Taylor & Francis, Abington (2002)
9. Davis, F.D.: A Technology Acceptance Model for Empirically Testing New End-User - Information Systems: Theory and Results, Cambridge. MIT Sloan School of Management, MA (1986)
10. Davis, F.D., Bagozzi, R.P., Warshaw, P.R.: User Acceptance of Computer Technology: A Comparison of Two Theoretical Models. Management Sciences 35(8), 982–1002 (1989)
11. Davis, F.D.: Perceived Usefulness, Perceived Ease of Use, and User Acceptance of Information Technology. MIS Quarterly 13(3), 319–339 (1989)
12. Schepers, J., Wetzels, M.: A meta-analysis of the technology acceptance model: Investigating subjective norm and moderation effects. Information & Management 44(1), 90–103 (2007)
13. Holden, R.J., Karsh, B.T.: The Technology Acceptance Model: Its past and its future in health care. Journal of Biomedical Informatics 43(1), 159–172 (2010)
14. Organization for Economic Co-operation & Development (OECD): Engaging Citizens Online for Better Policy-making. Policy Brief, Paris, France (2003)
15. Organization for Economic Co-operation & Development (OECD): Promise and Problems of e-Democracy: Challenges of Online Citizen Engagement. Paris, France (2004)

Do Voting Advice Applications Have an Effect on Electoral Participation and Voter Turnout? Evidence from the 2007 Swiss Federal Elections

Andreas Ladner and Joëlle Pianzola

Institutional Policies, IDHEAP Lausanne, Route de la Maladière 21, 1022
Chavannes-près-Renens
andreas.ladner@idheap.unil.ch, pianzola@nccr-democracy.uzh.ch

Abstract. Voting Advice Applications (VAAs) render a valuable platform for tackling one of democracy's central challenges: low voter turnout. Studies indicate that lack of information and cost-benefit considerations cause voters to abstain from voting. VAAs are online voting assistance tools which match own political preferences with those of candidates and parties in elections. By assisting voters in their decision-making process prior to casting their votes, VAAs not only rebut rational choice reasoning against voting but also narrow existing information gaps. In this paper we examine the impact of VAAs on participation and voter turnout. Specifically, we present results on how the Swiss VAA *smartvote* affected voter turnout in the 2007 federal elections. Our analyses suggest that *smartvote* does have a mobilizing capacity, especially among young voters who are usually underrepresented at polls. Moreover, the study demonstrates how VAAs such as *smartvote* do affect citizen's propensity to deal with politics in general.

Keywords: e-democracy, voter turnout, electoral participation, Voting Advice Applications (VAAs).

1 Introduction

Low voter turnout is a familiar phenomenon in most advanced democracies. Switzerland, in particular, is among those countries that finish last on the voter turnout ranking list. Since 1975, electoral participation has never been higher than 50 percent.[1] The reasons for low voter turnout are often attributed to indifference, disenchantment or even approval towards current politics, but empirical research has not yet been able to find consensus on the matter. Scholars are divided on the reasons for decline of voter turnout and speculate on approaches to enhance participation. Disagreement even exists on whether low voter turnout is in fact a problem for democracy (e.g. [1]) or simply a systemic side effect (e.g. [2]). In the end, most scholars do, however, agree that low political participation does counteract those

---

[1] http://www.bfs.admin.ch/bfs/portal/de/index/themen/17/02/
blank/key/national_rat/wahlbeteiligung.html

E. Tambouris, A. Macintosh, and O. Glassey (Eds.): ePart 2010, LNCS 6229, pp. 211–224, 2010.

concepts of democracy which have inclusive participation among their funding normative principals.

Switzerland does not only deal with low levels of political participation, it has also been identified among those countries with low levels of political knowledge among its citizens, especially among the young [3]. That lack of participation in the democratic process and lack of knowledge and interest in politics is not necessarily favorable for democracy goes without saying. Dalton [4] underlines this argument with paraphrasing Thomas Jefferson who stressed that a well-informed electorate is the most important constraint on government. Thus, from a normative perspective, it can be argued that an informed electorate matters for reasoned vote choices and accordingly for the quality of representation. Empirically, it has been indicated that non-voters tend to have less information about politics than voters [5]. Hence, higher voter turnout could be achieved by raising information and interest. But how can this be achieved? One step might be to bring the electoral process closer to the citizens and motivate them to engage in it. As this paper will stress, one potential answer to this challenge could lie within the use of new internet tools which help citizens to gather information and support them in their decision making process during elections.

The coming of age of modern communication technologies not only immersed itself into our daily lives, it also gave leeway to modernize the process of casting ballots. The implementation of remote electronic voting (e-voting) was hoped to boost electoral participation, especially among the young. But these high hopes have so far not been met by reality. First of all, the introduction of e-voting systems has been limited to a few countries, since implementation difficulties have been greater than expected. Second, those countries that did implement e-voting procedures did not experience significant higher voter turnout ([6], [7], [8]). The following reasons serve as an explanation for this: First, the so called "preaching to the converted"- effect. In other words, the introduction of e-voting only reached those voters who were already interested in politics and would have gone to the polls anyway [9]. Second, e-voting was supposed to minimize voting efforts and hence attract those who, according to rational choice theory, do not vote because the cost-benefit ratio of voting does not pay off [10]. It is questionable which part of the voting process causes voters to invest time and might therefore restrain them from voting. It seems that e-voting does not necessarily reduce costs to voters in comparison to the traditional act of voting. This holds especially true in countries where postal voting is the standard, such as Switzerland [11]. Or as Norris [6] puts it, "the simple Victorian postage stamp beats the high-tech microchip hands down". It can be assumed that the *process of decision-making* prior to casting the vote is much more time consuming and costly than the actual act of voting. To gather information about politics, candidates and parties and their respective programs, evaluate and discuss the different policy stances is what asks for time investment. The so-called "pre-voting sphere" (process of gathering information and opinion formation before the election day) should therefore not be neglected when assessing the effects of e-democracy on voter turnout [12]. Research efforts on this matter, however, have so far been scarce.

Voting Advice Applications (VAAs) are such e-democracy tools which aim to assist voters in their decision-making process. VAAs have become astonishingly popular in a large number of advanced democracies in recent years. For example, the

Dutch *Stemwijzer* was used by 40% of the Dutch electorate in 2006 and the German *Wahl-o-Mat* has attracted more than 10 million users since its introduction in 2002 [13].[2] In order to gain more empirical insight on the effects of these tools on electoral participation, a particular VAA and its impact will be examined. This paper will focus on *smartvote* (www.smartvote.ch), a well-established Swiss VAA which helps voters to select candidates and parties on the basis of their own political values and preferences. Since *smartvote* is meant to support voters in their decision-making process, the question is whether the VAA can serve as a means of increasing interest in politics in general, support voters in gathering information and eventually affect participation and voter turnout.

The paper is organised as follows: first, theoretical considerations and evidence from other countries with regard to VAAs are discussed. Second, *smartvote* and its users are introduced. Third, results on its effect on participation and voter turnout in the 2007 Swiss federal elections are presented. And last, results will be discussed with an outlook on future research opportunities.

2   Theoretical Considerations and Evidence from Other Countries

Can VAAs such as *smartvote* motivate citizens to cast their vote? Do they increase interest in politics and consequently affect electoral participation? Before getting to the bottom of these questions, it is helpful to dissect why citizens abstain from voting. For the case of Switzerland, Bühlmann et al. [14] compiled six different types of non-voters based on a post-electoral survey of the 1999 Swiss federal elections: the uninterested citizens (33%), the alienated citizens (7%), the social isolated citizens (10%), the incompetent citizens (14%), the protesting citizens (17%) and the alternatively participating citizens (19%).

Fivaz [15] sees potential for the following three groups of non-voters to be positively affected by VAAs. First, the uninterested citizen: The uninterested citizen has problems finding a party that fits its preferences. Since VAAs allow voters to match their preferences with parties, such tools could return the uninterested citizen to politics. Second, the social isolated citizen is marked by a low level of income and education as well as low social status resulting in an overall social disintegration. VAAs offer simple access to information and allow comparisons of own opinions to those of the political class, independent of knowledge, social or financial status, and personal network. Hence, they increase the possibilities of bringing socially isolated

---

[2] Further VAAs; in Holland: Stemwijzer (www.stemwijzer.nl), Kieskompas (www.kieskompas.nl); in Germany: Wahl-o-Mat (www.wahlomat.de). Further examples for VAAs are Austria: Wahlkabine (www.wahlkabine.at) and Politikkabine (www.politikkabine.at), in the United Kingdom: Who Do I Vote for? (www.whodoivotefor.co.uk); in the United States: Project vote smart (www.votesmart.org), Glassbooth (www.glassbooth.org) and On the Issues (www.ontheissues.org); in Italy: Openpolis (www.openpolis.it); in Lithuania: Manobalsas (www.manobalsas.lt); in Bulgaria: Koimipasva (www.koimipasva.bg); in Canada: *smartvote* Ottawa (www.smartvoteottawa.ca); for general supra-national level: Political Compass (www.politicalcompass.org) and EU-Profiler (www.euprofiler.eu); and there is a VAA in Iraq as well: Niqash (www.niqash.org).

citizens back into politics. And third, the incompetent citizen, who does not feel competent enough to participate in voting: The main reason for abstinence here is lack of information. VAAs' principal asset is bundling and offering information on politics and policies which are otherwise hard to gather. Again, VAAs might give the incompetent citizen the information needed to re-enter politics. Taken all together, VAAs might be appealing to about half of the citizens who tend to abstain from voting. Although these propositions are highly speculative, there is evidence that VAAs do attract a specific group of voters who are usually underrepresented at elections: the young. Although voter turnout among the young has been steadily increasing over the last years in Switzerland, their relative participation rate is still low [16]. Studies on VAAs in the Netherlands, Finland, Germany and Switzerland conclude that especially the young are prone to use VAAs and that awareness and usage of VAAs is generally highest among the young and the well educated ([17], [18], [19], [20]). Since young citizens tend to be part of non-voters, electronic tools such as VAAs might offer a chance to mobilize its most frequent users into politics.

Further indicators for the mobilization capacities of VAAs are their ability to increase motivation and interest in politics among its users. A study on a German VAA called *Wahl-O-Mat* found that almost half of the users were motivated to gather more political information after they had used the VAA [19]. For the 2006 parliamentary elections in the Netherlands, Ruusuvirta and Rosema [17] found that the local VAA *Stemwijzer* helped those voters to make a voting choice who did not know in advance if they were going to vote. The survey data from the Netherlands suggest that voters do use VAAs to guide them in their vote decision-making [17]. Moreover, VAAs have become the most important source of information for younger voters in Finland ([17], [21]).

Although several studies suggest the mobilizing capacity of VAAs, it has to be kept in mind that figures are always subject to controversy. All data rely on the correctness of submitted answers by users, which may or may not be accurate. Whether users mobilized by the use of VAAs actually cast their vote cannot be determined with certainty. Furthermore, Ruusuvirta and Rosema [17] point out that the effects of VAAs on electoral participation are hard to prove. The difficulty lies in the causal mechanisms - whether the use of the VAA motivated to cast a vote or whether the motivation to vote led to the usage of a VAA is hard to distinguish. Nevertheless, it seems that VAAs do have an effect on electoral participation, but we have yet to figure out the extent of it.

From a theoretical perspective there are substantial arguments in favour of VAAs' impact on electoral participation. What gives rise to optimism with regard to VAAs impact on voter turnout is its main attribute of offering political information. VAAs render the unique possibility of gaining access to information about politics, political parties and candidates in a condensed and efficient way. This plays well with the rational choice argument. Acquiring and processing information is subject to costs, which, according to rational choice theory, individuals only accept if the benefits are promising [22]. Through increasing the amount of easily available information, VAAs reduce the costs of information gathering and thus increase the likelihood of voting (e.g. [17]).

Empirical findings also indicate that information is crucial for electoral behavior. Lutz [5] has analyzed low turnout in (direct) democracy. His findings underline the importance of information for democratic processes and outcomes. Especially in countries with multiparty systems, the complexity of required information to make an informed voting choice is high. As Walgrave et al. [13] put it, "the fact that VAAs seem to be popular, especially in countries with large and fragmented, and thus complicated, party systems, indicates that information is key". Lutz [5] finds that non-voters tend to be less informed and speculates that higher turnout could be achieved by raising interest and information. Previous literature on political knowledge has also come to this conclusion: higher levels of political information are linked to increased voter turnout ([23], [24]). Generally, political scientists have been indicating that a high level of information among citizens is a precondition for the well functioning and the stability of a democracy [25].

VAAs might furthermore add value to democratic processes for those aiming at the best possible integration of citizen's political preferences. Walgrave et al. [13] argue that VAAs spur issue-voting, in which voters cast their vote based on the "perceived proximity between their own position on an issue and the party they vote for". In other words, VAAs offer easy access to information about party and candidate policy preferences and can therefore lead to a voting choice based on issues. Since party affiliations have become weaker in all advanced democracies [26], voters tend to be more prone to seeking clues that affiliates them with a party or candidate in order to make a voting choice. The issue-matching module of VAAs might thus increasingly serve as an electoral guide for voters, allowing them to elect exactly those representatives that do share similar policy preferences. In other words, VAAs might even have an impact on the quality of electoral decisions and consequently representation.

3 VAA *smartvote*

Functioning and Use

The VAA *smartvote* (www.smartvote.ch) was introduced by Politools[3] in the forefront of the 2003 federal elections in Switzerland. Since then it was also offered on the occasion of more than twenty elections on regional and local level in Switzerland as well as in different foreign countries (most recently for the federal elections in Luxembourg in June 2009). The core of *smartvote* is, similar to most VAAs, the issue-matching module. In order to gather the necessary data for issue-matching, both the candidate and the voter answer a set of pre-assembled questions[4].

About six weeks before the elections the *smartvote* website for the specific election is made accessible to voters and leads them in three steps to their individual voting recommendation. The voters first have to specify their own political profile by answering the same questionnaire as the candidate did. For each question additional background information and explanations including pros and cons are provided on the website. Secondly, voters have to select the constituency in which they vote, respectively for which they want to receive a voting recommendation. Depending on

---

[3] Politools is a private association providing information about political processes for citizens: www.politools.net (German).

[4] The voter can choose between a "rapid version" consisting of 36 questions and a "deluxe version" consisting of 73 questions. Candidates answer a set of 73 questions.

the electoral system they can also decide whether they wish to receive a voting recommendation for lists/parties or for individual candidates. Finally, *smartvote* compares the answers of the voter with the answers of all candidates including the weighting factors the voter has given to the questions. The higher the congruence of the answers between a voter and a candidate, the more "matching points" a candidate gets. This process is repeated over all questions and for every candidate in the selected constituency and results in a voting recommendation in form of a list with a decreasing ranking of the candidates according to their total matching score. If a voter wishes to receive a voting recommendation for lists/parties the procedure is similar. Here *smartvote* uses the mean value of all answering candidates of a list or party.

Additional features are provided by *smartvote* to visualize voting recommendations and party or candidate profiles; the so-called smartspider (see Figure 1) and smartmap charts. Both analytical graphs are based on the candidates' and the user's answers to the *smartvote* questionnaire respectively. The smartspider shows the agreement or disagreement on eight major political issue dimensions formulated as political goals (e.g. more law and order, more environmental protection, or a strong welfare state) in a spider net graph. The values on the eight axes range from 0 to 100 – 0 standing for complete disapproval of the formulated political goal and 100 for full approval. The smartmap is based on a system of coordinates with two major ideological cleavages serving as axes – the "north-south axis" for the cleavage between liberal and conservative standpoints and the "west-east axis" for the left-right cleavage.

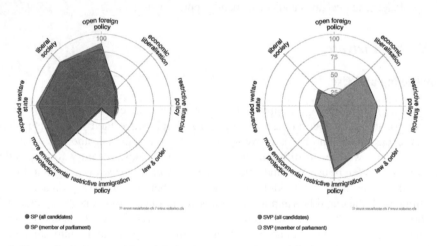

Fig. 1. Example for smartspider of Swiss Democrats (SP) and Swiss People's Party (SVP) for the 2007 Swiss federal elections
Source: www.smartvote.ch

smartvote Users

The use of *smartvote* increased severely since its introduction in 2003. In the 2007 federal elections absolute figures almost quadrupled and increased from 255'000 uses in 2003 to 938'403. This results in a *smartvote* use index[5] of almost 40% of voter turnout in 2007. These figures, however, have to be corrected for multiple counting's, where users have generated more than one voting recommendation. Hence, the estimation for the real number of voters using *smartvote* in 2007 is 375'000. This means that about 16% of those who went to the polls in 2007 were *smartvote* users. A similar trend can be observed by candidates running for office. In 2003, half of the candidates answered the *smartvote* questionnaire, while by 2007 85% of all candidates running for office participated on the *smartvote* website [20]. These statistics indicate the increased popularity of *smartvote* among the Swiss electorate.

Regarding socio-demographic characteristics, the typical *smartvote* users are male, younger and tend to have a higher education and explicitly more income (see Table 1).

Table 1. Socio-demographic characteristics of *smartvote* users, 2007 Swiss federal elections

Characteristics	*smartvote* users (in %)
Gender	
Men	67
Women	33
Age	
18-24 years old	21
25-34 years old	28
35-44 years old	21
45-54 years old	15
55-64 years old	10
65-74 years old	4
75+ years old	1
Level of education	
Low	3
Medium	54
High	43
Household income (in Swiss Francs)	
-3'000	5
3'001-5'000	11
5'001-9'000	40
9'001+	44

Source: NCCR "Democracy", IP16 "smart-voting", post electoral survey among *smartvote* users [15].

Selects[6] data on the 2007 Swiss federal elections indicated that voter groups with a turnout rate below average primarily consisted of women, young voters and voters with low or medium levels of education [16]. The young are the congruent part

---

[5] *Smartvote* use index: absolute number of voting recommendations per election in relation to voter turnout. Absolute voter turnout in 2007: 2'373'071
(http://www.bfs.admin.ch/bfs/portal/de/index/themen/17/02/
blank/key/national_rat/wahlbeteiligung.html).

[6] The Swiss Electoral Studies *Selects* is an electoral research project of several political science departments of Swiss Universities that started in 1995 (http://www.selects.ch).

between *smartvote* users and the voter group with low turnout rates. Hence, if VAAs manage to mobilize its young users, a particularly strong impact on turnout could be expected.

4 *smartvote* and Voter Turnout

For various reasons the impact of *smartvote* on electoral participation and over all voter turnout is not easy to evaluate. Only a part of the Swiss electorate uses *smartvote* and therefore representativity in our survey data is not given. However, since we are interested whether the use of *smartvote* affected electoral participation, presenting the survey data of users is sufficient.

The data presented here has been collected in a pre-voting and a post-voting survey among *smartvote* users in the 2007 federal elections. 27'000 *smartvote* users participated in our online surveys. To approach the question whether *smartvote* affected electoral participation and turnout, we will first have a look at evidence from aggregate level and then turn our attention to individual level data.

Evidence from Aggregate Level Data

As mentioned, voter turnout is extremely low in Switzerland compared to other countries. In the last few elections, however, there has been a slight increase from the all time lowest score of 42.2% in 1995 to 48.3% in 2007.[7]

Since *smartvote* was not introduced before the 2003 Swiss federal elections, it cannot be made responsible for the whole increase. However, there are some indications on the aggregate level that *smartvote* might affect overall turnout. In the two larger cantons of Zurich and Berne, where *smartvote* was particularly popular during the 2007 federal elections, the increase in turnout was above average. Furthermore, turnout among younger voters has severely increased over the years [16]. Since *smartvote* attracts especially the young, it seems interesting to trace whether the tool has a mobilizing capacity among this voter cohort. In order to evaluate in how far these trends are connected, evidence from individual data need to be taken into account.

Evidence from Individual Level Data

In general: *smartvote* is used by those who already participate, have a higher political interest and know more about politics than the average voter (see Table 2).

From the Swiss Electoral Studies Selects we know that of those who did use *smartvote,* 72.7% also participated in the 2007 elections, whereas from those who did not use *smartvote*, only 46.4% participated. Furthermore, among those who did use *smartvote*, 30% are very interested in politics and 50% are rather interested in politics. This leaves about 20% of *smartvote* users who consider themselves as not interested in politics, compared to about 38% of voters in general.

---

[7] Voter turnout 1999: 43.3%, Voter turnout 2003: 45.2%,
    (http://www.bfs.admin.ch/bfs/portal/de/index/themen/17/02/
    blank/key/national_rat/wahlbeteiligung.html).

Table 2. Political interest and knowledge among voters and *smartvote* users

	Voters (%)	*smartvote* users (%)
Interest in politics		
High	16.5	30.5
Rather high	45.3	48.0
Rather low	26.3	19.0
Low	11.9	2.5
Political knowledge		
High	6.6	16.2
Rather high	19.0	26.4
Medium	26.9	25.2
Rather low	29.9	16.8
Low	17.6	15.3

Note: N=4392 for voters and 333 for *smartvote* users
Source: Swiss Electoral Studies 2007

The theoretical argument has been put forward that VAAs ease access to information about parties and candidates and should therefore be a catalyst for turnout. *smartvote* users have been asked whether the VAA improved their basis of information, whether it motivated them to search for more information about political issues, candidates and parties and whether *smartvote* motivated them to discuss politics, candidates and parties with other citizens. Almost 55% of the users claimed that *smartvote* improved their basis of information and for an additional 30% this was a least partially true (N=17331). Quite important parts of the users got particularly motivated to search for more information about specific political issues (16.4% true, 32.6% rather true, N=17382) and about specific candidates or parties (20.7% true, 35.9% rather true, N=17376). And over 65% of the users claimed that *smartvote* motivated them to discuss political issues (28.3% true, 37.2% rather true, N=17410) or parties and candidates (31.2% true, 36.9% rather true, N=17364) with other citizens. *smartvote* users stated that the VAA was the most important instrument for getting information about parties and candidates for the 2007 elections among a list including all sorts of media channels, political events, advertisement and other online channels [27]. Similar results were found in a study on the German VAA *Wahl-O-Mat*. Almost 50% of users were motivated to search for more information on political issues after using the tool, 45% claimed that the VAA made them particularly attentive for special issues on the federal level and 70% stated that the use of the VAA motivated them to discuss the results of the voting recommendation with friends and family [19]. These results indicate that VAAs are not merely toys used by tech-savvies but rather make citizens more attentive for political issues, motivate them to search for more information and makes them discuss politics with other citizens.

Since the motivation aspect can positively affect participation and consequently turnout, this aspect deserves closer attention. Our survey data of the *smartvote* users indicate that *smartvote* most likely had a positive impact on participation. 15.6% (N=17641) claimed that *smartvote* had motivated them to take part in the elections. Another 25% reveal that they have at least been partially motivated. The motivation effect of *smartvote* was significantly stronger among younger voters (see Table 3).

Table 3. Impact of using *smartvote* on the decision to vote or not (in percentage) in the 2007 Swiss federal elections

	Definitely motivated me to vote	Rather motivated me to vote	No influence	Rather prevented me from voting	Definitely prevented me from voting	N
Total	15.6	23.6	60.1	0.6	0.2	17'641
Gender						
Men	12.7	23.7	62.6	0.5	0.2	12'214
Women	22.1	23.4	53.7	0.6	0.1	5'391
Age Groups						
18-24	20.8	25.6	52.9	0.6	0.1	3'874
25-34	17.5	24.0	57.7	0.6	0.2	5'086
35-44	13.7	23.2	62.5	0.5	0.2	3'633
45-54	11.9	22.7	64.7	0.6	0.1	2'505
55-64	10.1	21.8	67.4	0.5	0.2	1'677
65+	9.5	20.3	69.5	0.5	0.1	739

Source: own calculations

It is interesting to note that those who have been motivated the most by *smartvote* to vote in the elections are the young. We cannot rule out that other factors caused our respondents to cast their vote, however, since we did ask them directly if *smartvote* was the reason for their participation, we can deduce causality.

That high interest in politics results in participation is supported by the fact that in our sample more than 80% of those entitled to vote in 2007 also took part in the 2003 federal elections. Thus, it is not surprising that a majority of the respondents stated that they have not been influenced in their decision to vote or not since they participate regularly. If we take a closer look at those who did not vote in 2003, however, we do find a much stronger motivating effect (see Figure 2). Among those *smartvote* users who were eligible to vote in 2003 but abstained from voting, 41.4% claimed that the use of *smartvote* motivated them to take part in the 2007 elections. In comparison, 10.7% of users who already took part in 2003 stated that the use of *smartvote* motivated them to cast their vote in 2007. Hence, the 41.4% of former non-voters constitute a voting group that could have been mainly motivated through using *smartvote* to participate in the elections. Based on these numbers and given our absolute numbers of *smartvote* users plus those that filled in the questionnaire and the Swiss voter turnout for 2007, we can estimate that approximately 0,6 – 1,1 % of the voter turnout in the 2007 Swiss federal elections could have been due to *smartvote*.[8] These numbers are estimates, but they might be even higher since we did not include

[8] These calculations are based on the assumption that those who filled out the *smartvote* questionnaire among users are representative for all *smartvote* users. Extrapolations lead to 14'368 – 25'127 additional voters out of 2'373'071 total voters in the 2007 federal elections in Switzerland thanks to the use of *smartvote*.

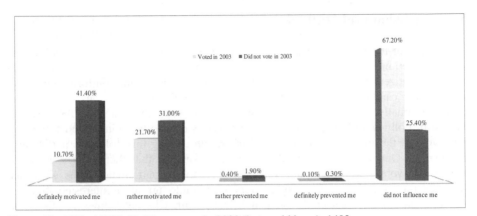

N voted in 2003: 12907; N did not vote in 2003 (but could have): 1402

Fig. 2. Did *smartvote* motivate you to take part in the 2007 Swiss federal elections? Comparing those who voted in 2003 to those who did not vote in 2003 (only those eligible to vote in 2003) Source: own calculations

the potential of new voters (young voting cohort)[9] and those who did vote at both elections but only due to the motivating effect of *smartvote*.

If we take a closer look at those who were not yet eligible to vote in 2003, the young voters, the motivating influence of *smartvote* is even stronger: 20.6% (N=2138) claimed that *smartvote* definitely motivated them to participate in the 2007 elections and 27% claimed that it rather motivated them to take part.

Overall, it can be summarized that *smartvote* does have a motivating effect; however, the effect is rather modest since most *smartvote* users are already motivated to participate in elections anyway. These findings are in line with results from other countries: A study on the German *Wahl-O-Mat* found that 7.8% of its users were motivated to cast a vote which they, before using the VAA, would not have done [19] and data from Finland's parliamentary election indicate that VAAs can mobilize voters with a low socio-economic status and increase the likelihood of voting by 21% for men and 23% for women [18].

Young voters with low education are particularly prone to abstain from voting. That *smartvote* is able to motivate this particular group of voters is promising for effects on electoral participation and turnout. Generally, at this stage it is difficult to evaluate the exact boost of *smartvote* on voting turnout – due to lack of representativity and possible self-selection in the survey and issues with casual mechanisms in the sample. Nevertheless, all indications point into the direction that VAAs – at least in the case of Switzerland – do have a positive impact on turnout, especially among those who do not participate regularly but are basically interested in politics. If the popularity of *smartvote* keeps on growing, the likelihood of its effect on voter turnout might increase. Even among those who are less interested in politics.

---

[9] The precondition for this calculation was that the respondent was already able to vote in 2003. Thus, young voters that did not meet the voting age criteria by 2003 were not included.

5 Conclusion and Outlook

The results of the analyses of the use of *smartvote* in the course of the 2007 Swiss federal elections show that VAAs do have an impact on elections. *smartvote* motivated citizens to participate in the elections, to search for more information about parties and candidates and to discuss politics with other citizens. The young disproportionally use *smartvote* and claim to have been motivated by the VAA to engage in politics and take part in the elections. Since young voters tend to abstain from voting, the mobilizing capacity of *smartvote* among this cohort is particularly promising. Our survey on the 2007 elections indicates that there was a group of former non-voters who were motivated by the tool to participate in the elections. Whether this group of former non-voters was made up of uninterested citizens, incompetent citizens or socially isolated citizens cannot be determined at this point, but leaves interesting opportunities for further research on the matter. If *smartvote* increases turnout of specific parts of society, it might be especially interesting to ask whether this favors specific candidates and parties.

Although we are optimistic about VAAs development, for now it has to be kept in mind that e-democracy tools such as *smartvote* are still young and are subject to further development. Yet, the data on its use is gathering up and, given its popularity, will soon offer the chance for longitudinal studies and more general conclusions. Favorably, similar data from other countries will soon allow comparative studies. For now, the descriptive analyses have produced first indications of an effect on electoral participation and voter turnout in Switzerland. Nevertheless, at this stage, cautiousness with regard to existing data has to be used. Further research is needed to investigate the casual mechanisms in our results. The potential of VAAs for affecting elections is, however, irrevocable.

That VAAs' potential might also bear negative aspects should not be neglected. Critics argue that VAAs might not necessarily be favourable for the democratic process since they offer the possibility of manipulating voting recommendations (by its developers or by parties) and thus distort the electoral process. Framing and fraud of such instruments might pose a threat to democracy, which makes scientific scrutiny indispensible. Especially since VAAs such as *smartvote* are developed by private actors - mostly on non-profit basis, however. The VAA under examination in this study is produced by scientists, proofed by experts, pre-tested in terms of its statement selections and transparent in its design. Hence, access to the calculation methods of *smartvote*, its financing sources and to the candidate answers on the *smartvote* questionnaire greatly reduce the aforementioned concerns. The ascribed negative potential of VAAs is further weakened through its monitoring capacities on political actors. Due to *smartvote's* transparency on candidate positioning, the voting behaviour of politicians once elected to office can be scrutinized, therewith strengthening accountability and consequently democracy.

For Switzerland, a main breakthrough for VAAs will come if e-voting will be standardized for voting processes. In systems like Switzerland, where voters not only send in party lists but take their time to customize their own list with cumulative and cross-voting, electronic devices that simplify these tasks will be very useful. Once you are able to copy-paste your choice of candidates – this can be up to 34 names in cantons such as Zurich – into the official ballot paper or send the ballot directly via remote internet-voting tools, the majority of citizens will eventually start to vote in the way they book their holidays nowadays.

But before this will become reality, today VAAs already render the possibility of bringing politics closer to the electorate. Through offering easy access to information they not only guide voters in their decision-making but might also spur changes in voting behavior. In the future, e-democracy tools such as VAAs will be easily accessible through a mobile phone or an ipad, offering a real chance of bringing voting decisions of citizens closer to their political preferences. With that, an increasing use of these tools will not only affect electoral participation, but also electoral campaigns and political parties. In other words, if voting decisions are increasingly based on issue stances, it will be interesting to analyze how political candidates will position themselves in the political space. VAAs not only make politics more accessible to citizens, they might also affect electoral processes and thus offer a new set of opportunities for electoral studies.

References

1. Lijphart, A.: Democracy's Unresolved Dilemma. The American Political Science Review 91(1), 1–14 (1997)
2. Kriesi, H.: Direct Democratic Choice. The Swiss Experience. Lexington Books, Oxford (2005)
3. Oser, F., Biedermann, H.: Jugend ohne Politik. Ergebnisse der IEA Studie zu Politischem Wissen, Demokratieverständnis und Gesellschaftlichem Engagement von Jugendlichen in der Schweiz im Vergleich mit 27 anderen Ländern. Zürich (2003)
4. Dalton, R.J.: Citizen Politics. Public Opinion and Political Parties in Advanced Industrial Democracies. CQ Press, Washington (2006)
5. Lutz, G.: Low Turnout in Direct Democracy. Electoral Studies 26, 624–632 (2007)
6. Norris, P.: Will New Technology Boost Turnout? Evaluating Experiments in UK Local Elections. In: Kersting, N., Baldersheim, H. (eds.) Electronic Voting and Democracy, New York, pp. 193–225 (2004)
7. Norris, P.: E-Voting as the Magic Ballot for European Parliamentary Elections? Evaluating E-Voting in the Light of Experiments in UK Local Elections. In: Trechsel, A.H., Mendez, F. (eds.) The European Union and E-Voting. Addressing the European Parliament's Internet Voting Challenge, London, pp. 60–90 (2004)
8. Trechsel, A.H.: Inclusiveness of Old and New Forms of Citizens' Electoral Participation. Representation 43(2), 111–121 (2007)
9. Norris, P.: Preaching to the Converted? Pluralism, Participation and Party Websites. Party Politics 9(1), 21–45 (2003)
10. Jeitziner, B.: Wahlen im Internetzeitalter. Informationsvermittler als politische Berater von Wählern und Politikern. In: Schaltegger, C.A., Schaltegger, S.C. (eds.) Perspektiven der Wirtschaftspolitik. Festschrift zum 65. Geburtstag von Prof. Dr. René L. Frey, pp. 47–64. vdf Hochschulverlag, Zürich (2004)
11. Leuchinger, S., Rosinger, M., Stutz, A.: The Impact of Postal Voting on Participation: Evidence for Switzerland. Swiss Political Science Review 13(2), 167–202 (2007)
12. Fivaz, J., Schwarz, D.: Nailing the Pudding to the Wall – E-Democracy as Catalyst for Transparency and Accountability. Paper Presented at the International Conference on Direct Democracy in Latin America, March 14-15, Buenos Aires, Argentina (2007)

13. Walgrave, S., van Aelst, P., Nuytemans, M.: Do the Vote Test: The Electoral Effects of a Popular Vote Advice Application at the 2004 Belgian Elections. Acta Politica 43(1), 50–70 (2008)
14. Bühlmann, M., Freitag, M., Vatter, A.: Die Schweigende Mehrheit. Eine Typologie der Schweizer Nichtwählerschaft. In: Sciarini, P., Hardmeier, S., Vatter, A. (eds.) Schweizer Wahlen 1999, Bern, pp. 27–58 (2003)
15. Fivaz, J.: Impact of "smart-voting" on Political Participation. Working Paper Presented at the Civic Education and Political Participation Workshop at the Université de Montréal, June 17-19 2008, Montreal, Canada (2008)
16. Lutz, G.: Eidgenössische Wahlen 2007. Wahlteilnahme und Wahlentscheid. Lausanne (2008)
17. Ruusuvirta, O., Rosema, M.: Do Online Vote Selectors Influence Electoral Participation and the Direction of the Vote? Paper Presented at the ECPR General Conference, September 13-12 , Potsdam, Germany (2009)
18. Mykkänen, J., Moring, T.: Dealigned Politics Comes of Age? The Effects of Online Candidate Selectors on Finnish Voters. Paper Presented at the Conference of Politics on the Internet: New Forms of Media for Political Action, November 25 , Tampere (2006)
19. Marschall, S.: Idee und Wirkung des Wahl-O-Mat. Aus Politik und Zeitgeschichte (APuZ) 51-52, 41–46 (2005)
20. Ladner, A., Felder, G., Fivaz, J.: Are Voting Advice Applications (VAAs) more than Toys? First Findings on Impact and Accountability of VAAs. IDHEAP Working Paper 2/2008, Lausanne (2008)
21. Carlson, T., Strandberg, K.: The 2004 European Parliament Election on the Web: Finnish Actor Strategies and Voter Responses. Information Polity 10(3-4), 189–204 (2005)
22. Downs, A.: An Economic Theory of Democracy. Harper and Row, New York (1957)
23. Palfrey, T.R., Poole, K.T.: The Relationship between Information, Ideology and Voting Behavior. American Journal of Political Science 31(3), 511–530 (1987)
24. Delli Carpini, M.X., Keeter, S.: What Americans Know about Politics and Why It Matters. Yale University Press, New Haven (1996)
25. Kirchgässner, G., Feld, L.P., Savioz, M.R.: Die Direkte Demokratie. Modern, Erfolgreich, Entwicklungs- und Exportfähig. Verlag Franz Vahlen, München (1999)
26. Dalton, R.J.: Democratic Challenges – Democratic Choices. The Erosion of Political Support in Advanced Industrial Democracies, Oxford (2007)
27. Ladner, A., Felder, G., Schädel, L.: From E-voting to smart-voting. E-Tools in and for Elections and Direct Democracy in Switzerland. Paper Presented at the Conference 'Direct Democracy in and Around Europe: Integration, Innovation, Illusion, and Ideology' at the Center for Democracy Aarau, October 3 (2008)

An Integrated Application of Security Testing Methodologies to e-voting Systems

Marco Ramilli and Marco Prandini

University of Bologna, Italy
{marco.ramilli,marco.prandini}@unibo.it

Abstract. Various technical bodies have devised methodologies to guide testers to the selection, design, and implementation of the most appropriate security testing procedures for various contexts. Their general applicability is obviously regarded as a necessary and positive feature, but its consequence is the need for a complex adaptation phase to the specific systems under test. In this work, we aim to devise a simplified, yet effective methodology tailored to suit the peculiar needs related to the security testing of e-voting systems. We pursue our goal by selecting, for each peculiar aspect of these systems, the best-fitting procedures found in the most widely adopted security testing methodologies, at the same time taking into account the specific constraints stemming from the e-voting context to prune the excess of generality that comes with them.

Keywords: eVoting, security, testing methodologies.

1 Introduction

Testing is important to ascertain the adherence of an implemented system to its specification, but even more to prove that it exhibits sensible reactions to unexpected stimuli. Even the best design process cannot capture the latter property, since no explicit requisite can represent it; thus, testing contributes in an unique way to the development cycle of secure systems [1–3], notwithstanding the impossibility of guaranteeing the absence of any problem through it [4]. The scientific and technical communities have made various attempts at defining detailed procedures for security testing. Clearly, the goal pursued in these efforts was to devise generally-applicable guidelines, while at the same time providing as much detail as possible regarding the proper way of performing each step. Two limitations affect the proposals found in the literature. First, their application could result quite cumbersome, requiring a non-negligible effort in the preliminary phase of mapping the suggested procedures to the specificities of the system to be tested. Second, the "perfect" proposal does not exist, each one exhibiting areas of excellence and more neglected sections.

We aim at a twofold result for the mitigation of the aforementioned problems. The paper is structured as follows. In sections 2 and 3 we briefly outline the most widely adopted testing methodologies. We proceed (section 4) to synthetically review the commonly adopted e-voting architectures and to summarize

E. Tambouris, A. Macintosh, and O. Glassey (Eds.): ePart 2010, LNCS 6229, pp. 225–236, 2010.

their common characteristics. By combining the elements of this preliminary exploration, we choose from the different methodologies the testing procedures that better suit the specific needs related to testing the components of e-voting systems. Taking into account the constraints that define the class of e-voting systems, as opposed to generic ones, we simplify those procedures by safely removing the unneeded details and more precisely driving the testing process.

2 Related Work

We deem useful to recall a few concepts related to the different approaches to security testing, to e-voting, and to the relation between the two worlds that emerges from the most significant experiences to date.

2.1 Security Testing Approaches

There are significant differences between the many papers, from the academic as well as the technical world, that deal with the subject of security testing. A possible classification organizes the various proposals into three broad categories:

Toolkits implement in a convenient package a set of testing techniques, usually aimed at discovering specific classes of security problems. Toolkits represent the operating side of security testing. They are valuable companions to guidelines and methodologies, which in turn provide the strategies to effectively use them. The Open Vulnerability Assessment System [5] and the BackTrack Live CD [6] are significant examples among countless others.

Guidelines organize the process of security testing, by collecting sets of best practices and comprehensively listing items to be tested; they often distill the experiences gathered on the field by the technical community, but usually lack the level of detail that allows to design a precise test plan. Some examples of well-known guidelines come from NIST, namely: the Common Criteria for Information Technology Security Testing [7] and the Technical Guide to Information Security Testing and Assessment [8]. The Open-ended vulnerability testing (OEVT) [9] is being devised starting from the experiences gathered by the Electoral Assistance Commission in the U.S.A on the Voluntary Voting System Guidelines (VVSG) [10].

Methodologies represent the most structured approach to security testing. To different extents, every methodology defines: (a) an abstract model for the system, (b) an abstract model for the process of finding its vulnerabilities, and (c) a procedure for realizing a concrete test plan from the models, given the details of the system under test. A detailed discussion of the most widely adopted methodologies is illustrated in section 3.

2.2 e-voting Systems

The need for technological aids to make the voting process more efficient and accurate predates the availability of sophisticated computer architectures, but usually the adopted solutions (for example, punch-card devices and optical scan machines) perform little more than substituting a supposedly more robust media for the traditional pencil-and-paper. More recently, comprehensive systems have been designed and implemented that exploit computers and networks to take care of every step of the voting process. The foreseen advantages have greatly increased, but the concerns raised by the trustworthiness and security aspects of such complex (and opaque) architectures have grown equally strong. Examples of commonly adopted approaches include:

Direct Recording Electronic Voting System (DRE). The voter chooses by simply touching the name of the candidate directly on screen and the machine casts the vote on its own storage device. At the end of the election, the machine produces an exhaustive report to be sent to the precinct for counting. The systems by leading vendors (Diebold, Election Systems and Software, Sequoia among the others), widely adopted for instance in the U.S.A., are mainly of this kind. However, they have harshly been criticized for the complete lack of independent correctness-checking capabilities, that leaves open the possibility of undetectable mistakes of malicious or accidental nature.

Voter Verified Audit Trail (VVAT) Electronic Voting Machine solve this problem by generating a proof which can be audited by the voter to ascertain the correct recording of her will. It can be a paper ballot which can be reviewed by the voter before confirming her intention to cast it, and then collected in a secure storage should a recount be needed, or a mathematical proof that pushes the concept even further, by allowing the voters to check whether their vote was accurately recorded by the electronic system (end-to-end verification), not only in the paper trail [11, 12].

2.3   e-voting Security Threats

Although security testing is an incomplete test, meaning that it does not ensure the absence of flaws, it is the *only* process able to prove threats. In sensitive systems like e-voting, the presence of threats might interfere with the correct election outcome compromising the democracy of the hosting country. Examples of the most important areas where security threats might be present are :

1. Secrecy. If the system does not assure secrecy, the system is at least vulnerable to covert channels attacks, where an attacker may buy or sell votes.
2. Integrity. If the system does not assure integrity, an attacker could compromise the election by replacing or modifying the integrity of the ballots or directly the integrity of the final counts.
3. Availability. If the system does not assure availability, the system can not assure the universal suffrage, becoming vulnerable at least to external quorum attacks, in which the attacker can modify the total number of voters denying the minimum voters requirements.
4. Authentication. If the system does not assure authentication controls, it is at least vulnerable to multiple vote attacks, where an attacker could vote multiple times for the preferred candidate.

Depending on the system implementation we may find different entry points where the security threats may appear. For example the integrity of the system might be threatened by malwares, or directly by the vendor introducing incorrect behaviors or backdoors on the voting platform; the authentication control might be threatened by wrong input validation, brute force attacks or buggy sessions. Since the range of the entry points is so large and so strongly platform dependent, the paper does not describe the details of each of them, but synthesizes the general features useful to devise an e-voting system testing methodology.

2.4   e-voting Systems Testing Experiences

Oddly enough, to our knowledge, there is no documented application of the most complete testing methodologies to e-voting systems. Certification for official use, where it is mandatory, commonly follows guidelines like the VVSG, that are quite country- and technology-specific. *A posteriori* security reviews skillfully exploit various toolkits and attack techniques, not adopting structured approaches (but producing interesting results nonetheless). Notable examples of the latter category were the seminal Security Analysis of the Diebold AccuVote-TS Voting Machine [13] performed in 2006, the California Top-to-Bottom Review [16], performed by various Californian universities [14, 15] on all the voting systems used in 2007 for state and local elections, and the similar Evaluation & Validation of Election-Related Equipment, Standards & Testing (EVEREST) program undertaken in Ohio in the same year [17].

3   Existing Security Testing Methodologies

In this section, we give a glimpse of the main security testing methodologies that we exploited to build a tailor-made testing process suited for e-voting systems.

3.1   ISSAF

The Information Systems Security Assessment Framework (ISSAF) [18] is a well-established penetration testing methodology, developed by OISS.org. It is designed to evaluate the security of networks, systems and application controls. The methodology outlines three well-defined action areas, and details the nine steps composing the main one, as follows:

- Planning and Preparation. The first phase encompasses the steps needed to set the testing environment up, such as: planning and preparing test tools, contracts and legal protection, definition of the engagement team, deadlines, requirements and structure of the final reports.
- Assessment. This phase is the core of the methodology, where the real penetration tests are carried out. The assessment phase is articulated in nine activities: (1) Information Gathering; (2) Network Mapping; (3) Vulnerability Identification; (4) Penetration; (5) Gaining Access & Privilege Escalation; (6) Enumerating Further; (7) Compromise Remote Users Sites; (8) Maintaining Access; (9) Covering Tracks.

- Reporting, Clean-up and Destroy Artifacts. During this phase, at the very end of the active parts of the methodology, testers have to write a complete report and to destroy artifacts built during the Assessment phase.

ISSAF has a clear and very intuitive structure, which guides the tester through the complicated assessment steps.

3.2 OSSTMM

The Open Source Security Testing Methodology Manual (OSSTMM) [19] is the de-facto standard for security testers. It describes a complete testing methodology, offering fairly good tools to report the result set. In the OSSTMM ontology, the complex made by the target and the logical infrastructure to access it is named *scope*. The scope of application of OSSTMM encompasses any interaction, with any asset within the whole operating security environment, including the physical components of security measures as well. The methodology mandates that all the threats within the scope must be considered possible, even if not probable. On the access paths side, the scope is organized in three channels: COMSEC (communications security), PHYSSEC (physical security), and SPECSEC (spectrum security). Channels are the means of interacting with assets, where an asset is defined as anything of value to the owner. Fig. 1 represents the scope extension. The three main channels are split into 5 sub-channels:

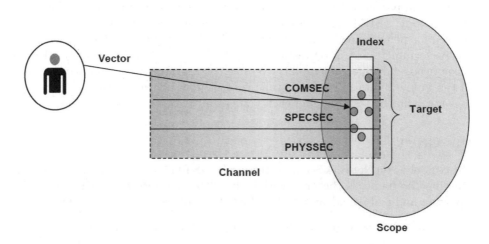

Fig. 1. OSSTMM: The Scope Process

- Human. It comprises all the human elements of communications
- Physical. It comprises the tangible elements of security where interaction requires physical effort or an energy transmitter to manipulate.
- Wireless Communication. It comprises all the electronic communications, signals and emanations which take place over the known EM spectrum.

- Data Networks. It comprises all the electronic systems and data networks where interactions take place over dedicated cables and wired network lines.
- Telecommunication. It comprises all the telecommunication networks, digital or analog, where the interaction takes place over shared network infrastructures, such as telephone lines.

OSSTMM describes 17 modules to analyze each of the sub-channels. Consequently, the tester has to perform 17*5 = 85 analyses before being able to write the final report.

3.3   Black Hat

Most attackers follow a sort-of-coded procedure to exploit systems, made of four steps, as described in the following list:

- Bugs Information Discovery. In this step the attacker, using automatic and manual analysis, gathers information about system bugs.
- Exploration. In this step the attacker filters the informations obtained in the previous step, obtaining a list of vulnerabilities (i.e. exploitable bugs).
- Assessment. The attacker figures out the most profitable vulnerability.
- Exploitation. The attacker, using both known and improvised techniques, begins the exploitation.

While the apparent order of this procedure has led many to call it "the Black Hat Methodology" (BHM), it is not formally defined anywhere, nor general enough to be used for penetration testing. The main difference between attacking a system and performing penetration testing is the final goal: to attack a system the attacker needs only one vulnerability, to protect the system the tester needs to find all the vulnerabilities. The non-cyclic control flow present in the methodology does not help the tester to find each vulnerability, but only the first one.

3.4   GNST

The Guideline on Network Security Testing (GNST) [20] issued by NIST, notwithstanding the name, is the first methodology to introduce a formal process for reporting and to take advantage of inducted hypotheses. It follows four steps:

- Planning. System analysis finds out the most interesting test targets.
- Discovery. The tester searches the system, looking for vulnerabilities.
- Attack. The tester verifies whether the found vulnerabilities can be exploited.
- Reporting. In the last step, every result is reported.

Each step has an input vector representing known facts and an output vector representing the complete set of results deriving from the performed actions. GNST introduces an attempt at considering inducted hypotheses, where the output vector from a step can become part of the input vector of another one.

4 Applying Methodologies to e-voting Systems

There are many different kind of tests to be performed on voting systems, for which the authors believe that a specific methodology is needed, such as: usability testing, performance testing, and proof of correctness. With an overall perspective, the tester needs to verify the good behavior checking each election requirement. Testing the election requirements mens checking:

R.1) Voter Validation. The voter should reach the state where he is authenticated, registered and he has not yet voted.

R.2) Ballot Validation. The voter must use the right ballot, and the ballot captures the intent of the voter.

R.3) Voter Privacy. The voter cannot be associated with the ballot, not even by the voter herself.

R.4) Integrity of Election. Ballots cannot change during the election time and the casted votes are accurately tallied.

R.5) Voting Availability. Voters must be able to vote, all enabling materials must be available.

R.6) Voting Reliability. Every voting mechanisms must work.

R.7) Election Transparency. It must be possible to audit the election process.

R.8) Election Manageability. The voting process must be usable by those involved.

R.9) System State Requirements. The systems must meet the State certification requirements.

R.10) State Certifications. The voting system must have the certification of the State where the election takes place (whether it considers the afore-listed requirements or a different set).

Focusing on the security aspects of e-voting systems testing, we may consider as the common and implicit *"testing goal"* of the process the overall security of the system. Considering that in security the composability property does not hold (security(a) ∪ security(b) != security(A ∪ B)), except in unrealistically simple situations and after an unusually complex design process, the tester must verify every component and the whole system in two separate views. This means that tester has to test at least a fixed object called *Voting System* and many different objects called *Voting Objects*.

4.1 Testing Voting System and Voting Objects

The voting objects vary according to the analyzed system, but for the sake of clarity some examples include: touch screen monitors, printers, network cables and routers, power supplies, software and so forth. For each defined Voting Object the tester needs to verify that it is not possible to:

– Compromise the Hardware, i.e. insert, remove, substitute or damage physical devices. An example of denial of service attack performed through the hardware occurs when an attacker cuts the edges of a resistive touchscreen monitor (RTM). The attack analysis shows that the vulnerability resides in the technology that place the touch sensors on the surface of the screen, and suggests to adopt as a countermeasure the substitution of RTM with capacitive touchscreen monitors, which have glass-hidden sensors.

– Compromise the Firmware, i.e. alter drivers, hardware BIOS or embedded code. An example of election hijacking performed through firmware alteration occurs when the attacker modifies a router, choosing it because it is a rarely tested COTS component, substituting its firmware with a custom one which allows to dump or to manage the network communications between machines and the ballot box, thus greatly increasing the chances of compromising the election system.

– Compromise the Software, i.e. insert new code, modify the existing code, delete existing code or force an unexpected behavior. For example, an attack vector of this kind on the Unix platform could be an unsecured boot process allowing an attacker to find a privileged login through single-user-mode, or an unsecured terminal where by shutting down the graphic user interface the attacker can operate on the local file system.

Assessing the absence of the afore-listed attack opportunities does not mean that the analyzed system can be considered safe. The best way for a tester to identify all the possible flaws is to consider the most favorable situation for the attacker (the worst situation for the system), assuming a White Open Box point of view, where everyone knows how the system works (through documentation), how the system has been written (through source code) and where the tester can simulate both internal and external attacks. We define the posture of tester as *"Voting System Tester Point of View"*, which is unique for all the systems. Flaws hypotheses and induction flaws hypotheses may be applied in the same way as most of the methodologies show. Properly documenting the evidence regarding what the tester has found, and reporting every relevant action performed during the test is a common provision of most of the methodologies. Summing up, the new methodology should have three new basic assumptions as follow:

A.1) Testing Goals = the entire security of electronic voting system
A.2) Testing Objects = Voting System + Voting Objects
A.3) Tester Point Of View = Voting System Tester Point of View =
       Internal/External Open White Box

Adding assumptions means decreasing the procedure's complexity because the final methodology has three less steps to follow. Fig. 2 shows the transition from the discussed methodologies assumptions to the new ones. On the left of Fig. 2 *"testing goals"* are defined. ISSAF defines the testing goals in the "Planning and Preparation" section, OSSTMM in the "Scope" section and GNST in the "Planning" section. The meaning of the arrows between left boxes and the central one is that each *"testing goal"* is an instance of "Security of Voting System" as previously discussed. On the right of Fig. 2 *"Testing Objects"* are defined. ISSAF define the testing objects in the "Planning and Preparation" section, GNST in the "Planning" section, while OSTMM classifies the testing objects in the

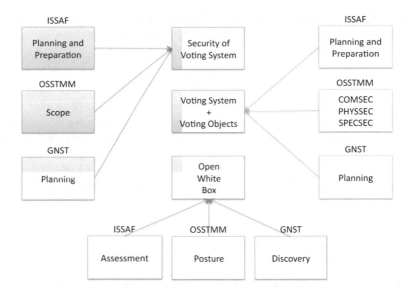

Fig. 2. Transition from old to new assumptions

three known channels. The meaning of the arrows between the right boxes and the central one is that each "*Testing Objects*" should be collapsed into "Voting System + Voting Objects". Finally on the bottom of Fig. 2 "*Voting System Tester Point of View*" is represented. ISSAF defines the Voting System Tester Point of View into the "Assessment" section, OSSTMM in the "Posture" section and GNST in the Discovery section. Again, the meaning of the arrows between the bottom boxes and the center one is that each "*Voting System Tester Point of View*" should be fixed to "Open White Box" to ensure a safe, worst-case-scenario analysis.

5 Tailoring the Methodologies to the e-voting Context

In this section we finally discuss how to choose the most appropriate procedures from the illustrated methodologies, adapting and simplifying them to fit the scenario of e-voting systems testing. The description is necessarily kept at a rather high level of abstraction, because the amount of details involved in the accurate description of each set of procedures could never fit a conference paper.

5.1 ISSAF Adaptation

ISSAF can be exploited as follows, taking advantage of the three new assumptions introduced in section 4. Referring to the Fig.2 the main ISSAF "Planning and Preparation" steps are:

– Identification of contact individuals from both sides.
– Opening meeting to confirm the scope, approach and methodology.
– Agreement on specific test cases and escalation paths.

By fixing the assumptions A.1 and A.2, the tester does not really need to perform the first two steps, which are time and money consuming and often require organizational skills that do not belong to the tester. In the presented scenario there is no way to discuss the scope of the security test; it cannot be other than "the entire security of electronic voting system". Similarly, there is only one set of testing objects that must be tested, as shown in point A.2, thus freeing the tester from the need to define agreements of specific tests cases and escalation paths. Fixing assumption A.3 simplifies the process shown in section 3.1, allowing to avoid the following 3 steps out of the proposed 9:

– Information Gathering.
– Gaining The First Access.
– Privilege escalation.

Notice that the tester does not need to verify the absence of privilege escalation or of remote/local access to the machine, not because these are irrelevant; on the contrary, the starting assumption means that the tester directly operates on the worst-case scenario assuming the attacker already owns this information.

5.2   OSSTMM Adaptation

OSSTMM provides a comprehensive concept of scope, allowing a vast variety of scenarios. For its application to the e-voting domain, it is possible to reduce the space of possible testing procedures by taking into account the assumption A.1 and A.2 as described in section 4.1. These allow to prune the the Scope Definition process, composed by the regulatory phase (cfr. page 25, sec. A.1 and A.2, OSSTMM light edition) and definition phase (page 26, sec. B.4 to B.7, ibid.). Another simplified step regards the information phase (cfr. pages 26-27, sec. C.8 to C.13, ibid.) where the tester should acquire as much information as possible about the system. According to the section 4.1 we reduce the information phase into the assumption A.3, freeing the tester from to the heaviest part of the information gathering task.

5.3   GNST Adaptation

GNST does not provide a detailed set of actions to define what it calls "Planning". It suggests to define rules, to acquire management approvals, to find financing and finally to set up the testing goals and testing objects. Although no strong guidelines are presented, each of the aforementioned steps is superfluous in the e-voting domain, where testing is clearly mandated and financed and testing objects have been previously clarified: the entire GNST Planning phase can be substantially collapsed by applying the constraints deriving from A.1 and part of A.2. GNST's discovery phase has been defined as follow:

- Network Scanning.
- Domain Name System (DNS) interrogation.
- InterNIC (whois) queries.
- Search of the target organization's web server(s) for information.
- Search of the organization's Directory server(s)for information.
- Packet capture (generally only during internal tests).
- NetBIOS enumeration (generally only during internal tests).
- Network Information System (usually only during internal tests).
- Banner grabbing.

By assuming a tester point of view according to A.3, the whole "discovery phase" can be taken as an assumption, allowing insider and external security tests. Following the general methodology, if the tester cannot find a way to remote access the system, he skips all the insider attacks. Assuming A.3, even in this case the tester will perform the tests related to threats originating from a potential insider attacker.

6   Conclusion

Security testing is a fundamental phase in the life cycle of almost any system. Sensitive systems like those used for e-voting undergo particularly severe testing to attain certification of their security properties before usage into a real election. This exacting process should be based on one of the state-of-the-art methodologies described in section 3 of this paper. These exist to manage the planning and execution of testing procedures, taking into account the complex interrelations between the different parts and the huge amount of detail involved, on any kind of system. However, before being usable on peculiar systems, any methodology has to be adapted to the specific context. This paper described the common-denominator aspects, constraints and problems that characterize the whole class of e-voting systems, across their different instantiations (DREs, VVPATs, etc.). With this knowledge, it was possible to identify the procedures of the different methodologies that are most fit to this specific domain, and to provide some guidelines to instantiate them in the most effective way, by removing as many unnecessary steps as possible. A key step in this direction was fixing some unequivocal assumptions, as described in section 4.1. Assumptions work by explicitly stating the context elements that the tester can assume to hold without the need for verifying them, thus removing some degrees of freedom that otherwise leave manifold testing paths open, and eventually allowing to reduce the complexity of the testing phase. The (inital) result should be of help to prospective testers, strongly kick-starting the unavoidable phase of adaptation to the exact system they are dealing with. The ongoing work regards the refinements of practical details and the preparation of a case study to demonstrate the effectiveness of the proposed work on a real system.

References

1. Arkin, B., Stender, S., McGraw, G.: Software penetration testing. Security & Privacy, IEEE 3(1), 84–87 (2005)
2. Bonver, E., Cohen, M.: Developing and retaining a security testing mindset. Security & Privacy, IEEE 6(5), 82–85 (2008)
3. Potter, B., McGraw, G.: Software security testing. Security & Privacy, IEEE 2(5), 81–85 (2004)
4. Thompson, H.: Why security testing is hard. Security & Privacy, IEEE 1(4), 83–86 (2003)
5. Brown, T., Anderson, W., et al.: Open vulnerability assessment system (December 2009)
6. Moser, M., Aharoni, M., Muench, M.J., et al.: Backtrack (June 2009)
7. Horlick, J.: HB 150-20 Information Technology Security Testing: Common Criteria. National Institute of Standards and Technology (October 2005)
8. Scarfone, K., Cody, A., Souppaya, M., Orebaugh, A.: SP 800-115 Technical Guide to Information Security Testing and Assessment. National Institute of Standards and Technology (September 2008)
9. Technical Guidelines Development Committee (ed.): 5.4. In: Voluntary Voting System Guidelines Recommendations to the Election Assistance Commission. U.S. Election Assistance Commission (August 2007)
10. U.S. Election Assistance Commission (ed.): Voluntary Voting System Guidelines. U.S. Election Assistance Commission (2005)
11. Chaum, D., Essex, A., Carback, R., Clark, J., Popoveniuc, S., Sherman, A., Vora, P.: Scantegrity: End-to-end voter-verifiable optical- scan voting. Security Privacy, IEEE 6(3), 40–46 (2008)
12. Adida, B.: Helios: web-based open-audit voting. In: SS'08: Proceedings of the 17th conference on Security symposium, pp. 335–348. USENIX Association, Berkeley (2008)
13. Feldman, A.J., Halderman, J.A., Felten, E.W.: Security analysis of the diebold accuvote-ts voting machine. In: EVT'07: Proceedings of the USENIX Workshop on Accurate Electronic Voting Technology, p. 2. USENIX Association, Berkeley (2007)
14. Bishop, M., Wagner, D.: Risks of e-voting. ACM Commun. 50(11), 120–120 (2007)
15. Balzarotti, D., Banks, G., Cova, M., Felmetsger, V., Kemmerer, R., Robertson, W., Valeur, F., Vigna, G.: Are your votes really counted?: testing the security of real-world electronic voting systems. In: ISSTA '08: Proceedings of the 2008 international symposium on Software testing and analysis, pp. 237–248. ACM, New York (2008)
16. Wagner, D.: Report of the california voting system review (USENIX Security Symposium (2007), http://www.usenix.org/events/sec07/tech/
17. Ohio secretary of state (pub): Evaluation & validation of election-related equipment, standards & testing -
/SOS/elections/voterInformation/equipment/VotingSystemReviewFindings.aspx, http://www.sos.state.oh.us
18. Open Information Systems Security Group: Information systems security assessment framework (2006)
19. Institute for Security and Open Methodologies: Open source security testing methodology manual (2009)
20. Wack, J., Tracy, M., Souppaya, M.: SP 800-42 Guideline on Network Security Testing. National Institute of Standards and Technology (October 2003)

Author Index

Printing: Mercedes-Druck, Berlin
Binding: Stein + Lehmann, Berlin